Do You Hear
What I Hear?

Minna Proctor

Do You Hear What I Hear?

Religious Calling, the Priesthood, and My Father

VIKING

VIKING

Published by the Penguin Group
Penguin Group (USA) Inc.
375 Hudson Street, New York, New York 10014, U.S.A.
Penguin Group (Canada), 10 Alcorn Avenue, Toronto, Ontario, Canada M4V 3B2,
(a division of Pearson Penguin Canada Inc.)
Penguin Books Ltd., 80 Strand, London WC2R 0RL, England
Penguin Ireland, 25 St. Stephen's Green, Dublin 2, Ireland
(a division of Penguin Books Ltd)
Penguin Books Australia Ltd. 250 Camberwell Road, Camberwell, Victoria 3124, Australia
(a division of Pearson Australia Group Pty Ltd)
Penguin Books India Pvt Ltd, 11 Community Centre, Panchsheel Park,
New Delhi—110 017, India
Penguin Group (NZ), Cnr Airborne and Rosedale Roads, Albany, Auckland 1310, New Zealand
(a division of Pearson New Zealand Ltd)
Penguin Books (South Africa) (Pty) Ltd, 24 Sturdee Avenue,
Rosebank, Johannesburg 2196, South Africa

Penguin Books Ltd., Registered Offices: 80 Strand, London WC2R 0RL, England

First published in 2005 by Viking Penguin, a member of Penguin Group (USA) Inc.

1   3   5   7   9   10   8   6   4   2

LIBRARY OF CONGRESS CATALOGING-IN-PUBLICATION DATA
Proctor, Minna.
Do you hear what I hear? : religious calling, the priesthood, and my father / Minna Proctor.
p. cm.
Includes bibliographical references and index.
ISBN 0-670-03326-X
1. Proctor, Gregory, 1941– 2. Episcopal Church—Clergy. I. Title.
BX5995.P75P76 2004
283'.092—dc22
[B]   2004052621

This book is printed on acid-free paper.

Printed in the United States of America ∞
Set in Dante
Designed by Francesca Belanger

For my father

CONTENTS

Thou hast counseled a better course than thou hast permitted.

—AUGUSTINE

. . . THERE WAS THE WORD

*S*everal years ago, my father told me that he wanted to become a priest. "Oh," I said, and that bland monosyllabic utterance constituted the sum and extent of my reaction to the news. I was effectively struck dumb—by nothing so simple as horror, excitement, bewilderment, or grotesque fascination, but by ignorance. As for many of my generation, religion had only skirted my life.

A few weeks passed before a follow-up question occurred to me: "What kind of priest?" Episcopal, I was told. "Is it okay for you to be married?" I asked. The question was gratuitous, conversational, because I assumed that, happily married for a second time and with two small children, my father wouldn't qualify for celibacy. I should have asked what an Episcopalian was.

I like to organize my thoughts, both the emotional ones and the intellectual ones. It's probably better described as a compulsion to organize, ascribe, and explain: to process. I don't know whether this compulsion is the writer in me, or if it's why I'm a writer, but in my small way, I'm always tracing the butterfly effect, from that first airy flap of the wings in the Amazon to the tidal wave in Japan. For years, I didn't sleep at night because I was too busy analyzing my dreams— lying there in the dark, eyes wide open, preoccupied with thoughts like, *Okay, the half-eaten fish in the swimming pool is my master's thesis, and the sleeping lifeguard is my adviser*—until a wise neurologist gave me some sedatives and told me to "just stop thinking so much." I sleep better now, but I'm still fanatical about trying to connect the dots.

When my father told me he wanted to become a priest, my dots were challenged. There was my life, my father, and the Episcopal priesthood—with no conceivable lines to be drawn between them.

For me, writing about something is the best way to attack apparently unconnectable dots. I'm more rigorous and more courageous on paper. Unsent love letters are my favorite genre. In writing, you can analyze and meditate, even research, and begin to fill in some of the white space. I thought about writing an essay describing how a person gets to be a priest and why—hopefully, that way, edging toward an understanding of how my father would get to be a priest and why. My basic religious illiteracy meant that I was sounding out each new word letter by letter, and parsing out concepts like an eighth-grade grammarian. I'd barely started researching the nuts and bolts of becoming a priest in the Episcopal Church when my father received word that his application had been remanded. At only the third phase in a forty-five-phase ordination process, my father was told he needed to "work on the articulation of his calling" before he would be given license to proceed. Suddenly my connect-the-dots process had mutated into a riddle. There was this idea of "calling," a mysteriously powerful "Vocations Committee," a process referred to as "discernment," and my father—hurt and angry because someone wasn't going to let him do this apparently generous and marvelous "thing" that he wanted to do. This thing that I still didn't understand.

The rules of the game changed. I extended my essay, and decided to try to figure out what this calling is that my father had been told he either didn't have or couldn't express. Why do some people have a calling and other people don't? What in the world was this discernment process that had special powers to identify who had a calling and who didn't? I wondered if it was at all like my own process, or whether it was some "way of knowing" that only people who know God have access to. My father knows God—why didn't he know whether or not he had a calling, if there were other people who did?

What is a calling? How does it manifest itself, and what does it mean? What is the difference between wanting to serve God and wanting, say, to be a fireman? By whose authority is a calling recognized or denied? Is the discernment process, whereby the church authority appoints a person to religious vocation, bureaucratic in nature, or is it mystical? Is it a combination of both? And if so, to what degree?

Everyone has access to the notion of being called, of feeling an impulse to something beyond simple will. Calling is a metaphysical state—whereas "the discernment process" is both the specific ritual by which the church appoints a leader and a description of the kind of knowledge by which each and every person recognizes his purpose in life, his "vocation." When that impulse concerns one person's individual relationship with divinity, however, perhaps not everyone has access to it.

If I were a world-class historian, I'd trace the idea of calling through the ages. In 1936 A. O. Lovejoy traced the idea of the "great chain of being" from Plato up to Darwin, and the result is a deliciously complex survey of cosmologies, featuring brilliant philosophers such as Leibniz and Spinoza and dripping with untranslated citations in Greek and French, promising even more insight into the history of ideas—if only I could read French and Greek. As it is, I'm painfully aware of not being a world-class historian, and with my methodology, it would probably take me another decade or so just to gain a comprehensive understanding of the intricacies of the Protestant Reformation—a period that would be critical to the story of calling. And I don't know then whether I'd be closer to solving my father's personal riddle. From what I've come to understand, that history of calling would begin with the ancient Israelites and run through the construction of the Catholic Church, into the Protestant Reformation, up to early America and the revival movement of the second Great Awakening, and then it would stop—the way Lovejoy stopped at evolution—because after that, "calling" sort of slithers away from the architecture of an idea and becomes a question of common usage. That common usage isn't, of course, divorced from history, and so my process takes account of history and common usage, of my father, and my own faculties of discernment. I certainly can't claim any superpowers where discernment is concerned, but I believe that whether or not everyone has a calling, no one would argue that understanding the idea of calling is reserved for a privileged few. And so my humble discernment is theoretically as good as anyone's.

I don't go to church for this book. That would be another book—a sort of "stranger in a strange land." The land of religion isn't my territory; it would be distracting and false for me to trespass upon it. I did go to the church—in this case, the Episcopal Church—and I asked everyone who would talk to me what they meant by calling, if they had one, if they knew someone who had one. I also asked them to tell me about how you get to be a priest, and about the "discernment process," sometimes called the "ordination process" or "vocation process," and often referred to as "the Process." The semantic inconsistency is not irrelevant, but I'm getting ahead of myself.

My father's calling didn't come to him in a vision or a bolt, but rather evolved over the course of a sixty-year tempestuous relationship with God. For faith is not only an intimate relationship with the invisible. It is also reconciliation with the visible, the actual, world and how one lives in it. A calling is, in effect, a description of that process of reconciliation between the visible and invisible, between what you believe and how you act on it. And discernment is not simply the moment in which one man or woman identifies the Spirit moving through another man or woman; it is the question that accompanies us through life: *what are we supposed to do now?*

PART ONE

My Father

Whoso would be a man,
must be a nonconformist.

—RALPH WALDO EMERSON

The Reverend Charles Ransom, "Father Chuck," is a compact man with neat, rugged features, flashing blue eyes, and a full head of soft white hair, which he wears in long waves over his ears. He's a little like a lion in a zoo—fierce, gentle, regal—the most popular attraction. A hobby actor with a magnetic personality and a TV evangelist's knack for dropping perfectly calibrated nuggets of the gospel into conversation, Father Chuck is a small-town charismatic.

Soon after my father joined Saint Paul's Episcopal Church in Mount Vernon, Ohio, just over twelve years ago, Chuck ascended to the pulpit. Their fast friendship is a pivotal element to my father's story. Typically, there are two "pivotal" priests in the narratives of people who have decided they want to become a priest. The first is a symbol: the definitive priest, often from childhood, the iconographic person whose sepia-toned image, bearing, and character means *priest*. He (or increasingly, she) is the unalterable portrait of the priesthood, an accumulation of qualities and interactions, and experience of church itself—an archetype whose feet, lodged deeply in the past, don't quite touch the ground. The second is a figure from the present, a tangible hero and confessor: a role model. This second figure is the stark illustration and reminder that priests aren't born—don't appear incarnate at the altar—priests are made. Priests are (of course) human, with an accumulation of their own experiences and ideas, steps and missteps, and system of choices, all of which they bring to bear on their relationships and on their vocation. This is the priest you can see yourself in, a glittering mirror reflection. (Women who grew up with an all-male clergy describe going back as adults—

post-Emancipation, Episcopal Church, 1981—to worship with a woman priest and finding that the experience of seeing someone who looked like them at the altar awakened vocational urges to the priesthood they never knew they had.) This priest makes it look attainable—the priest who gives you the confidence to admit aloud to yourself and the public world that you think of being a priest, too. It is the luster of the ideal priest combined with the real-life promise of the mentor priest that carries a person along the distinctive interior path to ordained ministry. Chuck is that second priest in my father's story.

Almost twenty years ago, soon after my parents divorced, my father joined a church in Westerville, a suburb of Columbus, Ohio. A retired military officer was serving at Saint Matthew's as a volunteer assistant rector, and my father noticed him and thought vaguely at the time that maybe he'd like to do something similar when he retired. A decade later, after he'd bought a house out in rural Ohio, Amish country, remarried, and started regularly attending Saint Paul's, he met and befriended Chuck Ransom. My father says that during this period he "became aware" that going to church was a "good thing" for him (my father's understated way of saying that the church had become central to his life), and out of that awareness started nursing the idea of becoming a deacon and assisting Father Chuck. He mentioned his thought "offhandedly" to Chuck—not realizing, perhaps, that "offhandedly" is exactly the way many people first declare aloud their interest in this peculiar vocation where hubris and humility knit hopelessly together. It's an admission of uncommon vulnerability, and the fear is that your confidant will burst out laughing and say something like "You? You could never be a priest!"

Of course, Chuck didn't laugh (they rarely do) and like many skilled in listening, he didn't push the matter, either. In the end, it was for my father to lead the discussion. So the discussion lapsed— perhaps my father felt shy—and some time passed before Chuck brought the idea up again, wondering what had ever become of it. It was Chuck who set the wheels in motion, encouraging my father and his second wife, Elizabeth (who'd also grown curious), in 1997 to attend a diocesan discernment day for the diaconate—a sort of informational session organized by the local church authorities to help people figure out if they should consider becoming a deacon. My father came out of the meeting convinced that the diaconate, with a focus on outreach and advocacy, wasn't for him and that his talents lay instead in liturgy and preaching—the stuff of the priesthood. Within a couple of years he launched into the slow process of pursuing ordination.

Although my father had grown comfortable enough with his aspirations to begin exploring them openly in his church, he didn't tell me (for reasons I'll explain presently) what he was up to. We started discussing the whole process only after he'd entered it. By the time I arrived in Ohio, armed with a steno pad and tape recorder, determined to write about this mysterious thing that had happened to my father, he'd already encountered a major obstacle. The committee of three that had been formed to review my father's application claimed to be unconvinced that he had a calling to the priesthood.

This was the harsher equivalent of someone laughing and saying, "You? You could never be a priest!" There was no laughing; and somehow the committee had managed by implication to invoke divine authority—for if someone is "called" to the priesthood, we assume he or she is called by God. They weren't questioning whether or not my father's intentions were good; they were questioning his whole divine mission. When I arrived so shortly after this decision, my father was distressed, surprised, and confused. He didn't know how to begin explaining it all to me—so instead he threw his hands up into the air and said, "You should really talk to Chuck."

When I started this project, I assumed that getting anyone in any church to talk to me on the record would be a struggle. I had the

impression that all church organizations fiercely guarded their privacy (the way all organizations do), and I imagined myself wran-
gling with Opus Dei (the clandestine order of the Catholic Church
that polices the Vatican) in order to penetrate the secrets of how
priests get made—a fantasy that was somewhat justified by the
pedophilia scandal just beginning to break in the news at the time.
Although my fears have since been proven entirely wrong by any
number of generous interlocutors, at this my very first interview,
Father Chuck instructed me to put away my notepad and tape
recorder—"It's too formal," he explained. "Makes me nervous." It's
a testament to how out of my element I was that I interpreted his
gesture as either reticence or a promise to reveal dirty secrets about
the church, though it was neither.

My father's story starts here, because Chuck is the first person he
told that he thought about becoming a priest, and because Chuck
encouraged him. Father Chuck brushed away the tape recorder not
because he wanted to reveal top-secret information off the record,
but because he wanted to talk to me about my dad in a way that
reflected the kind of relationship they shared—an intimate one. He
wanted to talk about my father's hopes and disappointments, his
struggle to understand where God fit into his life, his courage to face
his aspirations, his compassion, and the profound impact that
accepting a religious path had on my dad's self-awareness as he faced
his seventh decade. He wanted to talk to me about something at
once so intimate and so alien to my own experience that I didn't
even know it existed: my father's spiritual life.

So my introduction to my father's story didn't begin with a
screening process or an unsympathetic priest; nor did it begin with
a dreamy childhood ideal of the priesthood, a fanatical mother, or a
colorful visitation from the Holy Spirit. It began with a friendship
safe enough to allow my father to reveal himself.

Pure friendship, speculated the French philosopher Simone Weil
in her essay "Forms of the Implicit Love of God," is a kind of sacrament, born from the words of Christ—"Love one another." It is the

fourth kind of religious love, she believed, after that of love of religious ceremony, the beauty of the world, and our neighbor—all ways of expressing love for God. Friendship is a perfect reflection of the Trinity—as Christ says, "Where there are two or three gathered together in my name, there am I in the midst of them." The core of my father's spiritual life is embedded in his notion of spiritual community, which builds outward from these kinds of religious love. And borrowing from Weil's portrait of devotion, I began to know my father through his friendship with Chuck in an entirely new light—as a religious person. That revelation was the most important outcome of my late-morning, martini-laced lunch with Father Chuck, and entirely unexpected to me, a voyeur into what it means to be religious, a newcomer to my father's rocky inner life.

An equally unexpected and curious revelation came forth toward the end of our meeting, as the liquor fueled another kind of fire. Father Chuck admitted bafflement over the committee's negative response to my father's application for ordination, allowing me my first glimpse of the wealth of gray area surrounding the discernment process, the shadowy stuff that would come largely to define my own inquiry.

I had walked into this with an open mind and, paradoxically, with the fuzzy, under-the-surface impression that the world of organized religion dealt in absolutes. Surely this was the telltale mark of an outsider I wore on my forehead. It has been twenty years since I last came to any personal conclusions about the subject of religion, when, first reading the Bible by way of studying Hebrew in preparation for my bat mitzvah (yes, I had a bat mitzvah—an elaborate though glancing two-year religious education), I determined, upon reading Exodus, that God is illogical. He performs miracles for his Chosen People in the desert, and then smites them with fiery panache when they misunderstand. God's operation manual is whimsical and uncontrollable, I thought. There are evidently rules, but they are irrational. Who wants to be subject to such a system? The infernal period of adolescence is already wracked by similarly

incomprehensible rules. I abandoned religion definitively shortly thereafter, and didn't think more on it.

Suspended thus in the philosophy of a thirteen-year-old, I
approached Father Chuck with the naïve assumption that the reasons
for my father's rejection were quantifiable and couched in absolutes.
To my astonishment, Chuck instead described how he'd gone to the
bishop of Ohio, a friend, the Right Reverend J. Clark Grew II (now
retired), and said, "You're really missing out on something special if
you don't meet this man." The response he received was something
along the lines of "You may be right, but my hands are tied."

Not only was I surprised to learn that Chuck shared my father's
confusion and sense of injustice, I was also taken aback at the notion
that the bishop—a bishop—could in one fell swoop admit there
might have been a miscarriage, and not be willing or interested in
rectifying it. This seemed neither absolutist nor authoritative.

Now, after having interviewed several bishops and church officials
myself, I understand Bishop Grew's reply more completely. There's a
process in place; it's based on years of experience, reams of surveys, a
comprehensive interpretation of doctrine, and subject to correction at
regular intervals on a churchwide basis. Though not ironclad, the system works only if you don't go around perforating it with exceptions.

Father Chuck would not have been the first "sponsoring" priest
to go to the bishop in anger. Despite the fact that sponsors are
embedded "in the system," they are in a unique position with regard
to bringing up new priests. Their recommendation and support are
required to start an applicant in the discernment process—but from
the moment the process starts, it's assumed that the sponsoring rector is "too close" to the applicant to be objective, and so the sponsors
are unceremoniously cut out of the loop. One church higher-up
later explained to me that sponsors "always have the most complicated relationship with the process." Her office makes a point of
reminding priests that when they put someone forward for discernment, "to some extent your own process of coming to the ministry
is going to be brought to mind—and to some extent, a person that

you strongly believe in is a part of you. So when they're turned down, you feel like you're being turned down, too."

But I didn't know all that then. I was impressed that Father Chuck could be (was allowed to be) angry at the system he was part of. I didn't know that the church could be thought of as a system that occasionally misfires—especially by someone who is part of the church. I thought that church was an all-or-nothing deal. "Of course we make mistakes!" a bishop reiterated to me almost a year later, emphasizing the validity of her point with impeccable composure. "Otherwise, we'd have to say we believe that the Inquisition was a good thing."

Sitting across the table from Father Chuck in the Village Inn, though, I had yet to learn how grounded in a theory of community that system is, and yet to learn a bishop's place in, and responsibility to, that community. The system wasn't absolutist, monolithic, or even mystic, but something else entirely. A something else that included a process whereby a small group of strangers were given the authority and legitimacy to evaluate—on behalf, somehow, of God—whether or not my father's earnest and quite remarkable offer to minister had divine approval.

The model discernment meeting opens with a prayer, followed by several minutes of silence (a manual suggests dimming the lights during the silence to set a mood of stillness and listening), after which the subject of the meeting, the person being discerned, makes some kind of opening remarks, explaining why he or she is there. I asked my father if his meeting followed that model, and whether he'd said an opening prayer, too. There was a prayer, but he didn't lead it. "That wasn't the mood at all," he answered. "I got the impression they would have been horrified at the idea of me leading a prayer." He paused, then added, "But I had one ready." How would my father have opened his own discernment meeting? "Something along the lines," he said, "of 'O Lord, may my mind be reconciled with yours, that I will know and understand and accept whatever will be.'"

For the record (because the record starts here), that prayer is a riff on Thomas à Kempis's invocation for the disciple in the *Imitation of Christ*: "Lord, give me heavenly wisdom, that I may learn to seek You in all things and find You, to relish You in all things and love You, and to understand all things as they are and as You in Your wisdom have ordained them."

In the early fall of 1999, my father filed the paperwork with the diocese of Ohio that formally initiated his application to the discernment process for ordained ministry. That first step involved submitting a spiritual history and statement, and obtaining the sponsorship of a priest. Chuck Ransom was my father's sponsor. Next, an official from the diocesan staff, a canon to the ordinary, formed a vocations committee on his behalf, made up of parishioners and a priest selected from churches in his district but not from his own congregation—the idea is to involve people who can appreciate local concerns but who have never met the candidate and so don't come to the process with preconceived notions. The vocations committee is charged with discerning a person's suitability for the ordained ministry, and with their approval, the candidate will move on to the next step—evaluation on a diocesan level.

My father's vocations committee was made up of a priest (the "convener") and two parishioners in good standing. The first of three formal discernment meetings was called for November. It was held in the rectory office of the priest leading the process. Over the course of that meeting, which did not open with my father's prayer, he was asked a series of questions about his motives. Some of the questions were drawn from the instruction pamphlet provided by the diocese to vocations committees, and might have included questions such as "Who has had an impact on your decision to seek ordination, and why?" or "What role has the church as a community had on your decision to seek ordination?" or "How is your public life a reflection of your faith?" Other questions directly related to the written material my father provided to the committee in his application, and focused on his work as a professor at Ohio State University, how he related that to his sense of calling, and what, specifically and personally, had brought him to pursue ordination.

My father is sixty years old this year, six foot two, and about 255 pounds. He is an imposing presence, with his broad Slavic features, almost vulgar, almost noble in their distinctiveness. A bumpy wine-colored hemangioma cuts across the right side of his face—it's the first thing you notice and the first thing you forget about him. Though his hair is still the same ashen brown slick it has always been, the whiskers I've never seen him without have gone snowy gray. For the first thirty years of his life he was a gawky, hollow sort of man, while now he's robust and has the appetite and stature of a farmer. He shattered his ankle once in a freakishly violent slip on the ice and they put an iron pin in his leg, for which he walks with not a limp so much as a list. He's got a sciatic hip and so rather than standing, he leans—a pose that for many years I mistook as an affect of teaching, the sort of passive swagger of someone who knows more than you do. He's unapologetically generous with his knowledge and unless you mistake it for trivia, the vastness and flexibility of what he knows is a constant reminder that conversation is a kind of grace. He figured out how to read in perhaps as many as fifteen languages, and plays at dropping grossly mispronounced foreign words into his sentences. He wears reading glasses from Kmart of an approximate magnification, the arms of which are invariably too short to reach from the bridge of his nose to the back of his ear. For years he walked with his head thrown back, his face up toward the sky. He didn't look where he was going, nor did he care who he passed. People just assumed he was deep in thought and shouldn't be disturbed. This peripatetic style was a way of privileging his musings, keeping on blinders to the mundane landscape around him. Now he leads with his belly rather than his chin when he walks, looks you in the eye as you approach, and refers to those solipsistic years in which he carried his head in the clouds in terms of regret.

There's something so earthbound about my father—the limp, the hemangioma, the way he always smells like pimientos, brewer's yeast, and Ivory soap—that it's hard for me to associate him at all with the transcendental. The idea of him wending heavenward on a spiritual quest strikes me as precarious and completely unlikely.

What *did* bring my father, a musician, a hobby farmer, a parent of four, an active member of his church, to that unfamiliar room in a shady country parish, to sit around a table with a small group of strangers to whom he was expected to offer up for stark evaluation his spiritual journey? What marked the passage from one stage in his life story, one version of his identity, to this entirely new one? What brought him from here to there?

The great twentieth-century spiritual autobiography *The Seven Storey Mountain,* by Thomas Merton, begins:

> On the last day of January 1915, under the sign of the Water Bearer, in a year of a great war, and down in the shadow of some French mountains on the borders of Spain, I came into the world. Free by nature, in the image of God, I was nevertheless prisoner of my own violence and my own selfishness, in the image of the world into which I was born. That world was the picture of Hell, full of men like myself, loving God and yet hating Him; born to love Him, living instead in fear and hopeless self-contradictory hungers.

My father was born in January, twenty-six years later, on the eve of a second great war, in the shadow of the Cross Island Parkway in the immigrant neighborhood of Rosedale, Queens, on the border of Nassau County, which was open country then. Unlike Merton, whose bohemian parents had no religion, my father was born into the Catholic faith. And though he might characterize the Christianity of his youth as compromised by idolatry, lo-fi heresy, and a cold, monarchical papacy, religion in his family was practiced with passion and sincerity. The youngest male of five children (the oldest of whom died of scarlet fever in 1934), my father was—according to the then typical second-generation immigrant model—destined for the Roman Catholic priesthood. He would be his mother's "sacrifice" and salvation. The priesthood then was among the most noble of ambitions. It was "the highest life a boy could aspire to," explains one priest who was brought up during the same period. "It meant being a real Christian, it meant being called to serve Christ and his church, it meant being respected and revered almost as Christ himself."[1]

The diversity of my father's childhood neighborhood is probably unreproducible today, except in an airport or in the green-card line at the federal building. He grew up surrounded by Irish, Italians, Poles, Germans, Jews, Norwegians, and a very few fellow Ukrainians. That world, far from the bombs and the genocide in Asia and Europe, wasn't the picture of hell, but of industry, scrappiness, discipline, and the melting pot—the seedbed of the American dream. The "fear and hopeless self-contradictory hungers" that Merton wrote of— perhaps the fruit of that same American dream—were yet to come for that generation.

Sometimes I'll tease my father for being a dyed-in-the-wool city kid who bought the farm. Where he lives now, in the rolling hills of eastern Ohio, a fifty-mile commute to work in the "big city" (Columbus), couldn't be more different from Queens, New York, where he was born and bred. He always debates the premise of my teasing, which is apparently wrong. We're not city folk at all, he tells me, we're farmers from way back. Moreover Queens was New York City, he explains, but it was as rural as you could get back then. Booth Tarkington or Mark Twain "sounded familiar to me when I was a kid," he says. "I knew what they were talking about." His rustic sensibilities were fed by visits to his grandparents' Connecticut farm. They were dairy farmers, originally from Galicia in western Ukraine, who found their way to Lebanon, Connecticut, which still had dirt roads in the 1940s. His grandfather used draft horses to draw a sickle bar mower across his land. My father says that when he looks across the street from his house now and sees the Amish farmers, they look just like his grandfather, except his grandfather wore white and the Amish wear black.

Memories of preurban New York aside, my father is also taking into consideration our true rural ancestry when he rebuffs my teasing. For generations extending back into the centuries, his families on both sides were hearty, provincial Ukrainian peasants. My paternal grandfather, Hryhoriy Mykhaylovich Prokhorovich, who arrived at Ellis Island in 1923 (and was renamed George Michael Proctor), hailed from a town in the Poltava district outside of Kiev called Bolotnytsa, a town so small it doesn't appear on most maps—the name itself means "muddy place." According to my father's formulation, the fifty or so cumulative years that he and his family lived in the city, plus the eight or so that I personally have added onto the Proctor legacy, do not a family tradition make. Effectively, every generation of my paternal family (myself included) has migrated. The Proctors are probably better described as being of the Diaspora than of either the soil or the asphalt. To wit, my grandfather published in 1925 a chapbook of poetry written in Ukrainian and composed while he was living in exile in Turkey. The book's title is *Na Chuzhyni,* which my father translates as "In a Foreign Land." The poem called "Tuha za Rodynoyu" ("Homesickness") opens: "It is already the fifth year that I have been traveling, that I have been wandering the wide world. I am the prodigal son. What am I looking for? What am I helplessly seeking?"

But my father's real formulation—if you'll bear with the mounting digression—goes deeper: born in 1941, he is over half a century old in 2000. That means he's lived through Roosevelt, Truman, Eisenhower, de Gaulle, the Cold War. "I know what Eisenhower looked like," he explains. "I can hear de Gaulle's voice." But then he calculates backward. What if he lived the same fifty-nine years in the other direction from 1941? That takes him back to 1882: one lifetime of Gregory Proctor carries you to Grover Cleveland, Brahms, Wagner, Marx, Darwin. If you repeat those fifty-nine years back, Beethoven is still alive. My grandfather lived seventy-nine years and was born in

1895. If you take his life span backward from 1895, that brings you to 1816—a few years before Haydn was on his deathbed—just one person's life span ahead of my grandfather. Go back again, and you get to Bach and the Baroque period. "Lay people's lives end-to-end," suggests my father, "and twenty-six people brings you back to Jesus. How much farther back to Ra, the sun king? Not a long time when you look at it in terms of historical spans that are comprehensible because you lived through them. It's kind of scary," he says, "to think it wasn't that many thousands of years ago when we were crawling around."

My father's return to the soil, in other words, is more than just nostalgia for his grandparents' way of life. "Sometimes to move away is to return," he tells me; "that's what happened in this case. Other times I've moved away just to run away, but sometimes to move away is to return to the foundations." It might be different, says my father, if we were from Mount Vernon, Ohio, where the names on the gravestones in the cemetery are the names of people who still live there.

For an essentially rootless family such as ours (scattered by politics, economics, divorce, and mobility), it makes more sense to take the long view of history. It makes much more sense to me personally because, if with religion he's going back to *his* foundation, I'm of course left wondering what in the world my foundation is supposed to be. Can noncommittal even be a foundation? What am I supposed to be able to return to when I'm sixty? Whereas if I think of my foundation in terms of the human project, I am in fact not entirely untethered.

Rabbi Ismar Schorsch, an eminent figure in Conservative Judaism, recently spoke to me about the passing down of religion from one generation to the next. He was speaking specifically of Judaism and Jewish identity, but his model transposes because the subject is ritual, or practice. Certain fundamental values can be communicated or taught as can history, according to Schorsch, but religion—with a unique set of "theological" values—is harder to pass on. Hard to teach

children, harder still to teach grandchildren. Religious practice, rituals are "vessels," explains Schorsch, that contain and give shape to
these values, making it possible to pass them from generation to
generation.

What my father has to pass along, what he has passed along, is
very different for me and my sister, who were brought up without
religion, than it is for my half brother and half sister, who are being
raised in the Episcopal Church. My secular, academic upbringing
privileged reason—by no means an unpleasant lot. Many formerly
religious people and atheists alike joyfully embrace the clarity, the
legible justice, of a reasonable world. Consider the firm, logical
lucidity of Mary McCarthy's ex-Catholicism in *Memories of a Catholic
Girlhood:*

> As a lapsed Catholic, I do not trouble myself about the possibility
> that God may exist after all. If He exists (which seems to me more
> than doubtful), I am in for a bad time in the next world, but I am
> not going to bargain to believe in God in order to save my soul.
> Pascal's wager—the bet he took with himself that God existed,
> even though this could not be proved by reasoning—strikes me as
> too prudential. What had Pascal to lose by behaving as if God
> existed? Absolutely nothing, for there was no counter-Principle to
> damn him in case God didn't. For myself, I prefer not to play it so
> safe, and I shall never send for a priest or recite an Act of Contri-
> tion in my last moments. I do not mind if I lose my soul for all
> eternity. If the kind of God exists Who would damn me for not
> working out a deal with Him, then that is unfortunate. I should
> not care to spend eternity in the company of such a person.[2]

My father would agree with McCarthy, even though he is no longer
a "lapsed Catholic" but a churchgoer. He is fiercely contrary to
wagers and contracts where salvation is concerned. The quid-pro-
quo Catholicism that McCarthy describes resembles the religion
that my father was raised with, and he, too, rejected that version of
faith. His first love, on the other hand, was ritual—the same ritual

that Rabbi Schorsch describes, the same ritual that he has returned to in the high Protestantism of the Episcopal Church. His Catholic education was shaped by that love. Mass was said in Latin when he was an altar boy; as a seminarian in his teens, he sang the offices a cappella according to the ancient rules of plainsong. Antiquity was alive, a vital part of his expression of faith as a child.

Today when he speaks of salvation, he locates it in the spirit of community and tradition that the church offers. "Heck, I would go to church even if I didn't believe in God, because it's important to uphold the traditions—it's critical to the survival of a society to stay in touch with its tradition." He recognizes the church as a moral center, a firmament of communicable values that stands in opposition to the relative anarchy of a world defined by free will. "I think it's more important to have continuity, respect for the way things always have been done, than almost anything else," says my father. The center of his church's service is Holy Communion, the celebration of the Eucharist, representing a union of saints and believers joined together in the ritual of sacrament—the outward symbol of invisible grace. This celebration ties us back in time to Jesus, to the people you're part of, he explains. "That's the religion." World without end. Such ideas, with their emphasis on continuity, living tradition, and an ethical code, are central to my father's spirituality today, and perhaps make sense only when measured against his past—and mine, too.

That said, my father's return to religion is hard to reconcile with my formation. It was by his instigation that I was brought up without it. By his instruction, I was raised without God. An educated secularist, I'm left with a voyeur's romanticized vision of faith, a tourist's flirtation with ritual, an amorphous sense of God's will, a historical account of what Darwin meant to Christianity, and insufficient intellectual apparatus for navigating the concept of Jesus. And though there are questions of doctrine I can comprehend (or apprehend) in abstract terms, the history and governance of the church is complicated, and often too political to be abstract. I could say that my father set me on a path to godlessness—and then abandoned me there. For I wasn't taught to think in terms of right and wrong, but in terms of defendable and undefendable. My father's church is the body of Christ, the family of God, the pillar of the community. I was brought up to think of the family as expendable, and the father as unavailable. "Don't do that to kids!" my father says now. "Just don't do it."

The less things are part of a continuum, the easier it is to witness them. Even one's own life can take on a theatrical shape, organizing itself into scenes and acts. Time between events passes elliptically when you are not wholly part of the action. Because of my parents' separation, I never had the luxury of a continuous relationship with my father, the regularity of daily life that muddles the distinctions between one event and the next. Our encounters over the years have been so sporadic that each one distinguishes itself, each a precious piece of some borderless puzzle.

Ideally, then, my father's path back to church should be traceable—for me, watching from afar. Each step should have the bold delineation of a rung on a ladder—or a trail of bread crumbs. In truth it's more like the ancient musical notation for the Gregorian chants in my father's *Liber usualis,* where the fat, square notes pile vertically, or slur diagonally across the staff in the broad stroke of a quill pen, and you have to learn the code in order to know which note follows which, and when.

When I was thirteen I had a bat mitzvah and he stood with my mother behind me as I chanted from the Torah in Hebrew. When I ran away from home at fifteen and bottomed out, I ran to him. When I was sixteen, he bought me my first car, a metallic pea green 1972 Skylark coupe with a 450 cc engine and a white vinyl roof. On my eighteenth birthday, he brought me to Family Court in Columbus and I signed papers attesting that I was an adult, so that he would be formally released from financial responsibility for me. When I was twenty-two, he remarried. In the long decade since then, I've driven out to Ohio once or twice a year for a week to visit with him, Elizabeth, and my little brother and sister.

Those visits to the cluttered farmhouse in the washed-out yellow countryside of central Ohio stand out from the rest of my life. It's not my home; I didn't grow up there. I'm detached and rootless in every way. I'm even ageless there—an adult in language, responsibilities, and opinion; a child, vying with everyone else for Daddy's attention. I devour detective novels I would never have time to look at in my real life, watch children's movies on the VCR with my little sister, and cook and clean because I'm accustomed to being too busy, not aimless, and I talk and talk, trying to fit a year's worth of relationship into five days. I tag along with my father on any kind of random errand—to the farm equipment store, to the vet, to the nearest bank machine (twenty miles down the road), to get milk—just so that I can sit next to him in the car, feel him near my left shoulder radiating his peculiar musty heat, and stare out the window at the unfamiliar landscape that he sees every day and probably knows by heart.

Somewhere along this stepping-stone relationship, we became together two individuated adults. That sounds funny. My father has been an "adult" for a long time—just not from my perspective. He was twenty-nine years old when I was born—I was a baby then, and a child, and a teenager, of course—and for all of that time, he was "Daddy," a blustery, brilliant enigma, an occasional parent and perennial point of reference. But he wasn't an adult in my world, and now he is. I understand that better than ever since I passed the age he was when I was born, and today I can comprehend fully in some strange perversion of my way of seeing the world how he's grown as much as I have since then.

There is my father beating the high score at Space Invaders in the game room of a mall across the highway from a depressing apartment complex in the outskirts of Columbus while my sister and I hover jealously nearby. It's 1982; we go through packs of quarters meant for the laundry, but can never beat him. Then there is an ellipsis, change of scenery. Eighteen years later, there is my father in the function room of a church in a shady country town, sitting around a table with a retired schoolteacher, a merchandising representative, and a priest—none of whom he knows terribly well. In the silence before the conversation begins, the four of them pray that God will guide them, that God will help them all to discern whether or not my father has a calling to the priesthood.

George Proctor was an adventurer as a young man and had lived nine lives before he even arrived at Ellis Island in 1923. He fought in the civil wars that followed the 1917 Revolution, dodged an assassin's bullet, sailed the world—putting down in Siberia, Odessa, Greece, Hoboken, Constantinople—and survived two shipwrecks before he decided to abandon the merchant marine to emigrate to America after a fortune-teller predicted that he wouldn't live through a third shipwreck. In New York, he worked in a research laboratory, taking care of the animals, and was always very active in the Ukrainian community. He was a poet, newspaper columnist, actor, and theatrical director; he contributed enormously (and with the scantest acknowledgment) to the first Ukrainian/English dictionary. He was an Esperanto activist, and in a closet in Ohio, my father still keeps the reams of notes he was preparing for a Ukrainian/Esperanto dictionary. He was instrumental in building the Orthodox church on Second Avenue in Manhattan. Out in Queens, however, there were no Ukrainian Orthodox churches, and though he was a "strong believer," according to my father, George preferred not to go to church at all rather than worship with the papists in their language and tradition.

My grandmother Nancy (baptized Anastasia) was a devout Catholic and famously seized every opportunity to baptize my sister and me. I was baptized seventeen times (eighteen by some accounts) along with my little sister under Nancy's ministrations (a demonstrated lack of faith in the process itself that my father equates with heresy). It wasn't that she was really terrified our innocent souls, Jewish on my mother's side, would be seized by the devil, but she did think it wouldn't hurt to make sure. She stole us away to the church whenever she could, secreted a little vial of holy water in her purse, and on one occasion pronounced my two-year-old sister as my "sponsor," in other words, my godmother.

Nancy, unlike her husband, was Ukrainian Catholic, a Uniate, as were most of the Ukrainian immigrants in New York at the time, who hailed principally from Galicia. The Ukrainian Catholic liturgy is almost identical to a Roman Catholic mass: though they accept the pope, they are theologically divided over whether the Holy Ghost proceeds from the Father, or from the Father and the Son. My grandmother felt at home in the Roman Catholic Church—the closest to her home out in Queens. My father was raised in this Latin-rite church. He served as an altar boy, acolyte, and choir member. His last year of high school he entered seminary with the Friars of the Atonement (Graymoor), in Montour Falls, New York, a Franciscan order that originated in the Anglican Church but turned to Rome in the early twentieth century. The order had attracted him because it professed to understand all Christians as part of one body—that is, the oneness of the body of the church. In the spirit of ecumenism, the seminary chapel had a mosaic design set into the floor under the altar describing a crucifix and a Star of David intertwined. At seminary, my father received his minor orders (as acolyte, exorcist, lector, porter), and he took the name of Saint John Chrysostom.

After only half a year, however, he left the seminary, bitterly disappointed by what he perceived as an endemic attitude of divisiveness, precisely contrary to what had attracted him to the order in the first place. A predominantly Irish-Catholic population, the students divided themselves into camps—the Irish Catholics and the "other guys." My father was with the Italians, Germans, and Slavs in the "other guys" group. The animosity was ferocious enough, he remembers, to nurture spies and counteragents running between the camps. The Irish Catholics claimed a moral majority, and the other guys were troublemakers, "anarchists" by default. The behavior was entirely unpriestly, explains my father, and the competition and politicking was antithetical to the monastic environment. "It was like *Lord of the Flies* in there!" he says of his fellow seminarians.

Entering seminary in the Catholic Church was then, and remained until 1981, a very different process than it is now. It was assumed that by mere virtue of their application, boys felt a genuine call to the priesthood. My father remembers that the hallways of his Catholic high school were papered with recruitment pamphlets, emblazoned with the military-style motto "Are you prepared to answer the call?" His mother would leave similar pamphlets on his pillow every night. The seminary entrance exam was nothing more complicated than an informational interview with the dean of students, at which "discernment" as used today was hardly the program.

In his book *The Changing Face of the Priesthood,* Donald B. Cozzens, formerly president-rector of Saint Mary Seminary and Graduate School of Theology in Cleveland, a Catholic institution, candidly contrasts today's admission process with that of less than a generation ago. He describes his own interview in 1957 as "brief and superficial" by comparison; it would fall under the now denigrated category of discernment referred to as "having lunch with the bishop."

The "ordinary drill" required for admission to priestly studies today includes letters of recommendation, psychiatric and psychological assessments, criminal record checks, standardized tests, as well as a series of interviews. He admits that the data reviewed in the admissions process is both "considerable" and "essential," but explains:

> We still struggle, looking for signs of the reality and mystery of grace as well as for indications that the candidate has the temperaments and personal strength to meet the demands of priestly ministry. Is there evidence of a genuine aptitude for priesthood? Does the applicant possess the magnanimity required for the covenant commitment at the heart of priestly service? Is he spiritually mature and intellectually capable of preaching God's word with conviction and imagination? Will the candidate under consideration aspire to be a compassionate, enthusiastic servant-leader of God's people?[3]

When I visited a Catholic seminary in Weston, Massachusetts, not long ago, I was almost startled by the contagious sense of goodwill and community pervading the cafeteria at lunch. Anything but *Lord of the Flies*. The tables were filled with smiling, gracious men who seemed—as far as I could tell as I circulated—to be contentedly discussing their theology lessons. Today's intense and broad screening process not only values compassion and commitment, but also seems to teach it at some level. Perhaps if such a process had been in place in my father's day, he would have found more camaraderie. But it's a different matter and a difficult thing to project forty years back if you take into account (which you must) the environment of the Catholic Church in those years.

The Catholic Church was in fact thriving in the 1950s when my father was in seminary. Religion was on an upswing in postwar America, with statistics for church membership estimated anywhere from 60 to 73 percent of the adult population during the Eisenhower administration.[4] These are particularly startling statistics in light of the massive exodus from the Catholic Church soon after, in the wake of the Second Vatican Council. Ordinations to the priesthood are half of what they were at midcentury, the population of women in religious life has dropped 40 percent, and only 1 percent of Catholic nuns today is under thirty.[5] In other words, the church my father knew changed definitively and dramatically very soon after he left it.

The church my father grew up in was dominated by Irish-style Catholicism. The English-speaking Irish, who'd flooded into America in the early nineteenth century, held a kind of consolidated cultural power—which was only ever significantly challenged by the German Catholics in the early twentieth century in a tug-of-war over whether the American Catholic Church should be an immigrant church, populated by a variety of distinct nationalities, or an entirely assimilated New World church. Some of the factionalism that my father experienced—between the English-speaking Irish kids and the "immigrants"—may very well have been residual ripples of this debate.

"The Irish," wrote Richard Hofstadter,

> taking advantage of their knowledge of English and their prior
> arrival, constructed the network of political machines and
> Church hierarchy through which most Catholic arrivals could
> make a place for themselves in American life. And more than any
> other group, the Irish put their stamp on American Catholicism;
> consequently the American Church absorbed little of the impres-
> sive scholarship of German Catholicism or the questioning intel-
> lectualism of the French Church, and much more of the harsh
> Puritanism and fierce militancy of the Irish clergy.[6]

My father describes the intellectual mood of this dominant brand of
Catholicism as unnuanced and vaguely tyrannical, likening it to the
fervor depicted in James Joyce's *Portrait of the Artist as a Young Man.*

Religion stakes its claim early in a child's formation. Based on
rhythm and ritual, certain practices become as engrained, natural,
and *essential* as brushing your teeth or shaking someone's hand that
you've just met. Writing about his Catholic childhood in the 1940s,
Garry Wills describes the deep bond of ritual:

> The habits of childhood are tenacious, and Catholicism was first
> experienced by us as a vast set of intermeshed childhood habits—
> prayers offered, heads ducked in unison, crossings, chants, chris-
> tenings, grace at meals; beads, altar, incense, candles; nuns in the
> classroom alternately too sweet and too severe, priests garbed
> black on the street and brilliant at the altar; churches lit and dark-
> ened, clothed and stripped to the rhythm of liturgical recur-
> rences; the crib in winter, purple Februaries, and lilies in the
> spring; confession as intimidation and comfort (comfort, if noth-
> ing else, that the intimidation was survived), communion as
> revery and discomfort; faith as a creed, and the creed as cate-
> chism, Latin responses, salvation by rote, all things going to a
> rhythm, memorized, old things always returning, eternal in that
> sense, no matter how transitory.[7]

My father, too, was steeped in this ritual, embraced by the familiar comfort of its seemingly eternal continuity. He loved his church, loved it deeply enough to be disappointed by it. It wasn't the tyranny (or reassurance) of ritual that drove my father out—as it might drive out more adventurous or individualistic souls. Rather, he became irrevocably frustrated by the breakdown between the ideas expressed in the liturgy, the ideology of the church, and the expressed ideas of lived Catholicism—in his words, the tacit understanding, for example, that "heaven is split in two. Jesus owns one half, Mary owns the other."

The academic work at seminary was in fact a significant improvement over his Catholic day school, which was run by the Christian Brothers, a French order of strict anti-intellectuals. The kids at my school, jokes my father, "were all destined to become policemen . . . or criminals." With his interest in music and languages, my father was an anomaly from the outset. He hadn't, however, expected to continue being an anomaly at Graymoor, where the second-generation immigrant children who knew other languages from their parents were disparaged by the Irish contingent at the seminary—they were chided for being un-American.

Midcentury Catholicism is a highly lampooned period—from the brilliantly bitter, bumbling priests of J. F. Powers's novels, to the tragic stories of the Magdalene laundries, to the image that historian John Cornwell provides in *Hitler's Pope* of Pius XII, all alone in his garret late at night trying to exorcise Hitler. Religion here is often portrayed as cruel, greedy, power-hungry, and afflicted by the symptoms of its own desperation.

Some of the most cartoonish aspects of this kind of religiosity are the fruit of literal and extremely enthusiastic readings of medieval devotional texts like Thomas à Kempis's *Imitation of Christ,* which enjoins the religious to cast aside all earthly attachments and affections and to cultivate an impression of the self as the lowliest creature of creation: "Direct your anger against yourself and do not allow puffed-up pride to get its hold on you. Show that you are humble and lowly by permitting everyone to walk over you and trample you underfoot *like mud in the street.* . . . What have you to complain about, you *shallow man?* You soiled sinner, what answer can you give those who criticize you, since you have ever so frequently offended God and many times over have deserved hell?"[8] Kempis promoted a kind of anti-intellectualism that, like many varieties of anti-intellectualism, saw the movement of the mind exclusively in terms of the pursuit of status— "Certainly, when Judgment Day comes we shall not be asked what books we have read, but what deeds we have done, we shall not be asked how well we have debated, but how devoutly we have lived."[9]

In *A Portrait of the Artist as a Young Man,* there is a conversation between the protagonist, Stephen Dedalus, and his college dean that exemplifies just how stultifying such literalism can be in the context of Christian teaching:

—For my purpose [explains Stephen], I can work on at present by the light of one or two ideas of Aristotle and Aquinas . . . I need them only for my own use and guidance until I have done something for myself by their light. If the lamp smokes or smells I shall try to trim it. If it does not give light enough I shall sell it and buy another.

—Epictetus also had a lamp, said the dean, which was sold for a fancy price after his death. It was the lamp he wrote his philosophical dissertations by. You know Epictetus?

—An old gentleman, said Stephen coarsely, who said that the soul is very like a bucketful of water.

—He tells us in his homely way, the dean went on, that he put an iron lamp before a statue of one of the gods and that a thief stole the lamp. What did the philosopher do? He reflected that it was in the character of the thief to steal and determined to buy an earthen lamp next day instead of the iron lamp.

A smell of molten tallow came up from the dean's candlebutts and fused itself in Stephen's consciousness with the jingle of the words, bucket and lamp and lamp and bucket. The priest's voice too had a hard jingling tone. Stephen's mind halted by instinct, checked by the strange tone and the imagery and by the priest's face which seemed like an unlit lamp or a reflector hung in a false focus. What lay behind it or within it? A dull torpor of the soul or the dullness of the thundercloud, charged with intellection and capable of the gloom of God?

—I meant a different kind of lamp, sir, said Stephen.[10]

Through the Narrow Gate, religious historian Karen Armstrong's caustic memoir of convent life during the same pre–Vatican II period that my father was at seminary, depicts a particularly harsh environment of endemic anti-intellectualism and cruelty—conceived of in a literalist mode and designed to thwart independence of spirit and capacity for nuance. Here, the young novices were forbidden to form relationships, to read, to talk; they were denigrated and cajoled into self-flagellation; they were bullied into a state of utter disconnect from their bodies and from their minds.

Armstrong, who entered the convent as a very young sixteen-year-old, had been first attracted to the simple purity and apparent serenity of the nuns who taught at her Catholic day school. Her youthful faith was ignited early on by the frightening experience of almost losing her little sister to a dangerous illness, and not a little sense that God had intervened on her sister's behalf, so she felt that she was in some kind of debt. And by her own account, the decision was also something of a fugue from the frightening world of adolescence, as well as adolescent rebellion. Her parents considered her vocation to be a tragedy—not a gift—and pleaded with her not to go. After three years, physically and emotionally debilitated, intellectually stifled, Armstrong fled the order.

Seminarians fared quite a bit better than the nuns of the same period—women in traditional Catholicism simply represent the flesh incarnate, in all of its dirty legacy and horror. The historian Garry Wills, who was also a novice, training to be a priest, in a Jesuit seminary in the early 1950s, and who also defected, offers some insight into what challenges a young man like my father would eventually have faced. Entering his second year of priestly studies, Wills balked at the prospect of taking two specific vows: chastity and obedience—distinct vows that each presented very different but significant obstacles to a young Wills.

As for the first, Wills apprehended the inherent loneliness of celibacy and wondered quite simply whether he—who had grown up in a large Catholic family and whose primary experience of religion was in community—was personally capable of negotiating such an isolated lifestyle. We've barely begun to appreciate the psychological nuances that make a celibate life not only possible but successful, explains Donald Cozzens. *Confusion,* he writes, is the principle reaction of a celibate to that fundamental human impulse for companionship. "Should a priest come to believe that he has 'fallen in love,'" writes Cozzens, "he easily concludes that he is in the grips of a vocation crisis, and in a certain sense he is. But the real question is not whether to leave and marry, rather it is to discern if he and his beloved can commit to a celibate friendship. In other words, is he experiencing a vocation crisis or an intimacy crisis?"[11] Writing shortly before the pedophilia scandal exploded in the Catholic Church, Cozzens goes on to anticipate the issue that would consume discussions of a celibate priesthood: "For the priest convinced that his truth is indeed the priesthood, crises of intimacy sometimes lead to exploitative relationships with a number of women or men."[12]

Garry Wills, who did fall in love and marry shortly after leaving the Jesuits, was stymied to an equal degree by the physical submissiveness of celibacy and the intellectual submissiveness of obedience. The syllabus of a Jesuit education as he describes it was incredibly categorical. Students "learned" spirituality (blind faith) before theology, which was at that point considered a *lesser* branch of religious knowledge. On this subject, Cozzens writes,

Religious obedience has quite an exceptional dignity. In its absolute form, we owe religious obedience to God alone. But just as God's revelation comes to us only when mediated, so too, the truths of faith reach us only when mediated. The meaning of faith and the authenticity of religious obedience confront a crisis when religious authorities . . . demand all too much submission to an obscure package of doctrines.[13]

Today my father claims that he could have "gone either way" on the celibacy issue. At sixteen years old it never occurred to him that it would ever present a problem—and certainly not a crisis. He loved the monastic rule of life, and celibacy was an inextricable part of that. Furthermore, he explains that celibacy was attractive, and easy to contemplate within the monastic environment of the seminary. After attending single-sex elementary and secondary schools before going to seminary, the all-male environment was actually more familiar than threatening. It was almost a year and a half after leaving seminary before my father began to feel comfortable in the normal, public world. He didn't start dating until he was a sophomore in college.

But there was a siren beckoning my father away from seminary: music. Studying the organ and medieval music notation, he had grown increasingly interested in music scholarship—an interest that quickly began to extend far beyond what was available at Graymoor. That quickening passion, combined with his disappointment over the splintered community, fed his decision to leave.

The hardest part of leaving, he remembers, was convincing his mother that it wasn't a tragedy.

He put himself through college at the Mannes College of Music on Rockefeller loans and by working as a cashier and stock boy at King Kullen. He was an industrious, even brilliant student and won a fellowship to the master's program at Queens College, CUNY. It was during that period, in his mid-twenties, that he met my mother.

Religion was still central to his sense of himself when they married, in 1965—and central to my mother's conception of their marriage. They celebrated two separate nuptials, first in a Jewish ceremony with a rabbi, and then with a Uniate priest. The wedding diptych was not merely a gesture toward ecumenism, but a way of celebrating the equal importance of the two separate faiths they were bringing to the union. It was also a way of reassuring their families. For Nancy, a couple wasn't married if a priest didn't perform the ceremony—whereas in the Jewish tradition, marriage marks the establishment of a new household, where children will be brought up Jewish. In order to be married by a rabbi, my father had to vow to bring us up Jewish. His own private agreement with my mother was that they would teach each other about their respective religions rather than actually adopting as a family either one.

My life span, counting backward, equals just over half of my father's life. I have now passed the age he was when I was born. It would take fifty of me (not twenty-six) to get back to Jesus Christ.

We weren't raised Jewish. In fact, for most of my life, I've operated under the impression that my parents had left religion entirely up to me—it was for me to choose between Judaism, Christianity, and secularism, whenever and however I was to so decide. That put me (once upon a time) more or less in the center of the curve of a 4 percent minority—based on a nationwide 1989 survey of tenth-graders who, when asked to identify what religion they'd been brought up with, responded, "I don't know."[14]

At twelve years old, soon after my parents' divorce and during my mother's brief incursion into practicing Judaism, I distinctly remember explaining to my friends that I was preparing for a bat mitzvah in order to "even out the celestial score." My Catholic grandmother had baptized me—often—and now, in honor of my Jewish grandfather, I was going to be bat mitzvahed, I would explain. Summoning the full ironic acumen of a twelve-year-old, I would say that in this way I would be sure to get into heaven by the front or the back door. I didn't then, and I don't now, believe in heaven. I believed in the symmetry of my reasoning, the way I believe in the symmetry of vaulted ceilings. My identity has always been secular—secular by default, but secular.

My mother recently challenged this long-nurtured impression of mine that I was expected to choose my own religion. "I don't doubt for a minute," she said, "that when you were little you had the *idea* you could choose your religion, and I don't doubt you came by this idea legitimately—but was this something someone told you, or something you just *gathered*? Because," she continued, "as far as I was concerned, you were never anything but Jewish."

I should admit that my initial reaction to my mother's question wasn't far short of panic. It's troubling to contemplate the idea that you've utterly misunderstood yourself for over thirty years. (And I do have the tendency to embrace radical conclusions based on the most visceral of experiences.) But memories are a prism; my mother's vision is as multifaceted and fractured as my own. For all practical purposes and according to Jewish law, I am Jewish. There was nonetheless a legitimate reason why my sage twelve-year-old self didn't recognize this as the last word. That reason was, of course, my father.

Today my father insists: "You went with your mother to temple; you went to church with me. . . . You were always respectful. No one ever made you do those things. Remember, no one ever forced you to go to church." I hadn't exactly remembered it in those terms. For one thing, my father's presentation makes it seem like there was a time in which I'd spend Friday night at temple with my mother and Sunday morning in church with my father—contemporaneously. Since neither of them practiced religion while they were still married, this religious tag-teaming that my father describes could not logistically have happened. On the other hand, it's true that once they independently became interested in religion, they didn't force it on us. If anything, religion was offered gently, noncoercively, and not in very much detail. Which leads me to wonder: Was I going out of genuine curiosity, or was I going to please my parents? Did I want to impress them, or simply spend more time with them? I moreover suspect that as my father paints the picture of me as a well-behaved little girl tag-ging along to services, he's telescoping twenty years into one. If I tagged along to church at the age of fourteen, for example, during visits to my father, who by then lived twelve hundred miles away from me, then I can say with confidence that I went in order to spend more time with him. Later in the same conversation, my father also reminds me that when I was little, I happily gobbled up plates of calves' liver braised in butter and wine: another inconceivable notion.

Even if I did independently embellish a theory of religious free choice, I embellished it from something. I might have been encour-aged by Grandma Proctor, who was still alive then, who still hoped to save us, and who dragged us out to Easter services, where I counted ladies' hats because I had read in a book that this is what bored little girls did in church. I wouldn't have had any notion of what the resurrection was, or how it concerned me, or who Christ was—prophet, savior, or God—which at least serves to lend credibil-ity to my assertion that when we celebrated Christmas (which we did with all the trimmings and fuss of a typical American family), it was without religious intent or content. Yet I certainly wouldn't have understood either the point of going to church or the point of Christmas if it weren't in some way a bid for the Christian cause— which I'll speculate led me to the notion that my religiosity was something to be *bid* for.

Whether or not the secular parameters are explicit, the celebra-tion of a religious holiday is a form of endorsement, especially where children, prone to literalism, are concerned. Thus, even if my mother contends we were Jewish, I was being courted by Christianity—a mixed message, and a matter I reconciled by assuming that I was meant to choose one, both, or neither.

You simply can't bring children up in a religiously ambivalent household—toeing the line between nothing, and something Jew-ish, something Christian—without expecting them to attempt to resolve the paradox, to build a reassuring logic as protection against this very big world of abstractions. But I think my father nourished the idea that we were in fact *both* Christian and Jewish despite the fact that we were effectively nothing and he was lapsed. Or, sort of lapsed. Perhaps in my earliest years, his then-latent Christianity had certain telegraphic expressions that none of us comprehended or identified. The complexities of a person's mind are beautiful in retrospect and murky in the moment. In those deep metaphysical conversations between toddler and father, hashing out the whys and wherefores of Easter with Grandma and of Christmas, I formulated the impression that I was meant to choose my religion as an adult. Now, an adult, I know I don't have the tools to make any such decision. My father didn't contradict me, then. He didn't say, "No, you girls are Jewish." As always, he talked to the smallest child as if she were the most practiced philosopher. He agreed that my position was baffling. He agreed that he contributed to the confusion—for he wasn't ever going to tell me how to think. Now he says, "I'm sorry I put you there, dear. I didn't mean to make you lost. Well, of course I did everything I could to help you along the way. . . ."

> Kansas City Octopus
> Is wearing fancy slacks
> Bell-bottoms,
> Just got 'em
> Fifty bucks including tax.
>
> —CALEF BROWN, *Polkabats and Octopus Slacks*

My father talks about the 1970s, my early years, as his "experimental period," and he means it in the most negative way possible. This was the decade of his life in which he strayed, lost sight of his values, and lost perspective, the period in which he felt most outside of himself, untrue to himself. It was a decade that culminated for him in divorce and the breakup of a family, loneliness, and the depths of the crisis that would eventually bring him back into the church.

It was devastating to learn that my father characterized the 1970s as a mistake. As difficult as it is for a child to bear the idea that her parents are suffering or have suffered in the past, it's even more difficult to accept that they suffered when she was happiest. The seventies, as banal as it may seem, were my golden years—my lovely, exciting childhood, my blissful experience of a happy family. Right up until the moment my parents separated in 1979, I had no idea that anything whatsoever was wrong. Once it had happened, I assumed that the divorce was inevitable. And although I probably entertained fantasies that it was reversible, I also intellectualized it and developed rationalizations that enabled me to accept it. And yet, more to the point, when I imagined how things might be better again, I imagined everything going back to how it was before.

When I asked my father why he wanted to become a priest, I was stunned that his answer didn't originate in the present, or even in his distant childhood, but in mine—it originated in the horrible mistakes of my "golden years," and the upheaval of the divorce and our shattered family.

There isn't a single moment or declaration representing my father's departure from the church. He simply got busy with graduate school and his career, got married, had children. My parents are both musicians and academics; sexism in the ivy tower made it difficult for a married couple to find work in the same institution—rather, made it difficult for my mother to find a fulfilling position in the same university where my father was hired. They commuted a lot, split positions; we moved five times in the 1970s—from Oberlin to New Haven to Austin to Wellesley to Columbus. In his application to the diocese of Ohio, my father writes: "As so often happens in early adulthood, my regular attendance at services fell away." That's it. Nothing too terribly complicated.

But falling away from the habit of church, according to the more detailed account he offered me, gave way to a new habit of indifference. My father let himself drift into what he calls a period of "unfocused moral expectations." He claims that "from the late sixties through the early eighties there were virtually no common expectations of moral behavior in our society. In such a media-driven, self-centered environment," he continues, "it is no trouble at all to experiment and a good deal of trouble to maintain the high standards of decency that allow a society to prosper."

I imagine that people just a few years younger than my father—students (rather than junior faculty) in the late 1960s and early 1970s involved in the peace protests and youth uprising—would counter that on the contrary there were very high expectations of moral behavior. These were expectations that were being put successively to the Johnson and Nixon administrations, expectations that were not met—*after* which standards of decency famously fell apart. It's true that to a large extent, the remarkable heroics of the civil rights movement initiated a shift of "moral" attention away from the family and community (where the church could extend its guiding influence) out into the public sphere. In that sense, yes, everything was more mediacentric. Heroes were public figures, celebrities, not model citizens.

Writing in 1973, Tom Wolfe, that notorious bard of a generation, claimed:

> A hundred years from now when historians write about the 1970s in America (always assuming, to paraphrase Céline, that the Chinese will still give a damn about American history), they won't write about it as the decade of the war in Vietnam or of space exploration or of political assassinations . . . but as the decade when manners and morals, styles of living, attitudes toward the world changed the country more crucially than any political events . . . all the changes that were labeled, however clumsily, with such tags as "the generation gap," "the counter culture,"

"black consciousness," "sexual permissiveness," "the death of God" . . . the abandonment of proprieties, pieties, decorums connoted by "go-go funds," "fast money," swinger groovy hippie drop-out pop Beatles Andy Baby Jane Bernie Huey Eldridge LSD marathon encounter stone underground rip-off. . . . This whole side of American life that gushed forth when postwar American affluence finally blew the lid off. . . .

In the groundswell of the youth revolution, people kept looking for repeat performances—kept waiting for another Reverend Martin Luther King Jr. or JFK to step up to the podium. They got a drunken Norman Mailer at the podium instead. A bold poet to be sure, but not a hero.

Social critic George Lipsitz describes the glitter of the seventies as "sequins for beads, decadence for politics, and open plagiarism for originality." Professor Shelton Waldrep adds, "The unstable nature of the seventies era—its very ambiguity—provides the period with its generative and disruptive influences."[15]

"I was influenced," says my father, "by that insanely stupid and laughable seventies society. Of all environments to be influenced by—something so patently ludicrous: 'Kansas City Octopus's looking good tonight. Bell-bottoms: just got 'em, fifty bucks including tax.' It was comical, and we went for it. We said, 'Yeah this is cool, man. Do your own thing.'"

In this environment, according to my father's account of himself, he took the path of moral disorder, following a wayward society. He doesn't blame society so much as he faults himself for following it. Churchless, he says, he didn't have anything against which to measure his behavior. He lost perspective, "experimented" freely, lost track of his commitments, his vows. It's easy to become self-centered when you have nothing to keep you in check. More than one spiritual person has described religion as a means for extending beyond the self—reaching toward God from the folds of an ambitiously other-directed community—an antidote for egocentrism. "Every real revolutionary," wrote theologian Henri Nouwen in 1972, "is challenged to be a mystic at heart, and he who walks the mystical way is called to unmask the illusory quality of human society."

Father: This is more important than anything else to me. How did the church lead me to say, "Recognize that what you did was wrong"? Because I found myself embarrassingly influenced by the environment, by the way things were going in the social world. I found myself behaving the way radio and TV said I was expected to.

Daughter: When you say, "I found myself," when do you mean? When I was growing up?

Father: When you were growing up—your basic seventies time. You know, the ultimate period of, "Hey, check things out for yourself . . . forget your obligations." Talk about Satan walking the earth! I don't know if Satan is some Antichrist—that's a distortion—but I suspect Satan was doing Satan's job that God assigned him, which is to be a roadblock. Not to test for God's purposes but for *ours.* If there's a test, it's not for God to know anything, but for us to know. To focus on the way things really work as opposed to the way we would like them to work if things were as easy as we imagine, because things that we imagine as easy and good for us are no easier or better than all the other things. Why do bad things happen to good people? Bad things don't happen to good people. Things happen to people.

Daughter: All sorts of things . . .

Father: It's hard for me to get to the Christian style of dealing with this, because I love the Old Testament style here. When God finally loses his temper with Job, and says: "Where were you when I laid the foundations of the earth? How dare you ask me this! How dare you challenge me! You haven't the foggiest idea of what this is all about and you're questioning me. Shut up"—I'm very sympathetic to that. It's good stuff. Christians tend not to respond that way. They think of alternative approaches that have to do with transforming the whole thing into an embrace, into a warm bath—God really loves you and you just don't understand. But "you don't understand" is the primary message here. So my trick is, how do I get myself to understand?

In 1979, we lived in a drab suburb of Columbus called Upper Arlington. That year I read a hundred books and won a gold-toned medal from the library (which was stolen by burglars in 1990), including C. S. Lewis's Narnia series, which I read several times over. My best girlfriend had a cat named Baby Love, which I thought was a stupid name, even though my favorite board game was Candy Land. It was the year that my grandfather told me he was an old man and then tripped on a curb, so I believed him. My ice cream flavor of preference was bubble gum, and one time I managed to get eighteen gum balls out of one scoop, all of which I put in my mouth and then blew a giant bubble that popped in my face and over my hair in a sticky tangle and had to be *cut* out. Every Tuesday and Thursday morning at eleven-fifteen, I was excused from class to participate in a "gifted children program." I'd spend my gifted hour sitting on a windowsill, composing poems, which I'd copy into a hardbound black journal made in China. One poem began, "A desire is an evil thing / it burns from deep within." A girl in my fourth grade was raped and killed on her way home from school. The bogeyman was a pencil sketch who wore a navy wool cap. I remember being struck by the idea that at least in the drawing, he strongly resembled his victim. My parents broke up. My sister and I chased each other around the ugly narrow house one evening waiting for our parents to finish talking. We shrieked nervously and ran fast, trying to attract their attention. They were standing close together by the car and had been deep in conversation for a long time—it was way past dinner. We were told to go inside and leave them alone, in tones that even children recognize mean go inside. Then Mommy was crying, and Daddy was leaving in the car. After that, he was gone, along with all the pictures of him from the living room. That was it, the moment of departure. The introduction of absence into my childhood. The twilight of the seventies.

My sister and I are as different as apples and oranges (as the saying goes), but while we were growing up, we were responding differently to the same provocations. Both of us, I tell my father, bore a sense of shame throughout our teenage years that led us into frighteningly self-destructive behavior. "Breaking up a family," he answers coolly, "does tremendous damage. Kids automatically assume—and they have no reason to doubt—that it's their fault. For all I know, it *was* your fault." I interject a "Thank you." He continues, "Kids are perfectly justified to think that they caused it—and to be horrified by that possibility. It's scary for a kid to be thrown in that position. Don't put people into those positions. Don't do that to a kid. I had no right to do that. Society had no right to tell me it was okay to do that. And who was I, anyway, to listen to that bunch of schmucks?"

I know what went wrong during my adolescence, for I was practically conscious by that point. But my father isn't talking about the eighties, he's talking about the seventies—my happy decade—and he says he could have done better. What sickly hue does *that* cast over my cheerful days of oblivious innocence as I shoot a wary glance over my shoulder to early childhood? He should have done better. He knows that now. "The fact is," he says, "the seventies were destructive. By their fruits you shall know them." Not by their roots. It makes sense, you see, that my father finds such solace and security in roots, tradition, the religion that "ties us to the people we belong to."

It's not necessarily curative to be able to articulate your weaknesses. Knowing why you're messing up while you're messing up just serves to make you humiliated as well as wretched. It's the behavior that endures. Narrating past behavior puts it into context, but more important, it is a gesture to the future, a gesture of hope: what's past is past.

My father did not carouse with the devil, or do wicked, danger-ous things. He has not had a baptism of fire. He simply chose a course of negligence and failed to live according to his own precept: "There is more merit to all those who struggle to maintain an envi-ronment in which caring, loving behavior is not only normal but considered to be the moral standard."

Out of necessity comes the strength to be responsible. In adult-hood, you're prepared to tackle the idea of your parents' aging, you grow accustomed to the idea, whether manifest or imagined, that their health will get bad, their finances will change, they will become more dependent on you. You don't prepare yourself—though there's no reason why you shouldn't—for your parents becoming more articulate about their regrets. It is, however, that very articulation, coupled with the strength afforded by adulthood, that allows people to make peace with one another, to understand life as it was, rather than how it was meant to be.

In the earliest stages of this project, a neophyte, blustering into this unfamiliar world of religion, trying to piece together the puzzle of my father's story, I asked the current rector of my father's church whether she thought he'd been penalized in his application for his twenty-year-long absence from the church. Her answer: "Remem-ber, you can leave the church, but the church never leaves you." As I grew more savvy about these matters, I learned that if anything, my father's falling away and subsequent return actually stood in his favor. The church likes its ministers to come to the pulpit with some hard knocks behind them. "The great illusion of leadership," warns Henri Nouwen, "is to think that man can be led out of the desert by someone who has never been there . . . no God can save us except a suffering God, and no man can lead his people except the man who is crushed by his sins."[16] What's more, going away and coming back is proof positive that indeed, you can leave the church, but the church never leaves you.

Of course, it's natural (whether out of ignorance or egocentrism) that I would overemphasize the period that my father spent away from the church. Those are the twenty years that led up to and encompassed me: his marriage to my mother, my birth, my sister's birth, our formation. *My* life with father doesn't have church in it. My father, on the other hand, emphasizes those years for different reasons. Two decades out of six spent without church in his life represent a measuring stick against which he can say for certain that he is a better person when the church is in his life.

My mother has claimed that she married my father *because* he was a religious man—by which she means he was moral, by which she means he wasn't supposed to walk out. She didn't think to make the distinction between religious-Christian and religious-Jewish because she respected above all his capacity for faith and for conviction (a quality that, despite everything, never waned in him for a moment), and I think she married him because she was in love with him, too. I also think that he *is* moral. And now that I know that within two years of the divorce he started creeping back to the church—"in spurts," as he describes it—I wonder whether he wasn't having a religious experience all along. In other words, maybe he never really left Christianity but was living it in an entirely different mode. Admittedly, it's difficult to conceptualize the rejection of the church as an expression of Christianity, and yet it's somehow consistent. In "the Christian way of life," Henri Nouwen writes, religion

> does not take away our loneliness; it protects and cherishes it as a precious gift. . . . When we are impatient, when we want to give up our loneliness and try to overcome the separation and incompleteness we feel, too soon, we easily relate to our human world with devastating expectations. We ignore what we already know with a deep-seated intuitive knowledge—that no love or friendship, no intimate embrace or tender kiss, no community, commune or collective, no man or woman, will ever be able to satisfy

our desire to be released from our lonely condition. This truth is so disconcerting and painful that we are more prone to play games with our fantasies than to face the truth of our existence. Thus we keep hoping that one day we will find the man who really understands our experiences, the woman who will bring peace to our restless life, the job where we can fulfill our potentials, the book that will explain everything, and the place where we can feel at home. Such false hope leads us to make exhausting demands and prepares us for bitterness and dangerous hostility when we start discovering that nobody, and nothing, can live up to our absolutistic expectations.[17]

Perhaps my father needed to "strike bottom" in order to find his way out of the hole; needed to stray in order to recognize without a doubt what was his true path. The 1970s were for him what Saint John of the Cross described as "a long dark night of the soul," after which (we can be consoled) there is always a dawn.

For me, of course, the 1970s weren't quite so metaphysical. They were just a decade of childhood, after which adolescence dawns.

Off with my mother in Massachusetts in the early 1980s, my sister and I didn't know that my father was going to church in spurts. I don't think we would have known what to make of it. And in any event, when we came to visit, he devoted his time to us, and it didn't occur to him to drag us off to mass on Sunday morning—something he likely realized his prepubescent girls would have found burdensome, bewildering, and boring. Later, when we were teenagers and our visits grew less formalized, less dictated by the strictures of "visitation rights"—after we started driving ourselves from Boston to Columbus—he might have woken up early and gone off to church without us, leaving us to sleep late. But I didn't think of my father as "Christian." I knew where he kept his *Playboys,* and I was terribly impressed by his vast knowledge of Western civilization the day I emerged from the shower wearing a ratty bathrobe and he told me it was identical to the vestments of a twelfth-century Franciscan friar.

I certainly had opinions about religion even at that tender age. I recently found a scrap of paper tucked into one of my notebooks from that period onto which I'd copied this:

> It would seem, therefore, that the three human impulses embodied in religion are fear, conceit, and hatred. The purpose of religion, one may say, is to give an air of respectability to these passions, provided they run in certain channels. It is because these passions make on the whole for human misery that religion is a force for evil, since it permits men to indulge these passions without restraint, where, but for its sanction they might, at least to a certain degree, control them.
>
> —BERTRAND RUSSELL, *Why I Am Not a Christian*

No doubt attracted to the strong language and conviction of the sentiment, I hadn't seized on this little tirade as a response to my father. I made no association whatsoever between my father's spiritual life and Bertrand Russell's vitriol. In any case, I certainly wouldn't have intentionally pitted him against Lord Russell—I likely wasn't aware that there was any theoretical tension at all between my favorite philosopher and my father. For I adored the same qualities in both of them: ornery, stubborn, dogmatic, outrageous. I probably thought that my father should "do his thing, whatever that was"—while summarily and in ignorance loathing this abstraction, church, that didn't fit into my politics. Needless to say, nothing about my operative world at that point forced the issue. My father assumed I was utterly uninterested in church and let me sleep. Meanwhile, I wasn't frequenting anyone else who might have presented church, or religion itself, as something substantial with which to contend. There were, for that matter, much more immediate issues for me to contend with: sex, drugs, high school, my mother, the encroaching wormhole that was my future.

By the same token, my father wasn't connected to what was going on with my sister and me emotionally during those years, and I don't blame him. I'm not sure I knew, or know. Teenagers are egocentric. Teenagers in crisis are impossibly egocentric. I was just impossible. All those rages, compulsions, and expectations that come out of being a small sentient adult, intellectually prepared for independence but not mature enough for it! Distance didn't make knowing each other easier; and on the other hand, the time I spent with him inevitably constituted a vacation from all the "horribleness" of my regular life. He was an ineffective disciplinarian simply because he didn't know enough about the circumstances of my various rebellions, but he was and remains an astute judge of character and was probably the only one during that period able to appreciate the nice bits in my personality that I allowed to emerge when I was "on vacation"—when I was with him. I was, nonetheless, too self-absorbed to register and sympathize with what his life was like, what sorts of things he was going through.

I suffered my mother's loneliness because it was next to me; it was palpable—a constant balance against every check I claimed toward independence. I didn't at all recognize my father's loneliness. Whenever my sister and I visited him we were always in company—together—a fact that obfuscated what "daily life" might be like for any of us. Some perception that things were askew must have nonetheless penetrated my pubescent brain, for when I think back, I begin to make connections.

He wasn't always dating the most pleasant ladies, which—although single people may not recognize it—can be more alienating than being alone. He lived in apartment complexes across from malls with green shag rugs and shoddy built-in furniture that didn't reflect his aesthetic—something that was brought into woeful evidence when he'd take his *bandura* (a Ukrainian string instrument) out into the small garden and try to teach himself to play traditional folksongs above the roar of the eighteen-wheelers on the nearby highway and Michael Jackson blasting on the neighbor's stereo. He was too good at video games. He fed a handsome tomcat he called

Hey You! in the spirit of the cat's independence. Then a neighbor kidnapped Hey You! and dumped him out somewhere in the countryside—because he was leaving paw prints on his shiny Corvette. One day he told me over the telephone that he got drunk by accident and blacked out and woke up vomiting in the bathroom. I remember thinking, Now *that's* pathetic. As an adult, I now realize how easy it is to accidentally drink too much when you're alone and there's no one there against whom to measure your sobriety—or lack thereof. He went on salad, beer, and Hershey's chocolate diets toward the end of his paycheck cycle. He said poverty was good for his waistline. He did drink too much.

This was the fabric of my father's life as he lived it apart from us.

At some point during this early adolescent period, my father brought me along to a church picnic—really, the first solid indication I had that he cared at all about church. It's a testament to my resistance toward anything churchlike that I've hopelessly scrambled the chronology of that event—which now appears a critical revelation from my father's private life. I remember that it was all insufferably square compared to his usual haunts. They played Frisbee instead of softball. The menu included macaroni-and-mayonnaise salad, fruit punch, and actual straw baskets with pieces of fried chicken inside. Whatever dessert was, there were marshmallows involved. Everyone called my father "Greg" instead of Gregory, which he hates—they'd even written "Greg" on his *hello-my-name-is* sticker, and I seethed privately on his behalf.

I recently wrote him begging for clarification about this picnic, which I had originally placed too late, in 1985, and characterized as experimental. "I seem to remember," I wrote, "that it wasn't even an Episcopal church, but Lutheran or Presbyterian—and that you were just trying it out for a spell but weren't convinced." He answered, "You must mean Saint Matthew's in Westerville. I went there a lot in the early eighties. I didn't think of it as experimental, but as my church."

I had refused, it seems, to register that my father had a church—or did anything so apparently conservative or outside my own realm of comprehension—and so I misremembered this church, *his* church, as a lark. Everyone was, of course, very sweet to me at the picnic. "We like Greg a lot," they told me. "He's a good man. He's been through a lot."

I was probably thirteen the year of this picnic, which my father thinks was July fourth, because we watched the parade from the church lawn and he remembers that Bob Shamansky was U.S. representative that year and marched in the parade. My father called out from the sidelines, "Hey, Shamansky, I voted for you!" I might have asked my father on the drive home from the picnic why he wanted to hang out with all those square people, and I think he told me that he needed something more than beer and softball with graduate students. He needed some kind of family, something to keep him from feeling lonely. If he didn't articulate it that way, it must have been the subtext, because the one thing I haven't scrambled about the memory is that I associate my father going to church with his loneliness. That would have been the first time I had ever considered that my mighty father could have such feelings.

History is biased, my father recently noted, quoting from George Bernard Shaw's *The Devil's Disciple;* "of course it is. 'What will history say?' one character asks. The response? '*History will lie*, as usual.' " It's the historian's prerogative to see events through his own lens, and he isn't in fact obliged to anyone's version of events but his own.

As was the case in many divorced families, my mother bore the entire brunt of my and my sister's upbringing; while my father, the provider of vacations and hamburger dinners, got to be the "good guy." Consequently, my relationship with my mother runs deep. Every sewer we've slid into over the years, we've had to climb out of together. All the damage we've inflicted, we've had to face, resolve, and forgive fast and furiously—as if our lives depended on it, as if we had only each other. Our paths are inextricable. That's simply not how it is with my father. He's my friend and my lifeblood. I see him when I look in the mirror and I hear his inflections in my voice when I'm arguing some fervent point at a dinner party. But his life is extricable from mine. I consider that fact a personal tragedy, although it's not the kind of tragedy you can rectify. A clever historian can go back into time, identifying meaningful patterns, parallels, symbioses—but even the cleverest historian can't make paths cross where they didn't.

Over the past six years or so, my father's developed a new kind of game—out of the blue he'll posit a stunningly difficult question. This is new, sensitive Daddy. "You must be constantly terrified that men are going to leave you, after I essentially abandoned you. How did that affect you?" he might ask. Or one day, we're out in the drive-way replacing the disk brakes on the old white truck (rather, he's replacing the brakes, I'm just holding the ratchet wrench until he needs it), and he asks, "You're not jealous of your little brother and sister, are you? You know I love you just as much."

The generally self-referential nature of the questions leads me to believe they come out of (not a desire to torture me, but) his own interior process of evaluation, the looking back over one's life that any sixty-year-old man, even one not going through a discernment process, might be prone to. When I can, I answer his questions—anything less would be an obstruction to his self-examination. "Yes, I am jealous of Nicolas and Katyana—they get to actually grow up with you."

Despite the fact that the bulk of my relationship with my father has been conducted over the telephone, he is a sporadic telephoner (a trait I inherited). I realized at a certain point that there was no use waiting for a phone call. If I wanted to talk to him, I should call myself—a trick that's especially true for birthdays and holidays. I took it as a sign of neglect when I was younger, then I grew weary of the psychodrama. I understand well not wanting to get on the phone, especially after a busy day. Between the small children, the farm, the long commute, teaching, grading papers, and writing them, I know, he has busy days. It's also simply nicer to visit with people in person, and the phone should really be only a tool with which to set up appointments to see people in person. My sister likes the phone and wishes he would use it more. "A father should call his daughter," she insists, harping as always on her vision of a fantasy father.

"But ours doesn't," I tell her. "He's not Ozzie. If you don't want to build up resentment, you have to call him." You can't get mad at people for not being something they're not.

"Ozzie who? Anyway, he should call me," she says.

Their ongoing telephone standoff reached a crisis point in its periodic cycle the spring my father was meeting with his vocations committee.

"Your sister's mad because I didn't gush over her Web site," he told me.

"I think she's mad because you haven't called her," I answered.

"Well, I can't be expected to gush on command."

I explained to my sister that the vocations committee had sent him away, and he was going through a difficult period and needed our support. She said she didn't understand why he needed to become a priest; if he wanted to take care of people, he should take care of us first. As usual, she had a point. I started to wonder if maybe the vocations committee had read through the lines, had intuited, or even been told by God, that my father had a whole other family who felt neglected. Maybe they knew what I only suspected, which was that he was trying to make amends in the wrong place.

"You should call Martha," I told him. "It would make her happy."

"Why should I call her if she's mad at me?"

"I don't think pride has any place in family relationships," I answered, startling myself with my own heretofore latent predilection for meddling in other people's business. "And I'm sick to death of acrimony in our depleted family unit."

What I really wanted, but didn't articulate, was for him to act like a priest. I wanted him to prove that he could be there for someone who needed him. I wanted him to prove my sister wrong, and the psychic vocations committee wrong. I really didn't want to believe that God had participated in thwarting his application to the priesthood because God knew all his secrets, because God knew even bet-ter than my father that he wasn't cut out for the priesthood.

In point of fact, the vocations committee didn't get anywhere near God where my father was concerned. I'm not entirely con-vinced they bothered to learn his name in the course of their sum-mary judgment. And upon reflection, I don't think I believe in a God who sends psychic messages through bureaucratic processes. If any-one was judging my father, I was. And remarkably, if anyone was in a position to help him act more like a priest the way I thought a priest should act, I was. He did call my sister, and the standoff sub-sided.

One day my father offered to make me his World Famous Liver-wurst Sandwich for lunch. Since I'd never had one, I accepted. He asked my little brother, Nic, five at the time, if he would like a World Famous Liverwurst Sandwich, too, and Nic predictably responded with a grimace and said he'd like hot dogs better. Could Daddy make him hot dogs instead? At a certain point during the lunch prepara-tions, Nicolas discovered that Daddy wasn't cooking the hot dogs properly—they needed to be cut into little pieces.

"I'm not going to cut your hot dog into little pieces for you."

"No, no, you have to cook it in pieces the way Mommy does!" Nic insisted, his anxiety level peaking instantaneously, as it does in five-year-olds.

"Damn it, Nicky, you're not an idiot, you can cut it into pieces yourself!" my father thundered. Nicky's bright beautiful face went purple and squashy and then to my amazement he responded at nearly the same volume, "I'm *not* an idiot!"

It had never occurred to me that my father could be contradicted like that (with equal force and volume)—especially by a five-year-old, one-fourth his size. Of course, Nicolas was right, and my father was in perfect agreement.

"No, of course you're not an idiot, Nicky. I never said you were. You're just *acting* like one."

Argument over, love intact, and there was I (always in the corner), thinking, They're so intimate they can fight. My brother has the courage to disagree. I *am* jealous of my little brother.

To be sure, history is biased. One of the most interesting points that Dr. Judith Wallerstein determines to hammer home in her book *The Unexpected Legacy of Divorce* is that divorce is a different experience for adults and children. "To an adult," she writes,

> divorce is a remedy to an unhappy relationship. Yes, it's a painful remedy, especially when children are involved, but every adult hopes to end an unhappy chapter and to open the way to a better life that will include the children. Naturally, parents worry about their children when they decide on divorce, but they expect that the children will understand and support their decision and that they will adjust quickly and well to new family circumstances. They do not realize how little the child shares their view and how much help the child needs to even begin to accept the changes that divorce brings.[18]

Divorce is a "legacy," not a discrete event. What Wallerstein's twenty-five-year tracking research dramatizes particularly well is that the first ten or fifteen years of a child's experience are the most deeply affected, defined in a sense, by the divorce. In the 1980s, my family subdivided into four people, each living very individual emotional dramas, the burdens of which consumed us and drove us apart.

Although it seems I am harping on divorce, I should probably qualify that I am not a crusader against the institution. My father's surprising admission of regret notwithstanding, I am today more interested in what did happen than in whether or not it *should* have happened. My parents' separation is simply the event that triggered an extended period of abandonment. The luxury of time passed since then allows me to go back and participate a little more attentively to what my father went through in those years.

Furthermore, I can recognize and appreciate that the 1980s was a period of reckoning and recovery for my father. It was a period during which he struggled to come back into himself and redefine himself as an adult whom he could recognize and respect. It didn't happen overnight, as he had, by his own account, strayed far. It also wasn't a process that left him terribly available to us. As anyone who has gone through an extended soul-searching can attest to, it's not always the sort of solipsistic gibberish that's easy to share.

Loved ones might object that it is better to share—sharing pain and gibberish is an essential part of intimacy. But that's a hard call to make where teenagers are concerned. Teenagers are highly attuned to confusion, and since they're awash in it, they don't *necessarily* appreciate it in others. I can say with certainty that I would like to have been closer to my father, seen him and talked to him much more than we did. I can't say with certainty that I would have embraced his confusion—I simply don't know. I didn't embrace my mother's confusion. I ran from it.

There's another aspect that surely influenced my father's stoic privacy during those years—he didn't come from a family or a tradition where people shared their feelings or comforted one another. When my father says that at sixteen years old celibacy seemed to him like an entirely viable option, it's probably true; celibacy, a life without affective—emotional and physical—intimacy, would not have in fact been very different than what he already knew. Celibacy didn't constitute a sacrifice of anything, because he didn't have anything to give up. And the total self-containedness of celibacy must have seemed safer in a way than the prospect of an intimate relationship. It's generational, too. Intimacy and emotional sensitivity haven't always enjoyed the privileged position they do now. My father has had to learn it from scratch, had to learn how to be vulnerable. And each step forward along that learning curve has surely felt like stepping off the deep edge of an abyss. My mother bitterly remembers his constant enjoinder to her, "I don't care what you feel. Tell me what you think." That cruel gag order stands out from time past for her—a static portrait of their relationship. My father would take but an instant today to recognize that thinking and feeling aren't extricable. He knows now that life simply isn't that neat.

Intimacy is the cornerstone of a pastoral relationship. It's interesting to think that my father's soul-searching has led him so far along the learning curve that now he craves precisely that which was missing from his early life. Not only does he want to express it, but he wants to receive it.

It's easier to be a reformed man in an entirely new world. The tunnel that my father traveled during the 1980s emerged out in the countryside of Ohio, with a new marriage and a second family, a hearty church community. The stumbling block along my father's new path is made up of the remnants of his old path. Strangely, the stumbling block is my sister and I, living remnants of a former Daddy.

I say that cautiously, because I don't think that we represent any real barrier either to his being who he is today or to his aspirations for the priesthood. But as his daughters, we've flown behind him across his abyss without actually having experienced it as such—a consequence of distance and our busy adult lives. In other words, there's a leap, and I have a slight advantage over my sister because talking to my father about the priesthood has given me access to his evolution—a bridge backward. My sister, on the other hand, is left, sort of like my mother, with a picture of my father that's left over from "before," and it doesn't quite jibe with the "after."

Children write a different history than their parents of their shared life. Even two children from the same divorce write a different history from each other. My sister's book wouldn't be like this one at all—it probably wouldn't be a book.

My sister Martha is fiercely passionate. She's affectionate and earthy, generous to a fault, strong-willed, unflinching, and reckless. She dives into things with a contagious ebullience, and then surfaces in despair because the water is never quite as lovely as she imagined. She looks like my grandmother Proctor—tall and large-boned with startling Slavic features: high cheekbones, slanted eyes, and a wide, perfectly formed mouth. Her hands are big like a man's, and for as long as I can remember, they've been busy making things. Even during those distended afternoons of adolescent inactivity, as we were slouched down on couches staring at the floorboards, wondering what anything would add up to, her sturdy fingers would be busy threading minute colored beads that she kept sorted in egg trays onto invisible thread, then knotting and twisting the strands into intricate patterns, totally absorbed and oblivious to the almost comical juxtaposition of her largeness against her miniature task.

My sister doesn't choose the path of least resistance, which is why I think she tends to suffer fools. They don't resist her. She doesn't cultivate challenge and challenging relationships, in part because she's the only sheriff in her town, and in part because she hasn't ever (or yet) figured out how (or if) to integrate compromise into her life and her choices. I admire Martha's uncompromising side, and sometimes by comparison I feel like I'm a big pushover. My father is a challenge in her life that perhaps exhausts her for others. Not my father so much as the disparateness between my father and her ideal of "father." She doesn't like that he hasn't been there for the last fifteen years. And now, the problem is not that he left but that they've never made up. She's never felt (or been made to feel) as if the original act of abandonment has ended; it just perpetuates. As in Lawrence Ferlinghetti's heartbreaking poem "I Am Waiting," she too is still waiting for the dream deferred. And she will continue to hope for my father to conform to that abstract ideal of father, and continue to be disappointed—while I will continue to modify my expectations to conform to reality. Between the two of us, we have a point. What is love if not complicated?

When we first talked about my father's aspiration to be a priest, her initial reaction was predictably fierce. Based on our experience of him as a paternal figure, *priest* isn't the first word that comes to mind. "First he fucked up our family," she said, "then he got a new one. Now he wants to get a third one—and he still can't even take care of the first one!" My father is certainly not single-handedly

responsible for the marriage ending, and she knows that as well as I
do, but she's talking out of anger and some significant degree of bafflement. His ambition is a sudden upset of all the measurements
that we've been accustomed to dealing with. He wants to be a
"father" in a way that doesn't remotely reflect on us. It's another
strike against the fantasy that we're central at all to his existence.

Her argument sticks to me like a burr, and I think her anger is a
problem that my father should be able to resolve if he really is going
to be a priest. Priests can't perform miracles, they can't change history or who they are, they can't even make someone stop being
angry (nor should they try). But if I've understood correctly all that
the establishment has been telling me about the priesthood, a priest
should be able to demonstrate that he understands suffering, that he
can share the pain of the crucified Christ; that he's there to gather up
Christ's body, the church, in his arms. He doesn't "feel your pain"—
as my father would say—but he won't ignore it.

> Dear Gregory,
> The hope is that over the next year, you can work with a spir-
> itual director, or partner, who can help you strengthen your abil-
> ity to describe and clarify your sense of calling to ordained
> ministry.

The basic functional difference between ordained ministry and the
ministry of the laity is sacramental. The ordained minister enacts the
Eucharist. Religious preparation, psychological stability, and academic
credentials have everything to do with the ability to perform the daily
tasks of parish priesthood—administration and pastoring. They have
nothing, however, to do with the ability to celebrate sacraments—
divine rites. Many people have the religious, psychological, and intellectual wherewithal to perform the work of a priest—but there has to
be some kind of spiritual criterion. Thus the locus of a decision to
promote a candidate into the mechanism for becoming a priest falls

on the closest thing to divinity that a candidate can present—his or her calling.

If your application to the priesthood is remanded because your vocations committee deems that you need to spend a year working on the articulation of your calling, you turn to your spiritual director. Spiritual direction is an ancient ministry that was once described to me as "therapy where the focus is on your relationship to God." If you don't already have a spiritual director, you typically turn to your parish priest.

Immediately following the decision handed down by the vocations committee, my father scheduled a couple of meetings with Diane Cook, a young priest from Iowa, recently appointed rector of his church, Saint Paul's, in Mount Vernon. I asked her what kind of work they might do together, and she answered that she thought she would be able to help him get to the point "where he can articulate in a way that they are able to hear his call and his ministry." She had explained to him, "What I'm hearing and what you're saying may not necessarily be the same. So it might be helpful to sit down and talk so that people can hear your call the way it's really expressed." Different ways of saying: You need to change your language—you need to learn how to communicate better. But it's not just simply a matter of communication skills; it's a matter of learning a language that is common to the listener.

"It's being able to articulate how you find God in your life," Cook says, "and how you express your love of God, and God's love for you in your everyday existence. Sometimes that means being able to talk about your feelings—and that kind of thing isn't always easy to do. I think it's also just personalizing it so that people can actually see and hear that God is really at work in you. Even if you might know it up here," she says, pointing to her head, "it's nice to every once in a while hear it from the heart."

Articulation is the daily tool of a writer's craft; it's the daily tool of a thinker. In its secondary sense, *articulate* means "to pronounce clearly"—which is what Reverend Cook is talking about. In a primary sense, however, *articulate* means "to joint," that is, to connect two distinct elements with a third element, or article—to make a connection, to build. In literature, neither plot nor argument exists without the establishing of connections.* A *story* is a series of events (a pile of lumber and nails); a *plot* is a selected and organized series of events (a tree house). Elements or events in a story are variables whose unique and significant meaning comes out of how they're joined. You can make four in any variety of ways: as $2 + 2 = 4$; as $1 + 3 = 4$; as $1 + 1 + 1 + 1 = 4$; as, in fact $10 - 6 = 4$. The unity of action in a plot, claimed Aristotle, comes from parts that are "so closely connected that the transposal or withdrawal of any one of them will disjoint and dislocate the whole."[19] Articulation is making connections and delivering them clearly. If they're fulfilling their end of the bargain, writers do this in a short story, as professors do this in a lecture, as preachers do this in a sermon.

My father wasn't making connections that people could hear. If he were a novelist, he might be labeled "obscure" or "experimental."

> Gregory needs to develop his ability to speak directly and clearly. . . .
>
> Gregory has great difficulty answering direct questions in a way we can understand them. Even when prompted and coached, he has difficulty with a direct answer. . . .
>
> We believe that if he were to use this next year to clarify his calling, to explore his difficulty in expressing himself, and to grow in being able to speak openly about his spiritual journey . . .

*In his essay on Saint Ignatius of Loyola, Roland Barthes speaks of "articulation" as a separating out of elements, which makes "articulation" in Barthes's argument a synonym for "discernment." The difference between articulation as separation and articulation as jointing is only apparently irreconcilable. In the first case you are putting into evidence the disparateness of the elements that are connected. In the second, you are assuming disparateness and putting into evidence the connections. Both versions are relevant to Ignatian discernment; "the founding function of difference . . . is the basis of all language."

Gregory's answers to specific questions often involved too long descriptions of ideas, without the questions being answered. . . .

I've stumbled over this formulation, whereby one person's ability to clearly express himself must be met in kind by another person's ability to listen—to hear the different equations. A person's choice of words is not only sacrosanct but represents the shape of his thoughts.

The ability to traffic in the lingua franca, talking to the lowest common denominator, does not of course equal the ability to express oneself. And on the other hand it is foolhardy not to take account of one's audience—it is simply more efficient to adopt language and formulations that your audience is already familiar with. More efficient, that is, unless it's inaccurate. Wittgenstein would agree that a complex calling can't be expressed in simple terms. Ah, but there's that wrench again—the God component. If the calling is truly divine, who determines its degree of complexity—God or man? If calling is inherently simple, but the person called is unredeemably complex, in whose favor is the calling expressed? And what if a simple call is being expressed in difficult terms—but just isn't being heard, because the listener has no patience for difficult, because the listener thinks that difficult somehow precludes a calling, because the listener believes that calling should be simple both in effect and in expression? Who's to say which party isn't living up to their end of the contract—the listener, or the speaker? When you add God, or divine call, to the equation, you must also ask, which of the two parties is entitled to invoke God, and by what right?

"Gregory," the committee explained, "has expressed a deep commitment to God, a hunger for theological knowledge, and a sense of living as prayer. He might benefit from the guidance and feedback of a spiritual director to learn to express his spiritual life more clearly."

Gregory was not understood.

Calling, the locus of divine in the discernment process, is a catchall category representing not only that which a candidate cannot express about himself but everything that a discernment committee cannot comprehend about a candidate. It stands for the ineffable, the unquantifiable, incomprehensible. It stands for unconsummated communication.

This difficulty expressing one's calling is also, I am dismayed to learn, not custom-formulated for my father's case. It is rather, as one long-time counselor to seminarians, explains, "a category they have, a box to check off," that means "no." Which isn't to say that it's necessarily a *careless* verdict, but rather that it is a systematically unspecific use of the idea of calling by discernment committees—an intentional ambiguity. When it comes to calling (or lack thereof) definitions and resolutions seem to fall woefully short. There is a real need for poetry, room for interpretation, in an otherwise rigidly delineated evaluation process. The problem, of course, lies in *how* such a fundamentally oblique category is ultimately interpreted by the applicant.

"In any structure," explains Stephanie Paulsell, a minister with the Christian Church (Disciples of Christ) and a professor at Harvard Divinity School, "it's hard to accommodate the mystery of the human person—that's the dilemma—you want structures that are both fair *and* open to possibility, to uncommon gifts." Clearly, in a large organization such as the Episcopal Church, concerns like equal opportunity, canonical structure, and careful screening against sexual predators, are equally important elements built into the evaluation. Paulsell's own experience of calling is that "you live your way into it. You don't know what you're called to do until you're doing it." She admits that "for some people it might come as a bolt from the blue," but that for others "the sense of call comes from some deep place they didn't know was there"—an experience that's hard to reconcile with a respectively legitimate bureaucracy.

Reverend Cook characterizes my father's calling as unconventional. "I think that's very scary to the orderly church," she explains. "And I think that's probably where the greatest challenge is, because he's willing to go and be and do in a way that is not conventional, and that sometimes can be intimidating."

She has a canny way of putting it. There is a lot that is unconventional about my father, and there's a lot that's potentially intimidating. His delivery is strident. His sentences rise to climax. He makes his point with volume. But you don't feel like he's yelling at you. He thinks that a reading from the Old Testament bears a dramatic, fire-and-brimstone interpretation, and so he thunders and quivers accordingly when he delivers a weekly Bible reading. In his person—warm, large, bemused—he creates the same environment of acceptance that he considers the church's greatest gift to society. "The church says, 'Hey—it's a big umbrella—come on in. We'll take care of you if we can. If we can't, we'll pray for you.'" This notion of universal acceptance cuts to the heart of my father's calling. The emphasis he places on the big umbrella comes from gratitude—gratitude because the church welcomed him back from his extended absence and provided him with the stable moral code that allowed him to recognize, and come to terms with, his past—the "destructive choices" he made and the "sins" he committed.

The practical—not theoretical—side of this articulation equation is neither unfair nor tainted with God's supposed favor. My father uses big words, doesn't believe that questions must have answers, and is powerfully private. "There is," noted the committee, "a marked desire and tendency not to focus on himself, even when he is asked specifically to speak about himself. There is a theatrical aspect to the way he presents himself."

You wouldn't think privacy was my father's vice if you met him on the shopping strip in Newark, Ohio, where we were recently buying a new mattress. He stormed into the showroom brandishing a supersized foam cup (as a visual prop) and bellowed, "Where can I pee?" The store was empty except for its manager and a blushing clerk, who pointed to a back door and said, "Through there to the left." "Thank you," said my father, entrusting her with his hot chocolate, "Do you mean, just go to the left and pee? Or is there an actual toilet? Because in France, you know, they use holes in the ground. They have *pissoires*."

"I don't speak French," explained the manager as my father disappeared into the back room. Then, turning to me, he asked, "So, where're you folks from?"

He's theatrical, yes, they're right about that. From the very beginning, he's claimed that his strongest gift lies in preaching. It pleases him to no end when someone comes up to him after church and tells him that his reading that day from the Old Testament made the hair on her neck stand up. He's from Queens, he's New York verbal, he's a university lecturer, he's bold, he's not scared of people. But he is private—emotionally private. Only once I was an adult did he tell me that after dropping me and my sister off from our visits, and *after* the car turned the corner out of sight from our driveway, he let himself cry because he missed us. As little girls, we might have mistaken that heroism for indifference. For the first nine years he'd started going to church again, he didn't tell us. He didn't start saying grace over dinner when I was visiting until recently. He told me he wanted to be a priest, but never explained why until I asked if I could write a book about it.

It isn't surprising to me that in two and a half meetings with the three strangers comprising his vocations committee, my father didn't create a sense of intimacy. I don't doubt that he was friendly or sincere. I don't doubt he was theatrical. I do doubt that he told any secrets.

Telling secrets is a shortcut to intimacy—as any twelve-year-old girl at sleepover camp knows. The spilling of self is a kind of name badge—"Hello, my name is vulnerable to you"—that invites mutual vulnerability and promises emotional safety under the terms of a kind of blackmail. A confidence game. "I'll tell you a secret, so that you can tell me a secret, then we'll both have each other's secrets and we won't be likely to abuse that information"—a semireliable system at best.

Private is fine; it's dignified. Henri Nouwen, one of the greatest modern philosophers of Christian ministry, cautioned against the

ugly pitfall of spiritual exhibitionism.* But too much privacy, too
much guardedness, is considered privatism or inwardness. And that
is an obstacle. Reverend Douglas Brown, a spiritual director, describes
religion as "something intensely private and interior. It isn't a public
reality." Yet, he says, "it *is* a public reality but the cultural attitude is
that it's private, and so people aren't encouraged to express it." This
mandate, he says, broadly speaking comes out of the separation of
church and state, extending from the state to the marketplace. Since
we live in a market-driven culture, religious experience isn't part of
our daily, public experience. "But," he continues, "*intimate* doesn't
necessarily mean *private*. It's an illusion to think it does. Our spirituality, our relationship with reality, our relationship with God, our
relationship with ourselves, no matter how well- or ill-articulated,
determines how we are in the world. Whether I articulate it or not,
the way I live my life is the expression of my spirituality. Behavior
frequently goes unexplained and un-understood, because its religious,
philosophical, and emotional underpinnings are not revealed."

Many of the people I talked to about discernment said that they
were looking for "the way God moves in someone's life." But
there's a more concrete version of that sentiment. People look for
themselves in other people's experience. They want to be able to
relate to a feeling because, *Yes,* I've felt exactly that way, too! That's
how we understand something is important. Admittedly, there's

---

*Nouwen writes, "It would be very easy to misuse the concept of the wounded
healer by defending a form of spiritual exhibitionism. A minister who talks in the
pulpit about his own personal problems is of no help to his congregation, for no suffering human being is helped by someone who tells him that he has the same problems. Remarks such as, 'Don't worry because I suffer from the same depression,
confusion and anxiety as you do' help no one. This spiritual exhibitionism adds little
faith to little faith and creates narrow-mindedness instead of new perspectives.
Open wounds stink and do not heal. . . . Making one's own wounds a source of
healing, therefore, does not call for a sharing of superficial personal pains but for a
constant willingness to see one's own pain and suffering as rising from the depth of
the human condition which all men share" (*The Wounded Healer,* 88).

some narcissism in this; but there's also something larger that has to do with the way people acquire knowledge, the way we come to understand stuff.

"We tell ourselves stories in order to live," wrote Joan Didion in *The White Album*. "We look for the sermon in the suicide, for the social or moral lesson in the murder of five. We interpret what we see, select the most workable of the multiple choices. We live entirely . . . by the imposition of a narrative line upon disparate images, by the 'ideas' with which we have learned to freeze the shifting phantasmagoria which is our actual experience."[20] Ideas emerge from narratives.

If you simply say, "The moral rectitude of the church saved me," then you might invite nods of acquiescence—but you are not inviting your listeners to understand *how* the church saves. You are inviting them to rummage through their own personal experience to find an example of how the church might have saved them, and led them thus to the same conclusion. What if a saving church isn't part of their own narrative? Maybe something else saved them over the course of their lives, but they don't have the innate storytelling abilities to make that experience correspond to yours. Especially where storytelling is concerned, people are indulgent and compassionate listeners. If you tell them the story that explains your conclusion, they are likely to either sympathize with the character in the story or understand by virtue of example how it relates to their own shifting phantasmagoria. Storytelling is good rhetorical technique.

In the context of the discernment process my father was unable (or unwilling) to *personalize* his religious experience or make a story out of it. Ministry does not begin and end with the terrifying majesty of the Old Testament, the nobility of the New Testament, or the thrill of theology. The ability to realize and maintain faith comes out of something more visceral. The idea that God is among us, that the miracle of creation itself is revealed in the person sitting across the table from you, invites a purely emotional demonstration.

Sometimes, the scriptures make sense only when they can be reflected in something tangible. That is why homilies so often include personal anecdotes to demonstrate a scriptural idea.

That said, the imperative for the personal is relatively contemporary. "Ideas" in the abstract once had far more currency than they do now. But people have always needed an apparatus around ideas to digest them. The sermons of the Puritan minister Jonathan Edwards are studied today in American literature classes because he introduced lush metaphor into his fatalistic lessons ("O sinner! . . . you hang by a slender thread, with the flames of divine wrath flashing about it, and ready every moment to singe it, and burn it asunder; and you have nothing to lay hold of to save yourself, nothing to keep off the flames of wrath, nothing of your own, nothing that you ever have done, nothing that you can do, to induce God to spare you one moment"). In this postpsychological cultural environment, we're fluent in confessions, case studies, and the memoir. Today's journalism is littered with anecdotal experiences masquerading as information. Academia may in fact be the single realm where "the personal" is still regarded with some degree of suspicion, still considered the inverse of "fact" or "reason," and where abstract ideas are still a thrilling ride.

My father has been an academic for forty years. And his particular field, music theory, is not known for bucking the tide. The members of his vocations committee expressed concern in their evaluation that he frequently compared parishioners to students, and pastoring to counseling. They saw this as evidence of condescension—since parishioners are neither younger nor subordinate to priests as students are to professors. But, my father explains, they failed to understand that he works with and counsels graduate students. There may be a power dynamic at work, but there's not the inequity of maturity or intelligence that there might be between a schoolteacher and an eighth-grader. And while the committee saw this as a symptom of condescension, they complained that he spoke only in abstractions, and it was hard to understand what he was saying—a crass complaint from my father's perspective, because the very fact that he kept the conversation at the high intellectual level suggests anything *but* condescension.

Understandably, this last comment led my father to wonder if he wasn't being penalized for his higher education, whether he was a victim of a campaign to dumb down the church.* In fact, he was being penalized for his style. I know from grueling personal experience as a writer that finding a "style" that is both true to yourself and effective is a matter of nothing more glamorous than elbow grease and a resilience to failure. No one prepped or prompted my father before he went into this process. In good faith, he presented himself in the most illuminating and positive light he knew.

The spiritual autobiography my father wrote for his application to the priesthood is entitled "Apologia." I read that title a hundred times before realizing that even though he always referred to it in conversation as his "spiritual autobiography," on paper he'd renamed it. An apologia is "a written defense or justification of the opinions or conduct of the writer." In fact, this short essay is more of a defense than an explanation, and it's certainly not an autobiography. I'm not an expert in spiritual discernment, but I do know about literary forms and styles. My father's "Apologia" is unmistakably the work of an academic. The autobiographical material is scant, vague, and passive. "As so often happens in early adulthood," he writes, "my regular attendance at services *fell away*. Again as so often happens, it wasn't until the failure of my first marriage, twenty years ago, that

---

*I flirted with this suspicion, too, initially, especially when confronted with the tendency to talk about "the head" and "the heart" as binary opposites. Although the church endeavors to reach as broad a population as possible—and resorts to a market-friendly self-presentation to achieve that—I personally saw too much evidence of brilliant, highly educated clergy and an emphasis on extremely sophisticated theology of ministry in internal church documents to support this notion. I did not, however, interview my father's vocations committee. Based on their written evaluation, I would wager that they are less guilty of anti-intellectualism than they are guilty of impatience.

I found myself returning to the church." The essay treats religious experience as a foregone conclusion—as something essentially private that, as believers, we can all more or less agree on. Quite possibly he thought that he would sully the purity of the sentiment by trying ineptly to describe it. Little did he know they would have been happy with something less elegant, and more "sullied." My father recast the autobiographical form into a succinct, somewhat academic proposition: "Since at fifty-eight I am long past the age of ambition, I foresee myself using my gifts ministering to those passed over by ambition: churches struggling, churches with aging populations, churches in discord. In the spirit of Christ as I understand it, I offer myself as one who may help in embracing and healing. Along the way, I can share my vision of a moral—which is to say loving— society modeled at the parish level." I would venture to say that my father, the professor, had the best intentions but didn't understand (or didn't accept) the assignment.

In 1972 Henri Nouwen wrote that "the Christian leader is a man who is willing to put his own articulated faith at the disposal of those who ask his help. In this sense he is a servant of servants, because he is the first to enter the promised but dangerous land, the first to tell those who are afraid, what he has seen, heard, and touched." The Reverend Anne Richards admits that it's tough to be told the discernment committee didn't hear your call. "It leads people to believe that there is a *right* thing to say. . . . All I can tell people is that the committee can only work with what you give them. They cannot read the mind of God, nor can they read your mind. You need to get conversant with the language of your interior." Richards puts the emphasis on finding your own personal way to express yourself—not trying to figure out what the committee wants to hear. Clutching at her solar plexus, she adds, "You've got to learn how to represent yourself fully and in depth. For most people religious experience is so *primitive,* it's really hard to get out."

In other words, this articulation that my father stumbled over isn't easy; it doesn't come naturally. Everyone struggles with it. "It's a very primary process," explains Richards. "It's essentially the process of learning how to reflect theologically about everything that you have to do as a priest—learning how to run all your experience through religion as if it were a kind of filter. But the first thing you have to learn how to deal with is your own hope, your hopes about this call. It's a matter of finding the right words."

Preach always. When necessary, use words.

—SAINT FRANCIS OF ASSISI

Pope Benedict XV hailed Francis of Assisi as "the most perfect image of Christ that ever was."[21] No small acclaim, when you consider that living in the imitation of Christ is the sole common central principle of that variegated, multiform, and amorphous worldwide sect known as Christianity. In retirement, Saint Francis of Assisi received the first-ever stigmata, was visited by the Virgin Mary, and threw the devil over the side of a mountain. This was after a substantial career preaching the word of God, which had followed a reckless and pagan youth.

Saint Francis of Assisi was a powerful and charismatic preacher— his famously wretched and humble appearance notwithstanding. Responding to a vision he had, in which Christ implored him to "repair my church," he founded a religious order, tended to the sick and the poor, and endeavored to repair the church by setting a new example of ministry—wretched, humble, and indefatigably loving. He was, however, never ordained a priest.

Born into wealth, Francis came to believe passionately that the love of material possessions was the root of society's ills and man's estrangement from his maker.[22] The spiritual crisis that led Francis to cast off the material wealth of his legacy, to transform himself from prince to pauper, was gradual, "imperceptible" by one description. It didn't begin in a flash with the vision of Christ (that was later), but came to Francis as a dawning, an opening of his eyes to the misery, corruption, and warfare around him. Francis's religious practice consisted of living in the image of Christ, and offering this example of a living Christ to the world. "He didn't try to force his almost impossible ideal upon others," writes the religious historian Stephen Clissold, "who could not or would not, choose the hard road of voluntary poverty. He did not denounce or try to convince by argument. It was enough to live out his own vocation to the full. And in time others came forward to join in the strange venture, and soon the trickle grew into a flood."[23]

Beyond the experience of religious life as a gradual dawning, or enlightenment, my father shares with Saint Francis the idea that the heart-center of religious practice is providing a model of good. In the 1989 baseball movie *Field of Dreams,* a farmer hears a voice: "If you build it, he will come." "It" is a baseball field. "He" is the ghost of the farmer's father (who appears in the company of the disgraced 1919 Chicago White Sox team). My father's idea of the church is barely more complex than that. For him, if you build it, it will exist. "It" is goodness.

"For all the merit there may be," he says, "to surviving through faith the burning fiery furnace, there is more merit to all those who struggle to maintain an environment in which caring, loving behavior is not only normal but considered to be the moral standard. I take this to be the goal behind the formation of churches."

Community and a loving environment, centuries-old tradition, and a universalistic umbrella of welcome are the qualities that attract my father to the Episcopal Church. And as much as he may have a scholar's respect for the machinations of doctrine, he has a hobbyist's fascination with church history. His is a fascination that returns to the central idea of the church as tradition with all its rich, cluttered past. My father left the church and "lost his way" for twenty years, and it is therefore important for him to believe he's found the road home—and home is not a place but a tradition.

Which is not to suggest that my father's calling is simple—or even necessarily accessible. He's spent his working life walking a tightrope of complex abstractions, mathematical formulations, and rhetoric. The shift from twentieth-century music theory, which he has taught at the university level for the last thirty-seven years, to the more populist arena of the church does not mean he's embraced broad strokes, reductionism, or politic positions. He still likes thinking without a net. And though he prefers the colloquial delivery of Dr. Laura, what he's espousing often seems more like Kierkegaard with a tolerance agenda. "The more I can understand complex interrelationships and the value of oppositions as legitimate, the more I understand the way the universe works, and the more I am able to accept without losing my autonomy or my point of view. To be upset, and at the same time understand that you're never going to get it—you've got to stand up for your position, yet you're not right and you're not wrong. The guy who's fighting you tooth and nail has all the same justification you have. What you are trying to do is figure out how you fit into this complex system." Nonpartisan abstractions like that haven't curried him favor in the complex system—especially once you realize he's talking about Jesus.

I'll repeat, my father's calling isn't simple. I've been talking to him about it for two years now, and I couldn't reduce what he says to an advertising pitch or bulleted list. Yet I think that emotionally, or instinctively, it's clear. He wants to participate more fully in something that he loves and believes in. When you're convinced that something is good, it's difficult not to want to share it. The evangelical phrase "Go forth and share the good news" is a perfect expression of this idea. The church provided for my father when he was in need, and he wants to provide back to the church by giving himself in its service. He's an extraordinary lecturer—which makes him an extraordinary preacher. He has a deep, lifelong relationship with the liturgy and scriptures. He has a way of interacting that makes a person feel alive. And, you could say, he's been down a dark road and come back, so he speaks from experience. My father's "calling" is an offering. Like Saint Francis, he wants to offer himself as an example.

Gambier, Ohio, June 17, 2002—Two parked Ford Crown Victoria police cruisers went up in flames today while officers were investigating reports of an illegal marijuana crop.

"Gambier, Daddy, look!" I say, pointing to the somewhat confusing scene on the evening news. Framed: there's a tall early-summer cornfield running across the whole background, the edge of a red prefabricated shed, a tall tree behind that, and wet black smoke in the foreground. Maybe the faintest shadow of a firefighter flickers across the scene.

"Hey, that looks like it could be across the street," he says, coming into the living room from the kitchen, where he was preparing dinner.

"At the Siberian tiger farm?" I ask, referring to the outlaw petting zoo that was forced out of the Columbus city limits after one of their exotic lions mauled a four-year-old girl, and that recently took up residence on Deal Road near my father's house. This far out in the sticks, anything goes. On Deal Road alone, we have Siberian tigers, bloodthirsty pit bulls, and someone who raises cocks for fighting—their fenced-in front yard is stippled with miniature doghouses, each with a single rooster chained to it. Across the street from them is a little hand-built log cabin set deep into a natural arbor, with Swiss flower boxes at the windows and seven porcelain dwarfs decorating the lawn.

"No, directly across the street." The scene on the television switches to an interview with a police officer; the fire is in the background now, and it doesn't look like a rainy night anymore—in fact the sun is shining right into the officer's eyes and he's sweating. "We haven't ruled out arson," he says, "but we won't know until we do a complete forensic examination of the cars."

Directly across the street, there are about twenty acres of field, a narrow strip running flush from the road back. The field is bordered on both sides by hardwoods—cherry, oak, and maple trees. Two Mennonite families live on either side. I hadn't ever associated the field across the street with a neighbor—the concept of neighbor itself is already strained enough in this area, where houses are never nearer to one another than three-quarters of a mile—it is just an empty field and at dusk you can watch vultures diving into the clumped soil.

"I bet that's where Jack Hatfield* was camping out last summer," my dad speculates to Elizabeth, who doesn't look up from her book, *How to Build the Perfect Tree House* (she has the uncanny and enviable ability to read or grade papers with the television blaring and small children playing star wars or kitty rodeo on her head), and then he explains to me, "There's an old public right-of-way back there—behind the tree line."

"We were in the process of destroying an illegal marijuana crop when we noticed smoke coming from where we had left the cars," the policeman told the reporter.

"They were torched!" I say, delighted. This tit-for-tat destruction of property seems like the stuff of a Western movie to me.

"You never know," answers my father. "It was a hot day, they probably left the cars running with the air-conditioning on, and the catalytic converters might have caught fire on the grass."

"We're also investigating the possibility that the catalytic converters were faulty," continues the policeman being interviewed.

"See."

"Your neighbor across the street grows pot?"

"Probably not," he answers. "A lot of times kids plant it in the middle of someone's cornfield because its whole growing season is shorter than corn—they can plant it and get it out of there before a farmer ever needs to come check his crop. He probably didn't know anything about it."

*Not his real name.

"Catalytic converters my ass," I say, disappointed.

The next morning, my father and I and my little brother and sister make a pilgrimage to the hardware store. We're building a tree house—Daddy and Elizabeth's dream tree house, just like they used to make when they were kids, only better, with a shingled roof and a reinforced deck. They claim that it's a "family project," but they won't let Katyana color in the blueprints of the design they've hatched; and Nic's allowed only to hand my father tools—he's definitely not allowed to climb up onto the cab of the pickup truck to help me hold a support beam in place while my dad hammers. It's at least a forty-minute drive anywhere, and on the way home Katyana and Nic are arguing over airspace in the backseat. I try to distract Nicolas by telling him that when Martha and I were little she'd always get the better of me by crying first. It didn't matter who hit who or who hurt who—usually, she fought dirtier anyway—but she was always the first to cry, so she always got pity and I always got punished. I told him not to fall into that older-sibling stoicism trap. He is deeply grateful for my advice, and promptly punches his sister in the shoulder, and bursts out into fake wailing—"Wyah, wyah, wyah!" he screams with a big smile on his face. Katyana responds in kind, punching, giggling, and joining in the chorus, "Wyah, wyah, wyah!"

"Now you've done it," says my dad, turning unexpectedly off the main road onto a dirt road running through a cornfield. In the distance there's a tall, lone tree. The car is churning up a lot of dust, practically enveloping the tan family sedan. I imagine that from the road we must look like a small tornado charging through the tall corn. "I want to see if I was right," he says.

"Oh goody, torched cop cars!"

As we draw nearer, the outline of the prefabricated red shed from the evening news comes into focus. I wonder, "Are you sure this is public property?"

"The fields aren't—but this road up to the trees is a public right-of-way; at least, it is on the map—a municipal service road."

We approach exactly the scene from television the night before, except there's nothing left but two scorched parking spots and some orange police tape, broken and fluttering in the breeze. Otherwise, it's a hot, dry day and the wind is blowing strong enough to bend the corn slightly.

"Yep," he says. "Look how long the grass is!"

The scene of the latest local scandal is a little anticlimactic and seems consequently a little spooky, too. We don't stay long—five minutes and we're already back in our dust bubble, cutting through the cornfield. Katyana and Nic have resumed the new game I taught them. They're both laughing and hollering, "Wyah, wyah!" as we approach the main road and the dust starts to clear. There is a big, red, fancy-detailed pickup truck parked across the mouth of the dirt road. The driver's side window is open and the driver is watching us approach.

"Shut up," my father tells the kids. "Hmm," he tells me.

I'm scared, because I can start to see the driver now. He's about forty years old, clean cut, and hard like a bronze statue under his baseball cap with the insignia of a popular tractor. Those Farmall hats always strike me as friendly, "down home," when I see them in the farming goods store or on a man's head in the supermarket (something more practical and less partisan than the Yankees hats that you see all over New York). But today, I've never seen that hat look meaner. The man's leathered face is grimy, like he's been interrupted in the middle of serious labor, and his pale blue eyes seem to glow in the midst of all that grit.

"Shit," I say. Nic and Katyana are quiet in the backseat.

He's got one hand on the steering wheel and the other on the seat beside him. I am at once convinced that he's got a gun on his lap. I'm a city girl, and this is the wild, wild West—I'm sure that all farmers pack heat. Time goes into that molasses mode, and I have the impression that his fearsome eyes are drawing us helplessly toward him like a powerful magnet. He's roiling mad. My dad comes to a stop but doesn't cut the engine. He rolls his window just down below halfway and I shrink lower in my seat.

"What the fuck are you doing?" The man is already at a hundred percent hostility. There's no room for any further heightening of tensions. We're already there. He doesn't care that there are small children in the backseat, and me, a shrinking city lady with freckles cowering in the passenger's seat. He's mad; we are the enemy; and he has the right to shoot because we're on his property.

"What the fuck are you doing?" he says. "This is my property. This is not a fucking circus." He's not mad despite the small children—he seems to be mad *because* of the small children. We think that his misfortune and legal problems are a circus and he's going to shoot us.

"Sightseeing. We were taking a look up there by the shed," my dad answers pleasantly. "We saw it on the news last night."

"This is private property."

"This is a public road," insists my dad amiably, "at least on the map." He's *arguing* with the enraged man with a gun. (My thought would be to just apologize and leave.)

"No, it's not."

"So you must have bought it from the town—because I have a map, I don't know how old it is. It might be pretty old, over ten years. I bought it when I moved in across the way. I'm your neighbor over there," he points. "Gregory Proctor."

"This is my fucking property."

"So it was a public right-of-way, and you bought it?" My dad needs to clarify. "Because it looks like a town road on the map." I'm thinking that I've never heard my father at quite this level of pedantic—and that I can't imagine a worse time to needle a person, nor a worse person to needle.

"Yes," says the man.

Let's just apologize and leave.

"You should make sure they change that on the map," my dad says. There's no way he's going to apologize. "You know, there was a guy living in a tent up there last year. He thought it was a town road, and you don't want that guy living up on your property."

"No," says the man.

This is almost over, I think, and I might relax. But my father continues, because, I realize, he's determined to make this man understand that we are his *neighbors*.

"You know, I've been meaning to come over, to meet you, and to ask you . . ." The man in the pickup tilts his head ever so slightly, as if he's trying to figure out something, like which direction the wind is blowing. "Last summer this guy, an itinerant type, came by and wanted to do some work on our house—he said he'd done some work for you. And, well, he wasn't from around here, so I didn't know. So, is he all right?"

Then this sort of strange deflation comes over the enraged man in the truck—he seemed in a single instant to let go of something; his eyes lose their terrifying focus. "Yeah," he nods wearily, "I know who you mean. He's all right."

"All this trouble just when you're just trying to get ready for harvest must be a real hassle," my father says sympathetically. "Tough business." In that moment I remember that despite his warm tones, my father has been conducting this entire conversation through a half-opened window, and the engine is still running.

The man says, "Yeah, that's for sure."

My father waits a beat and then offers, "Let me know if I can do anything, and thanks for the advice about the roof guy. I'll think about it."

"Okay, yeah," says the man with a stiff half wave of his hand, and my dad starts to let the car roll, pulling slowly like a dopey large animal ambling out of hibernation around the pickup truck. The enraged man is diffused. He is now a neighbor (the kind you want); what's more, he knows that my father is his neighbor.

"See? Your old man knows how to act like a Christian," he tells me. "Put that in your book."

PART TWO

Calling and Discernment

Then the Lord put forth his
hand, and touched my mouth;
and the Lord said unto me:
Behold I have put my words in
thy mouth.

—Jeremiah 1:9

One is called to a vocation. A vocation is a job. In the classical period, there were only three vocations, teacher, priest, and physician. Vocation is not inherently passive, for *vocation* comes from the Latin verb *vocare*, "to call, to vocalize." One's vocation is a vocalization—the word expressed as a gesture, the action one takes in life. Whereas a *calling*, that free-floating verb turned noun, is more passive. One *is* called. To answer the call, one *expresses* one's calling in one's vocation. Vocation is, in a sense, practical, here and now, while calling is somehow eternal—hovering in the ether, something to reach out and grab.

In Protestant circles, the novelist Frederick Buechner is often quoted as saying, "The place God calls you to is the place where your deep gladness and the world's deep hunger meet,"[1] an artistic turn of phrase that I tripped over every time (of the many times) I read it, or had it repeated to me in the course of an interview. It's a distressingly vague definition wearing the costume of resonance. Yet it does serve to highlight the particular confluence of desire and need that *vocation* represents. And also, perhaps, in its vagueness, it represents the essential fluidity of the concept of calling.

"What is it to feel a calling for any thing?" wrote Florence Nightingale, who was called into God's service as a nurse at the age of sixteen. *Calling* is a word we use instinctively to define something vaguely that we feel specifically. I might claim that I have a calling to be a writer—meaning, I write because I want to, because if I didn't, I wouldn't know where to put all the words that haunt my brain. But it's also not simply that ephemeral. I've *decided* to write, rather than paint or become a physicist, and we can probably assume that with that decision, I've also cultivated a habit that means my thoughts construct themselves as sentences to be expressed with written words—the same words that I'll eventually describe as haunting my brain. Were I a painter or a physicist, we can also assume that my thoughts would construct themselves accordingly—to be expressed in plastic images or numerical formulations. Given that words are of considerably more common currency than images or numbers, I also share my habit with most everyone. The fact of my being a writer simply means that I am more compulsive about my relationship with words and their effective expression. Enter faith. (Or, rather, my experience of faith.)

Faith is the aspect of my "calling" that drives me to be a writer rather than pursue some other easier, more profitable, less neurotic livelihood: faith that I should be writing, faith that I can write, faith that at the other end of my keyboard there is a reader. Faith, in other words, that there is a need. The business of writing exacerbates the need for faith. For the business of writing (like that of many of the arts) precludes (not necessarily, but often) a direct, comprehensible reward system—a regularized order of affirmation. An article takes several weeks to write. An essay or short story takes several months. A book or novel takes several years. Along the way, there are few signposts of approval. As you forge your sentences and navigate your arguments, there is no single voice of authority acknowledging your success, acknowledging that your expression has indeed been effective, and that there will eventually be a reader. You lurch forward in your endeavor by virtue of desire, stubbornness, self-discipline, the illusion (often hard won) that you are supposed to be doing whatever it is that you are doing.*

This dynamic, this blind conviction, touches almost everyone in his or her endeavors: I am a good enough writer to be a writer. I am a good enough scientist to continue devoting my life to physics. My relationship is good enough to endure marriage. I am mature enough

---

*Faith is a kind of knowledge, a received but inexplicable conviction.

to be a parent. I am judicious enough to be a public official. I am sure enough of my information and consequent reasoning to make this (or any) assertion. From the ridiculous and superficial to the most important decisions we take on, we all have access in one way or another to that peculiar combination of will and faith that leads us to act as if according to a calling.

Simone Weil wrote, "I saw that the carrying out of a vocation differed from the actions dictated by reason or inclination in that it was due to an impulse of an essentially and manifestly different order; and not to follow such an impulse when it made itself felt, even if it demanded impossibilities, seemed to me the greatest of all ills."[2]

"Faith," says Saint Paul, "is the substance of things hoped for and the evidence of things not seen" (Hebrews 11:1)—bringing together again desire and illusion, or desire and conviction. To some extent, however, the calling of a nonbeliever to practice an art form, levy justice, hold a value to be good, can be measured in real terms. And the availability of those real terms emphatically contrasts with the demands of a faith in things unseen.

The real sacrifices of being a writer are things like job security; the real rewards can be things like respect, or popular acclaim, or simply more work (if you're lucky). None of which, however, has much to do with a writer's personal relationship to the blank page. In real terms: a good banker makes a lot of money; a good thinker is hard to contradict. Even the moral decisions we take on can be transposed to real or practical considerations. The decision of whether or not a person believes in the death penalty, for example, can conceivably be argued in real terms of deterrence, economic factors (jail time versus execution), and the statistics on rehabilitation, rather than on the equally compelling, but frustratingly invisible, moral terms of whether we should be the dispensers of mortal justice.

To be called to a religious life means to be called by God. The real sacrifices might include celibacy (in the Catholic Church), or having to live off a public-school teacher's salary (in the Protestant Church), and a genuinely hectic, sometimes harrowing workweek. The real rewards are myriad, and come primarily from a concrete sense that one is engaged in a worthy endeavor. The murky part of the equation remains the daily conviction that you are doing what you are *supposed* to be doing.

Any ongoing faith relationship with God can certainly include the perception of being summoned, or being guided to act according to a higher will. In the world of organized religion there is, however, another step—the terrestrial step, if you will. That step is literally the organization of the thing. God's messengers on earth (God's "princes" or "servants"), the arbiters of religion, must respond to the calling. He who is called must express his calling, locate his vocation. "As God has distributed to every man," wrote Paul, "as the Lord hath called every one, so let him walk" (1 Corinthians 7:17).

"In the most general sense," writes Rowan Williams, the archbishop of Canterbury and present leader of the worldwide Anglican Church, "vocation is God's summons into existence itself." He continues:

> God calls creation into being; every thing that is made is called and named; its identity lies in the purposive call of God. But for the Christian, this is more specific again: human beings are called to grow in community into the likeness of Jesus Christ. Their vocation is not just to exist, but to come into a life that shares in Christ's life. The Church's very name *(ekklesia)* means "a community that is called together"; but the Church is not only a called community, it is a community that represents God's call and invitation to all humanity.[3]

The community has a calling—or, in this case, a divine purpose. And one of the most basic tenets of monotheistic community is that people should be brought into it. Thus one component of calling involves the acceptance, or recognition, of an individual by the community—formal acceptance through ordination, conversion, or baptism. In the Christian tradition, "formal" is sacramental.

The reassurance that you are living the life you're supposed to be living—that you've found and realized your calling—is twofold in a religious context. If the church accepts you, seconds your vocation, consecrates your vow, then you can assume that you have been so called. This does not mean that realizing your true vocation depends exclusively on the church legitimatizing it. In principle, the finding of one's calling is an entirely individual, personal enterprise. Among the many calling stories that people tell, the most common characterization of "the moment of truth" comes as a great, unmistakable, and overwhelming sense of calm—an expressly interior state.

Recognition by the community, on the other hand, is the real acknowledgment of this abstract notion. And it's a complicated process. It is at once administrative, unscientific, inexact, dependent on trends, intuitions, hierarchies, interpretations—dependent on people who live here on earth, traffic in the invisible, and strive after truth, acknowledging a priori that it is the striving itself that is the only certain truth.

The most familiar use of *calling* is that of being called to a religious life. "He found his calling," one might say when a friend packs himself off to a monastery. Or, "She has a true calling," about a particularly talented preacher. But this is by no means the exclusive use of the word. One way to begin understanding the complexity of *calling* is to recognize that in the Anglo-Christian tradition, *calling* is a way of talking about God's will—a guiding force that to some degree or another holds everyone in its thrall.

Early Christians tended to speak more freely about God's will—invoking divine fiat was a less problematic concept back in the days when priests still had mantic functions, and when God never failed his prophets. Saint Ignatius of Loyola, for example, whose writings are often consulted in matters of vocation, assumed God's will was quite simple—simple enough that one didn't need prophetic or mantic abilities to know it. "The only end for which I am created," he wrote, "is for the praise of God our Lord and for the salvation of my soul." Entering religious life was essentially a "choice" in Ignatius's lexicon and it seemed in his view self-evident that anyone who could should in principle enter religious life. But, he stipulated, when one is actually seeking God's will with regard to vocation, "it is more suitable and much better that the Creator and Lord in person communicate Himself to the devout soul in quest of the divine will, that He inflame it with His love and praise, and dispose it for the way in which it could better serve God in the future." Today, a simple matter of common usage would dictate that same sentiment be expressed in terms of calling rather than "divine will."

But common usage is not accidental. *Calling* is a variant on the word *vocation*—an extension of the idea that God's will as to individual vocation is expressed, can be revealed. *Listening Hearts,* a widely used and highly regarded manual of discernment, explains that *calling* and *vocation* can be used interchangeably: "*Vocation,* however, often has a broad connotation, while *call* may refer to something more specific. A person might have a vocation as a choral director, for example, and a call to work with a specific chorus at a particular time."[4] In the fourth century Saint Augustine was dragooned (according to the practice of the day) into serving as bishop of Hippo—an administrative and political role that he did not automatically associate with his religious vocation. (For Augustine celibacy was the principal expression of his vocation.) And yet today, in contemporary American usage, one would say that he had a vocation as a religious leader and had been *called* to the bishop's seat.

Paul makes great use of the idea of calling as the revelation of God's will: "For ye see your calling, brethren, how that not many wise men after the flesh, not many mighty, not many noble, are called" (1 Corinthians 1:26). "Art thou called being a servant? Care not for it: but if thou mayest be made free, use it rather. For he that is called in the Lord, being a servant, is the Lord's freeman: likewise also he that is called, being free, is Christ's servant" (1 Corinthians 7:21–22). For the most part, though, *calling* was primarily a biblical reference in early

Christianity. God called the world into being; God called his people Israel to be a kingdom of priests and a holy nation; Jesus called his apostles to him, called his disciples to go out and spread the word.

In fact, there is something of a leap in the history of the Christian priesthood from biblical times to the third century. The very earliest practice of Christianity didn't really have priests per se; there were bishops (who were not *called* but assigned), and then the bishops eventually solicited the assistance of "presbyters" (elders)—who represented the first priests. *Calling* as it's used in the Bible faded out of usage during that formative period, and came back into the lexicon as a companion to the idea of vocation and became associated with the priesthood sometime early in the second millennium.

The idea of true vocation has generally been associated with monasticism and celibacy in particular. "Virginity is the one thing that keeps us from the beasts,"[5] claimed Saint Ambrose of Milan. Not everyone has the ability to live a celibate life. "It is true," wrote Ignatius, that "we may lawfully and meritoriously urge all who probably have the required fitness to choose continence, virginity, the religious life, and every form of religious perfection."[6] One priest I interviewed suggested that the word *calling* became associated with the priesthood in the eleventh century, when celibacy became associated with the priesthood. Not everyone is able to devote himself in this way to God—not everyone is asked to—but those who can, achieve a higher order of holiness. "By becoming a priest," wrote Thomas à Kempis in the fifteenth century, "you have not diminished your burden, but have taken on a stricter discipline, and are now obliged to strive for greater perfection and holiness."[7] The priesthood is a separate state of holiness: "Wherefore come out from among them, and be ye separate, saith the Lord" (2 Corinthians 6:17).

The idea of calling has a prominent place in the inclusive theology of the Protestant reformers. Both Luther and Calvin used the word *calling* in their writings, critically defending and defining the divine vocation of all believers. As theologian Alister McGrath writes, "The reformers rejected the vital medieval distinction between the 'sacred' and the 'secular.' There was no genuine difference of status between the 'spiritual' and the 'temporal' order. All Christians are called to be priests, and that calling extends to the everyday world. They are called to purify and sanctify its everyday life from within."[8]

This doctrine is central to the Protestant idea that everyone within the church is called to some kind of ministry—everyone has a calling, and that calling is sacred—it's what binds us to God and to the salvation of our soul. As Ralph Waldo Emerson wrote in 1830, "All the instructions which religion addresses to man imply a supposition of the utmost importance, which is, that every human mind is capable of receiving and acting upon these sublime principles." He continues, "It is the effect of religion to produce a higher self-respect, a greater confidence in what God has done for each of our minds than is commonly felt among men."[9]

The self-reliant, fiercely individualistic American sensibility obviously commanded a unique evolution of the idea of calling. Where the separation of church and state was the pivotal distinction between the Old World and the New—and paradoxically, where principles of freedom, justice, and human dignity derive fundamentally from Reformation values—American religious culture was born Protestant into an ideal of religious freedom. Religion in America embodies a critical middle ground between Old World absolutism (which leads to religious government) and devout practice (which relies on a significant degree of conviction and the belief in a personal God). In 1955, Will Herberg famously characterized the American paradox: "this secularism of a religious people, this religiousness in a secularist framework."[10]

Because the tyrannical European monarchies from which early Americans were fleeing had co-opted the principle of divine will for their own personal gain, colonialists at some level rejected, or resisted, the absolutist idea of divine sovereignty (God's will). This was an expression of both Reformation theology and evolving Americanism. *Calling* emerged as a way of talking about God's will in terms of an individual faith journey. It accommodated religious freedom (because you voluntarily joined a faith community if you felt so called), and embraced the notion of a personal, saving God. Rooted in personal choice and free will, individual *calling* is a perfectly American solution to the vexed notion of divine fiat.

The day the photographer came to Pope John XXIII National Seminary to take a picture of the 1989 graduating class, Svea Fraser stood off on the sidelines. Although she would be receiving her master of divinity degree that year, she knew that as one of only two women ever to graduate from this Catholic seminary in Weston, Massachusetts, she wasn't exactly a regular student. The seminary specializes in "late vocations"—men who come to the priesthood later in life—widowers, retirees, men just a little too old to comfortably fit in with typically college-age Catholic seminarians. Pope John XXIII Seminary had begun granting master of divinity degrees only several years earlier, and in an effort to assert the program's academic caliber among seminaries, Cardinal Bernard Law of Boston had recruited Fraser—an extremely active church member who had also been studying scripture at Andover Newton Theological School—to join the master's program. The group took their places for the portrait, and as the photographer was setting up his equipment, several of Fraser's fellow students noticed her standing apart and called her over to join them. "Come on, Svea," they insisted. "You're just as much a part of the class as we are!"

I went to visit Svea Fraser at her home in suburban Boston in 2001. She is one of the cofounders of the Catholic lay group Voice of the Faithful, formed in the wake of the Boston pedophile scandal. I had heard her speak, brilliantly, at the first national Voice of the Faithful conference that summer, and I wanted to talk to her about the group's work. As we stood in her library, perusing her books and discussing Thomas Merton, she pulled out a framed copy of her graduating class at Pope John XXIII. A tall, handsome woman with a happy, impulsive smile, she stands at the right end of the middle row—the only woman among about twenty-five men—next to one of her closest friends from the seminary, a Trappist monk. Fraser explained to me how delighted she was that day to be invited to join the group, and how honored she was at the prospect of being included in the official annals of the seminary. Then she took her yearbook off the shelf and opened to the official group portrait—an almost identical shot, minus Svea. In some diplomatic sleight of hand that day, they'd managed to take two formal portraits, to include Fraser in the festivities and scratch her from the record.

As we stood looking at the two portraits, Fraser revealed a sort of winning resignation. She is proud of having been one of two women to have penetrated that male stronghold, but she is also proud of how truly radical an achievement it was. It is as if the two versions of the class picture prove that the church was almost, but not quite, ready for her.

The Voice of the Faithful has an extremely well defined mission—to support survivors of abuse, to support priests of integrity, and to bring more governance by the laity to the church structure. They specifically do not take positions on controversial subjects, such as women in the priesthood, married clergy, abortion, or whether or not to bring back the Latin mass, because they don't want to compromise their goals with potentially schismatic polemics. Knowing this, I asked Fraser whether she personally had a position on women in the priesthood—or, more to the point, whether she had a calling to the priesthood. Besides holding an M.Div., she's been a church leader for over twenty-five years, building Catholic education and outreach programs in the far-flung countries (Singapore, Switzerland, Australia) where her husband's work brought the family; she's been a teacher and a campus chaplain—she's done almost everything short of ordained ministry. So her quick, unhesitating reply took me by surprise.

"Oh no," she said. "If I had a calling to be a priest, I would have left the Catholic Church long ago. I would have become Episcopalian, gone to a denomination where I could have been a priest—if that was what I was called to. No, I've come to realize that my thing is to be a Catholic, to live my religion in this difficult, confusing time—to *remain* a Catholic when there are a thousand reasons not to. That's my calling."

The idea of calling has been attached, detached, and reattached to the priesthood through the centuries as the role of the priest has sinuously evolved from the time of the early Israelites to the present day. It is difficult to understand how polemical the idea of *calling* is without also considering some of the polemics of the priesthood itself.

In *A Portrait of the Artist as a Young Man,* Stephen is told he might have a vocation and

> To receive that call, Stephen, said the priest, is the greatest honour that the Almighty God can bestow upon a man. No king or emperor on this earth has the power of a priest of God. No angel or archangel in heaven, no saint, not even the Blessed Virgin herself has the power of a priest of God: the power of the keys, the power to bind and to loose from sin, the power of exorcism, the power to cast out from the creatures of God the evil spirits that have power over them, the power, the authority, to make the great God of Heaven come down upon the altar and take the form of bread and wine. What an awful power, Stephen![11]

Written less than a hundred years ago, this description of the priesthood is already arcane—and yet traces of it linger in the shadows, feeding our impression of who a priest is and what divine powers he wields.

Skipping rope on the playground—"I want to marry a doctor, lawyer, Indian chief . . ." Here, the answer to the question "What is a priest?" seems simple. The priest is the guy who didn't make the list of potential suitors. But in certain other respects, too, the answer is simple. Priests are the spiritual leaders and conductors of ritual in a faith community.

Of American creeds, the Roman Catholics, Eastern Orthodox, Mormons, and Episcopalians all use the word *priest*. Most Protestant groups adopt alternative terminologies—*minister, reverend, pastor*—distancing the role from the word's past and present hierarchical and cultic associations, from the idea that there is a priestly, monarchical caste. Curiously, the need that many Protestant sects have had to distance themselves from the hierarchical associations of the word *priest* in modern history doesn't reflect the biblical meaning of the words *hiereus* (Greek, New Testament) or *kohen* (Hebrew, Old Testament): a minister, or servant, of God.

The idea of a priestly caste dates to the ancient Israelites, when high priests, or *kohen gadol*, served mantic functions in temple Judaism—they divined, healed, spoke prophecy, and performed sacrifices. Only incidentally did ancient high priests interpret or teach the Torah. The Jewish high priesthood and a priestly caste died out after the destruction of the second temple (70 C.E.), to be replaced by the rabbinic cult that evolved out of the populist Pharisees movement. Initially the rabbis were scholars; their function was to learn and interpret scripture. Talmud, the philosophical interpretation (or exegesis) of the Mishnah, which is the legal interpretation of the Torah, came out of this early rabbinic period, which lasted three centuries. It wasn't until the Middle Ages that the position of rabbi solidified into a figure we could associate with today's rabbi, the leader of a religious, synagogue-based community. In modern Judaism, the word *priest* is hardly invoked if not in reference to the corporate body of believers—to all Jews, the "priest people." "Now, therefore, if you will obey my voice and keep my covenant, you shall be my own possession of all the peoples, for all the earth is mine, and you shall be to me a kingdom of priests and a holy nation" (Exodus 19:5–6).

Conversely, in the Christian tradition, the priest is the evolved version of a presbyter, or elder—it is a postbiblical development. The presbyters emerged (or were selected out) from the community, but their role didn't take on a monarchical structure until well after the establishment of the papacy in the late fourth century. It wasn't until the eleventh century that the priesthood assumed a castelike appearance in Christianity. Castelike in the sense that it became a separate body, which was superior by birthright. Birthright—not by virtue of legacy or family—but by virtue of something resembling divine calling.

The Catholic theologian Richard P. McBrien explains that the priesthood isn't a revealed, eternal state that was delivered unto Christianity in biblical times. "Jesus didn't call his twelve apostles together one day," writes McBrien, "and announce, 'I've decided to establish a Church, a religion entirely separate from Judaism. I've also decided to give it a particular organizational structure. It will be an absolute monarchy, although it will appear at times like a modified oligarchy.' "[12] Just as the title *rabbi* never occurs in the Old Testament, the function of minister and the clerical structure of the church as we know it today never occurs in the New Testament. There are elements in kind, such as presbyters, deacons, missionaries, but Jesus, for example, didn't ordain anyone a priest.

The term *ordination* was coined by Tertullian in the late second century, and the practice of ordination wasn't described until the early third century. The ordination ritual consisted of a laying-on of hands, which expressed the idea of apostolic succession—that from the twelve apostles (Peter in particular) to the bishops who followed and the bishops who succeeded them to this day, there is an unbroken chain of communicated grace.

Early Christian communities were amorphous groups of disciples—students, seekers, idealists. The gradual reorganization of believers around leaders reflected the political evolution of the first three centuries of the common era. The Greek word for *church*—*ekklesia*—means "assembly," and was a political designation for city governance. The early terminology for administrative councils, *elders* and *youngers,* was common to churches and municipalities. Early bishops (*episcopoi*) were treasurers, who served the larger, wealthier churches. Eventually bishops became church leaders; they led the Eucharist exclusively, and were supported in their administrative work by presbyters (the elders). Toward the end of the fourth century, networks of bishops formed into synods, and those synods collected into patriarchates—the largest of those patriarchates was Rome, the seat of the empire and an important city in biblical history, so her bishop became pope.

Christianity grew and faith communities started cropping up in outlying rural areas—too many and too scattered to be served by one bishop—so the bishops began delegating presbyters to lead the Eucharist in their stead. These deputy presbyters were effectively the earliest incarnation of modern priests.

The importance of the community in the selection of priests and bishops in early Christianity was paramount. In the middle of the fifth century, the Council of Chalcedon in fact condemned "absolute ordination"—when a bishop (at his own expense) would ordain a priest to serve *him* rather than a community. This ruling was one of the earliest attempts to define the priest's role as a service to a *community*. Despite the prohibition, the practice of absolute ordination continued and flourished into the eleventh century. When, with the rise of feudalism and the "privatization" of the church, bishops began to assume prince-like status. These bishop/princes ordained men to the priesthood in order to bring them into their "courts," or immediate service—where there was no community at all to serve. Monarchs, similarly, began to hire priests into their courts—creating a titled priesthood. These priests bore the power to administer the Eucharist even without a faith community. Christian leadership thus became detached from territory. With this significant shift, the priesthood came increasingly to be understood as a sacred "way of life" instead of community service—a vocation with trappings of power.

Sixteenth-century reformers, both Catholic and Protestant, debated the practice of absolute ordination. According to the Protestants, absolute ordination was a corruption. From the beginning of his campaign, Martin Luther maintained that the role of the minister made sense only when it related to an actual congregation—a call to service of God and the church—whereas the Catholics considered it a legitimate function of the monarchical structure, and justified the practice in the Council of Trent.

The Council of Trent did, however, under pressure from the reformers, strictly limit the power of ordination to the bishops, so that although the titled, feudal priesthood was abolished, the pyramidal structure of the church (pope, bishops, priest, deacons, laity—in descending order) became doctrine. This was, in effect, when the clerical order of the Catholic Church went on the books— fastening monarchy into church law.*

The governance of today's Episcopal Church also maintains a hierarchical structure (from bishop down through priest and deacon, to laity)—though it is a much "softer" hierarchy than the Catholic one. Through the inclusive bodies of a triennial general convention, diocesan committees (standing committee and commission on ministry), and church vestry boards, the Episcopal Church runs what might better be described as a "representational hierarchy."

The Episcopal Church makes fewer claims on history and so avoids the kind of doctrinal battles that could (and sometimes do) compromise the integrity of the priesthood. Debates continue in Catholicism about whether the priesthood is a manmade or God-given structure, whereas Episcopal scholars simply recognize (with atemporal and incontestable logic) "Jesus as the great high priest and His body the church as His royal priesthood." The proclamation of Jesus as "great high priest" refers to any time after the birth of Christianity. The bishop, in this Episcopal structure, is the "high priest."[13] And a priest is a presbyter, or elder, who has been delegated the ability to perform sacraments.†

Bishops, who are consecrated under the rule of apostolic

---

*Even documents for the populist Second Vatican Council in the 1960s refer to the Council of Trent as a source authority for its model of the priesthood.

†The Episcopal Church is doctrinaire about liturgy, or ritual, not about history. The history of the ordination liturgy is carefully traced back to the first printed liturgies (*libelli*) in the fourth century. Early Anglicans developed their first prayer book in 1549 out of liturgical revisions to Roman and Gallican rites that were

succession, by which God calls them to the office of bishop, are told during the Episcopal ordination rite, "Your heritage is the faith of patriarchs, prophets, apostles, and martyrs, and those of every generation who have looked to God in hope." Here we see the word *heritage*—not *lineage* or *legacy*, which might suggest a birthright or a clerical succession back to Jesus. In their ordination service, priests are not included in this heritage, but instead are "called by God and his Church to this priesthood." That means that bishops belong to the apostolic succession, which gives them the power to administer the sacrament of ordination to the priesthood. But priests receive the sacrament but don't belong to the direct succession. Instead of a *legacy* there is divine calling—seconded by the "body of Christ," the members of the church.

"Calling is not a thing future with us, but a thing past," wrote the Reverend John Henry Newman in a sermon from the 1830s,* outlining one of the earliest modern interpretations of calling. We are called first in baptism and then many times again throughout our life, he explained. Christ walks among us, and bids us to follow him. "His call is a thing which takes place now"—in perpetuity. Baptism initiates a progression, often bringing someone to a higher

---

proposed by contemporaries and sympathizers of Martin Luther, in particular a German liturgy put forth by a man named Martin Bucer of Strasbourg in 1543. These revisions to the prayer book, the liturgy, and creed of the Anglican Church were numerous and political. Concessions were made variously to conservatives and radicals, to Calvinists, Puritans, Presbyterians, Scotts, Arians (early Unitarians), and older Eastern liturgies. The American prayer book, scripted and rescripted under the first American bishop, Samuel Seabury, contended with an equally complex variety of liturgical positions. The "final" product (soon to be revised, and revised again) was printed in 1789 and upheld "enrichment," "flexibility," and "political independence" as governing principles. A liturgical renaissance in the early twentieth century led to significant prayer book revisions in all Christian churches. The Episcopalians undertook a revision in 1928, which was completed in 1979—this is the version currently in use.

*Newman was still an Anglican and hadn't yet converted to Catholicism when he wrote this sermon.

state of knowledge and holiness: "We are introduced into a higher region from a lower, by listening to Christ's call and obeying it." This upward movement is a call. Newman qualifies that he is not "speaking of changes so great, that a man reverses his former opinions and conduct." Rather, "he may be able to see that there is a connection between the two; that his former has led to his latter; and yet he may feel that after all they differ in kind; that he has got into a new world of thought, and measures things and persons by a different rule."

Calling narratives, of course, abound in the Bible. A young Samuel was called one night, literally, three times by God. Each time he thought it was his master, Eli, summoning him, and he answered, "Here am I; for thou didst call me." And each time, Eli responded, "I called not; lie down again." The third time Eli realized that it was the Lord calling to Samuel, and instructed him the next time to answer, "Speak, Lord, for thy servant heareth." The fourth time the Lord called, Samuel answered accordingly, and the Lord delivered a prophecy to him—that Eli would be judged for the sins of his renegade sons, whom Eli had failed to discipline. The prophecy came to pass, proving that Samuel was indeed called to be a prophet: "And Samuel grew, and the Lord was with him, and did let *none of his words fall to the ground.* And all Israel from Dan even to Beer-sheba knew that Samuel *was established to be a prophet of the Lord*" (1 Samuel 3).

Abram was called when he was seventy-five years old: "Now the Lord said unto Abram: 'Get thee out of thy country, and from thy kindred and from thy father's house, unto the land that I will show thee. And I will make of thee a great nation, and I will bless thee, and make thy name great; and be thought a blessing. And I will bless them that bless thee, and him that curseth thee will I curse; and in thee shall all of the families of the earth be blessed. *So Abram went,* as the Lord had spoken unto him" (Genesis 12). Abram did as he was told because he "believed in the Lord" and the Lord "counted it to him for righteousness" (Genesis 15).

In the New Testament, Jesus similarly summons his disciples. He calls Simon (Peter), Andrew, James, John, and Matthew away from their families and their work: "Follow me." But it is Paul who most dramatically brings not only the idea of calling, but the word itself into the Bible. Paul's story in fact encapsulates the most salient elements of calling narrative—it is a prototype of sorts. He starts out a sinner of the baldest variety, a persecutor of Christians. On his way to Damascus to round up more believers to persecute, he is surrounded by light and he falls to the ground. And he hears a voice: "Saul, why persecutest thou me?" When Saul realizes that it is Jesus talking to him, he answers, "Lord, what wilt thou have me to do?" and is told to go into the city and wait for instructions. The vision has struck Saul blind, and he is led into Damascus, where he waits three days, without eating, drinking, or seeing. Finally Ananias comes to baptize him, fill him with the Holy Ghost, and cause the scales to fall from his eyes. Ananias, the Lord's messenger, is initially reluctant to go to Saul. He protests, "I have heard by many of this man, how much evil he hath done to thy saints at Jerusalem." Jesus answers, "He is a chosen vessel unto me, to bear my name before the Gentiles, and kings, and the children of Israel: For I will shew him how great things he must suffer for my name's sake" (Acts 9).

Paul's story has a before and after, a vision—rather, a voice—with instructions, and then a period of uncertainty (blindness), followed by baptism and salvation. But his story has two critical elements that we shall see set it apart from modern conversion narratives. First, he is not the only one to hear Jesus' voice: "And the men which journeyed with him stood speechless, hearing a voice, but seeing no man." Second, he receives a specific answer to his question "What wilt thou have me do?" The immediate answer, to be sure, is not definitive—he is told to go somewhere and wait. His purpose, instead, is revealed to Ananias—Paul is to be a "vessel."

Saints are similarly given instructions. Francis, for example was told to "repair my church." Others over the centuries came to crave such explicit instructions. In 1835, the Danish philosopher Søren

Kierkegaard wrote, "What I really lack is to be clear in my mind *what I am to do, not* what I am to know. . . . The thing is to understand myself, to see what God really wishes *me* to do."[14] Simone Weil, even after concluding that she was not called to convert to Catholicism, suffered a fate that condemned her to never know for sure what she was supposed to do. "The most beautiful life possible," she wrote, "has always seemed to me to be one where everything is determined, either by the pressure of circumstances or by impulse such as I have just mentioned, and where there is never any room for choice."[15]

Obedience is a luxury to these modern thinkers, a luxury afforded only to those whose callings come with specific instructions. "Since I gave up to God all ownership of my own life," wrote one nineteenth-century convert, "he has guided me in a thousand ways, and has opened my path in a way almost incredible to those who do not enjoy the blessing of a truly surrendered life."[16] For as Sir Isaiah Berlin once wrote, "Where there is no choice, there is no anxiety; and a happy release from responsibility."[17] As Paul himself explained, "God hath chosen the foolish things of the world to confound the wise; and God hath chosen the weak things of the world to confound the things which are mighty" (1 Corinthians 1:27). And both Kierkegaard and Weil were well aware of how such a challenge operated within their own belief systems. Saint Paul says: "Work out your own salvation with fear and trembling, for it is God that worketh in you" (Philippians 2:12–13).

Increasingly, as *calling* became a state that touched all Christians—not just the saints, apostles, and church fathers—the thorny question "What wilt thou have me do?" took center stage in the theology of vocation. It became the fear and trembling. Most people in fact are not blessed with a *moment* of revelation, but experience the summons as a gradual and unspecific desire—a yearning. Weil fell in love with Christianity through a George Herbert poem. Merton felt drawn to the churches in Italy while on vacation as a young man, then he read a book about mysticism, then he read more books—it was a long process of searching. Often the period of blindness lasts much longer than three days, and doesn't end with scales falling dramatically away from one's eyes, but is rather a defining period of confusion that melts into resolution once the "correct step" has been taken.

The Right Reverend Catherine Waynick told me that she knew at fourteen that she was called to be a priest, but says, "That was long enough ago, there was no point in mentioning it to anybody," because there were no female priests then. Bishop Bob Johnson explained that he was already in seminary, well along his way to ordination, before he ever had a calling experience: sitting in a chapel one night alone, he burst into tears and heard a voice telling him, "Bob, you're in the right place." My in-law Judy Walcott told me how excited she was when the Episcopal Church started ordaining women in the early 1980s, and she immediately entered the discernment process, only to discover in the wake of much deep discussion that it wasn't the priesthood she was called to at all, but to a life change of an entirely different order: a divorce. The Reverend David Lee Carlson explained to me that he had always wanted to be a priest, and even announced that fact to his rector when he was only eleven.

Jews don't have calling stories, but when I pressed my friend Andy Bachman to tell me what made him become a rabbi, he admitted that looking back, he could isolate calling *moments*—events that were formative in leading him eventually to commit his life to Judaism. He told me about when his grandfather passed away. Andy was in the fourth grade. His grandfather was a doctor and a respected, beloved figure in the community. He was a youth director at a park in Milwaukee where a lot of poor Jews lived, and they thought of him as a knight in shining armor. He was generous and charitable to a fault—terrible with money, he always treated people for free ("That drove my grandmother crazy!")—heroic, handsome, tall, athletic, charismatic. After the funeral, when Andy went back to school, his teacher, Mrs. Bernstein, had found the obituary that a young man from the park youth group had written for a Jewish newspaper. She explained to the class that Andy had been absent because his grandfather died and then she read the obituary aloud. "It was an incredible experience," says Andy. "I don't know if I would even be able to explain what kind of Jew Mrs. Bernstein was . . . but it took a certain kind of Jew to know how to convey these Jewish values: memory, honoring the dead, comforting the mourner. These were all mitzvahs. What a profound thing to give children—to teach them how to mourn and how to remember."

Early on in my research, I formulated the idea that calling stands for an intersection between religious desire and the real, daily world, and that this confrontation is motivated by an enhanced spirituality— the will to do something greater with your belief. "Oh," said the priest I was interviewing, "you mean conversion."

"No," I corrected her, "I don't mean changing religions." "Right," she answered. "I don't mean that either. I mean conversion in the sense that you've got a regular, normal person who goes through some kind of experience or series of experiences that are life changing or transforming, and that leads them to some kind of religious path."

In this sense, calling stories, like Saint Paul's, all contain a kernel of conversion, a desire to move forward with your faith. For people who feel a calling to ordained ministry, or religious life, this is an essential connection between biblical calling and calling as it's used by the church today. A person is not necessarily suffused in light, struck blind, thrown to the ground, and then given orders (though I suppose we shouldn't rule that out). But there is also a quieter, less explicit experience of calling, like reaching an intersection on a spiritual path.

"Some men," wrote Newman,

> do feel themselves called to high duties and works to which others are not called. Why this is we do not know; whether it be that those who are not called, forfeit the call from having failed in former trials, or have been called and have not followed; or that though God gives baptismal grace to all, yet he really does call some men by His free grace to higher things than others; but so it is; this man sees sights which that man does not see, has a larger faith, a more ardent love, and a more spiritual understanding.[18]

Conversion, or arriving at an intersection of faith, is in itself a small act of momentous obedience. William James, whose book *The Varieties of Religious Experience* vividly demonstrates that there is nothing essentially schematic in spirituality, also reminds us that "no chasm exists between the orders of human excellence." Inasmuch as calling is between man and his maker, or man and his conscience, there's not much point to assigning degrees of value to the call itself. As if he were responding to Newman's designations—"higher" callings, "larger faith," and "more ardent love"—James writes: "There are higher and lower limits of possibility set to each personal life. If a flood but goes above one's head, its absolute elevation becomes a matter of small importance; and when we touch our own upper limit and live in our highest center of energy, we may call ourselves saved, no matter how much higher some one else's center may be."[19]

The idea of *demonstrating* call entered and started changing the shape of the Protestant ministry in the late-eighteenth and early-nineteenth century, during the period of the Great Awakening—and that was through the practice of conversion testimonials. The spirit of revival and the importance of conversion grew out of the religious pluralism that distinguished America from its European ancestry. Pluralism led to voluntary church membership, which meant that denominations began competing for followers—and revival meetings were a huge popular success. Although the Episcopal Church was one of the more conservative stalwarts of this period (and its membership shrank, in consequence, compared to that of Methodist and Baptist groups), it didn't entirely resist the influence of evangelicalism. Throughout its history, American Anglicanism famously walked a middle ground between the burgeoning new style and its European roots in Catholicism.

Broadly speaking, this period of American history saw a significant shift in the perception of the minister. Richard Hofstadter has written, "As the evangelical impulse became more widespread and more dominant, the selection and training of ministers was increasingly shaped by the revivalist criterion of ministerial merit. The

Puritan ideal of the minister as an intellectual and educational leader was steadily weakened in the face of the evangelical ideal of the minister as a popular crusader and exhorter."[20] The evangelical sects agreed only that "he whose business it is to convert men to Christ should himself be converted; he who is to guide believers should be himself a man of faith . . . for the lack of this, no talents, however brilliant or attractive, can compensate."[21]

The notion of conversion zeroed in on real religious experience—"the sense of sin, the yearning for salvation, the hope for God's love and mercy." Early revivalists lobbied against the "crafty, cruel, cold-hearted, bigoted, faithless hypocrites" who were the "unconverted ministry." How could a congregation be awakened by an unconverted minister? wondered the revivalist preacher Gilbert Tennent in 1742[22]—whereas learned and regularly ordained ministers thought that the renegade revival tent preachers were heretical. They wondered how "one who was possessed of the Spirit could, without study and without learning, interpret the word of God effectively enough to be an agent of the salvation of others." It came down to a manufactured conflict between the word of God and the Spirit.

"The ultimate test of religious values," wrote the psychologist George A. Coe in 1900, "is nothing psychological, nothing definable in terms of how it happens, but something ethical, definable only in terms of what is attained."[23] One of the all-time most popular evangelical preachers, Dwight L. Moody, once said, "It makes no difference how you get a man to God, provided you get him there." Dwight Moody, like Saint Francis, was never ordained.

I wake and I discern the truth.

—TENNYSON

He who is called hears something. Those who recognize that call also hear something. All of this listening makes up the process of discernment, whereby, in the most mundane terms, a religious applicant is ordained to the priesthood or put on the pulpit, or a convert is baptized or welcomed into the community. *Discernment,* unlike *calling,* is not a strictly spiritual word; its function in religious jargon is rather localized. Protestants, especially the Episcopal Church, use it to mean the evaluating of candidates to the priesthood and increasingly to refer to a decision-making process. Quakers use it to mean the process of making a hard personal decision. Catholics use it with a more traditional bent: in the Ignation sense of perceiving spirits; in demonology, to diagnose possession; and in preparation for sacraments—marriage or the priesthood—the making of an "unchangeable choice." It isn't used at all in religious terminology of Judaism. "I am not familiar with your usage of this word . . . *discernment,*" Rabbi Schorsch sternly told me—the syllables of this *word* I had introduced into our conversation stumbling uneasily off his tongue. I might have well as asked this most venerated chancellor of the Jewish Theological Society and one of the leading minds in Conservative Judaism to try on a hot-pink leather jacket.

To discern: To perceive or apprehend something by the intellect: "To discerne the truthe from that whiche is false" (T. Wilson, 1551). To make a distinction: "Discernibleness involves negation. We should not know what warmth is, were there no cold" (J. H. Stirling, 1890). That is a concept familiar today in semantic terminology: a cat is a cat because it is not a bat or a rat. Discernment cuts to the heart of knowledge. We know nothing until we've discerned it.

Discernment, "or *discretio,* is an Ignatian term par excellence," according to Roland Barthes. Saint Ignatius of Loyola coined the term for spiritual use. His exercises are a series of guided meditations and role-playing designed to be used over the course of a four-week spiritual retreat with the specific aim of determining how best to realize one's purpose on earth. "Man is," according to Ignatius, "created to praise, reverence, and serve God our Lord and by this means to save his soul." That means that everything else on the face of the earth is "created for man to help him in attaining the end for which he is created." Ignatius's *Spiritual Exercises* are the single most influential model for Christian retreat and meditation practice. And they are the spiritual core of the modern discernment process.

Barthes—a semiologist, not a theologian—was intrigued by the remarkable ordering system that Ignatius formulated for his *Spiritual Exercises,* a roster of divided and subdivided meditations, considerations, and instructions, organized into progressive steps to be carried out in accordance with a strict schedule, all of which mimic in form the original myth of creation—"separating day, night, man, woman, elements, and species." The world was formed through the creation of difference:

> And God divided the light from the darkness. And God called the light Day, and the darkness he called Night. . . . And God said: Let there be a firmament in the midst of the waters and let it divide the waters from the waters. And God made the firmament, and divided the waters which were under the firmament from the waters which were above the firmament. . . . And God said: Let there be lights in the firmament of the heaven to divide the day from the night; and let them be for signs, and for seasons, and for days and years. (Genesis 1)

Discretio as separation, according to Barthes, "is the basis of all language, since everything linguistic is articulated." But the mystics used discernment—the separating out of discrete elements. They used Ignatius's guided meditations to get to the heart of inner language—to resolve "the discontinuity of inner experience."[24] That which is discontinuous can be distinguished into linguistic components; it can be expressed with language. "In the beginning was the Word, and the Word was with God, and the Word was God" (John 1:1).

The church takes up discernment in its pursuit of truth—both mystical and practical; perhaps not truth so much as the right answer. The wrong answer, says Ignatius, is the product of "inordinate attachment," which clouds the ability to discern. A retreat is designed to separate a person from daily attachments: "We must make ourselves indifferent to all created things," writes Ignatius. "Our one desire and choice should be what is more conducive to the end for which we are created."

In today's Episcopal Church, *discernment* is used to describe a decision-making process as well as the power one person or religious body holds over another to recognize or designate calling (to distinguish it from simple desire, for example): a screening process (in crasser terms). Across Christianity, *discernment* broadly describes a way of aiding someone in their endeavor to realize the right expression of their individual calling, their vocation.

"I have never wavered in my vocation," wrote the poet/priest Gerard Manley Hopkins, "but I have not lived up to it."

A theme that runs emphatically, and with utter sincerity, throughout the discernment process is that of praying in order to hear, or know what the "right answer" is. Since in practical terms God doesn't communicate by code, by symbols, readable messages, or miracles, this creates a situation in which everybody is listening hard for an answer that won't necessarily be given in decodable language. (Although Barthes might argue that discernment is highly codified precisely in order to compensate for the fact that the answer is entirely uncoded and undecodable.) Praying in order to hear truth is similar to psychoanalysis in which the aim of the exercise is not so much to be able to speak the truth as it is to be able to hear it, or recognize it once it's uttered. Truth in both disciplines is discrete. It doesn't depend on discovery in order to assert its existence.

Conversely, the academic philosophical tradition I was brought up in privileged the investigation itself. Truth is something one arrives at through analysis, interpretation, and reason. In other words, it's not a matter of hearing truth, but a matter of applying a process in order to arrive at truth. Or—just to be extra complicated— a matter of applying the process of investigation in order to be true to the pursuit of truth, without ever hoping to arrive there.

There are as many different callings, or descriptions of callings, as there are different individuals to be called. Common elements, as we've seen, recur in calling stories. The mystics: God tapping you on the shoulder, appearing in a vision, weeping in your ear. The emotionalists: a sense of anguish and restlessness leading to collapse, followed by great peacefulness. The empiricists: feeling your way into your calling. Such common elements could be evidence of a pattern of divine behavior. Or they could be explained by the symbolic and semantic lingua franca of religion, which forms a habit of interpretation and forges a path for expression. If one hears many stories of calling that take a certain shape, one is likely to express one's own calling story according to that familiar shape (codify the uncodifiable).

My father doesn't believe in visions. The testimony of his calling, thus, is void of visitations, and sounds to the naked ear quite like an interpretation of desire—his desire to be a priest. There is a demonologist in the Vatican who puts such high value on personal testimony that he seriously entertains alien abductions as divine visitations—to the consternation of more intellectually conservative Catholics. Calling, whether it follows a traditional pattern or a classical pattern or a subtle, unique, or sensational one, has many expressions.

Discernment, however is mantic; it is the art of divining. Its scope is far more limited. Discernment swallows the question whole ("What will you have me do?"), reframes it as "Am I called to be a priest?" (or a deacon or a nun, and so forth), processes it, and then spits it out again with scientific precision. There are only two possible answers: *Do this* or *Do that.* One is constrained to narrow one's options dramatically when the point of the exercise is to know the right answer from the wrong answer.

Many poets are not poets for the same reason that many religious men are not saints: they never succeed in being themselves. They never get around to being the particular poet or the particular monk

they are intended to be by God. They never become the man or the
artist who is called for by all the circumstances of their individual
lives.[25]

—THOMAS MERTON

Invariably, the best questions asked are the most obvious. What's to
stop anyone from presenting himself to the church, claiming that
he's been called by God to be a priest? By the same token, who is to
say that this person hasn't been called by God?

The paradox is, simply put, as old as the hills. In the first centuries
of Christianity, any number of disciples presented themselves as true
and legitimate heirs to the teachings of Christ, and to the correct
interpretation of God's word. Some were prophets and some were
charlatans—some visionary, others delusional. Of their various writings, some became the New Testament, and others were buried in a
six-foot clay urn on a hillside in Egypt and lost to history for sixteen
hundred years.

When faced with a crisis, Christianity has a tradition of returning
to "the source," to the early Christians, to the Bible, to the words and
life of Christ, in order to create a resolution. Lutherans, for example,
recognize only the sacraments traceable to the gospels. The Puritans
in the New World identified with the Israelites wandering in the
desert. Franciscans cast off their worldly goods and performed acts
of charity, like the first Christians. Thomas à Kempis authored the
Imitation of Christ, imploring fifteenth-century Catholics to meditate
on the life of Jesus Christ, as Christ himself exhorted us "to imitate
His life and His ways, if we truly desire to be enlightened and free of
all blindness of heart." To that end Kempis encouraged Christians to
cast off books and learning in favor of *feeling:* "I would rather experience repentance in my soul than know how to define it," he wrote.
And, "Christ's entire life was a cross and a martyrdom, and you look
for rest and pleasure? You are mistaken, O, you are mistaken if you
seek anything other than affliction, for *our whole mortal life is full of*
misery and surrounded by crosses." Ignatius believed that God's pres-

ence was in everything; "all things are creatures of the goodness of God and reflections of it."[26] In order to commune, then, with God, one had to release every attachment, making oneself in that way receptive to God's Spirit. Ignatian mysticism was the result of retreat and meditation—by visualizing and praying on the stations of the cross, the stations of Christ's suffering. Both of these theologians preached a religious practice based on looking backward to the most essential, most primordial expression of Christianity—the life of Christ.

Sister Catherine Grace is a nun at the Community of the Holy Spirit, up in Morningside Heights, right across the street from Columbia University. She's small but I had to race to keep up with her as she led me up three flights through the labyrinthine hallways of the convent town house. The layout of the convent reminds me of the medieval monastery in the film *The Name of the Rose*. Instead, Sister Catherine—tearing up the stairs in front of me, unlocking doors with giant iron keys, and spinning around corners—makes me think of Mary Poppins, especially when keys, pencils, and hands appear and disappear into her habit as if her whole person were a carpetbag of wonders. Our appointment was late in the evening, after dinner, and when she came to meet me at the door she said she was feeling somewhat high on sugar. Two of the sisters had turned eighty that month, and though they didn't usually mark birthdays (they celebrate the anniversary of their vows instead), an exception was made for a chocolate cake and champagne dessert.

I'd been told that the sister was "sharp as a tack," but apart from that, I wasn't quite sure why I'd been sent to Sister Catherine. (Yet I have gotten the impression that in the Episcopal Church, monastics are considered the resident "wise people"—perhaps because they have time to read. So, if you're asking hard questions, like "What is religious calling?" it makes sense that you get sent to the orders for thoughtful answers.) Sure enough, we'd barely started talking when Sister Catherine told me flat out that calling wasn't a Christian idea "or even monotheistic for that matter." She said she was sure that I, as a writer, would understand—"That's the joy of language!" she explained. "Words can mean whatever you need them to mean at the moment."

Calling is very multidimensional, admits Sister Catherine. Obviously, the word *calling* is used very specifically within the church: *calling* to the priesthood; *calling* to the diaconate; *calling* to a religious life. The calling to the priesthood in the institutional church, she says, "means you go through a process, where you must jump through fifteen hoops that are all flaming. Sometimes you get to go backward and sometimes you stop. Eventually you make it through all the hoops and you are ordained. There you are at the end of the process, looking back at all those fiery hoops, wondering, *Now what?*" She's not convinced that's a particularly useful way of thinking about calling.

Sister Catherine finds the deeper, inner sense of individual calling to be "more fascinating," and maybe even, "without being judgmental, more real."

According to Sister Catherine, there is calling in a broad context—"calling to a cosmological story within which all the rest of your life can be placed, viewed, looked at, compared to." And then there are what Sister Catherine terms "little callings," such as "What do I do with my life at this moment?" The cosmological story that Sister Catherine is talking about is the entire universe, which in her view, is "the profound and primary revelation of the divine. Not the scriptures—or all the rest!" she qualifies. "That stuff can become just so much gobbledy-gook."

At that point in our conversation I realize that I am talking to a nun who thinks the scriptures are gobbledy-gook. If the scriptures are gobbledy-gook, then, of course, any attempt to find the meaning of calling in the Bible is vexed. What she means more precisely is that next to the miracle of creation, the scriptures are *less,* and that as some biblical interpretations would indeed have it, creation was God's original call—the summons into existence.

"Everything," she continues, "from the birth of the stars, to the birth of the planets, to the birth of trees, to the birth of pigs and people, is connected. It's all part of the universe story." It's creation itself that begs a response, or "interaction" on our part.

Here is what Sister Catherine means about multilayered calling—cast into an ecological scheme. Sister Catherine is the crusader. (I guess that Mary Poppins was a crusader, too, but for the cause of happy little children, not for the green earth.) "The human species is one among many sharing the phenomenal blossoming of the earth. We're one species that has decided, because we're the self-reflective species, that we can *use* everything we find. We have a living planet and this one little species is using plant life, animal life, and the soil, water, and air. Humans are basically a cancer on the back of the earth." How does calling fit in to this argument? "I think we're sound asleep," she says. "We have become so disconnected from the awareness that it's all sacred, that we think all the *stuff* we've invented— boundaries, wars, machines, and the two or three companies that control the entire world—are real and important. This is a spiritual disconnect. We're fast asleep. So, how do *I* help people awaken?"

Calling, working off this example of responsibility to the miracle of creation, stands for responsibility. The question, she says, is "How do I not ignore it? What does it mean for me in terms of what I do and say, who I am? What am I willing to support? What am I willing to fight for? What am I willing to die for? Where is my passion? And what are my talents?" Those questions form the basis of a *discernment* process. But Sister Catherine's version of discernment has nothing to do with the church's system for screening applicants to the priesthood. It's a daily task. It's how you decide to spend your day each morning when you wake up. "I have a voice," she says. "I have eyes and the ability to reflect. I can look at this incredible creation and sing its praise. I can celebrate it and take action to preserve it."

That brings us, she explains, to the next level of calling—which is figuring out how to direct your passions in accordance with your abilities. "I feel called to be an educator for the spiritual life—in that everything is sacred and everything is a revelation of the divine."

Then you break it down further. Posing the question to herself, Sister Catherine thinks, "Well, Sister Catherine loves to speak to groups. She is good with computers. She likes handwork. She loves to bake." Her discernment process means taking all these daily skills and seeing how she can put them to work responding to the larger, "cosmological" calling. Where does that lead in practical terms? She would like to get her community involved with land preservation around their retreat center upstate, and maybe build an education center for the environment on the part of the protected land designated for development. "Calling," she says, "can become an explanation of the day-to-day. But it needs to come out of the larger calling of your sense of commitment, which needs to come out of the even larger calling of your own cosmology."

"Any action I take," says Sister Catherine, "toward healing, renovation, stopping destruction, any prayer I make and any time I'm with people in a way that is giving—it's as if I'm yanking one little thread of a web, and because everything is so interconnected the whole web moves. If I'm moving the whole web in the direction of life-giving, action, thought, whatever, then this alters the creative tendency of the entire universe in the direction of life—which is the natural yearning of the universe anyway."

Sister Catherine is not sure the church's discernment process necessarily represents this profound sense of call as a response to the obligation of existence. She thinks it works for some people, but in a sense the discernment process is a "way to circumvent" calling as she understands it—potentially, a way to ruin it. Her portrait of a draconian structure made up of flaming hoops certainly seems like a killjoy. And that's an important concern. Her version of calling is the identifying and responding to passion within the larger context of cosmology—how you understand why you are here on earth. If the passion gets stomped on, and the cosmology gets buried under paperwork, you're hardly left with a phenomenon at the end of the day.

The church ratifies a person's call when they allow them to proceed in the ordination process to become a priest. But as far as actually *discerning* call, in the sense that she intends—embodying all of the biggest and smallest life questions—Sister Catherine thinks the discernment process itself is a crapshoot. It can clarify for some people and obfuscate for others. What's more, when the church says, "Go away and reflect on the clarity of your call," the sentiment is right. Discernment is about finding clarity. "And," she objects, "I also think that's *precisely* what the discernment committee is supposed to be doing! You don't send someone off to do it on his or her own. Reflecting on the clarity of a call is exactly what a group should be doing together. Five heads and hearts are surely better than one—besides, if we were all that great at self-reflection, we wouldn't be paying all that money to therapists! In reality, then, concludes Sister Catherine, the screening committees aren't discernment teams, "but more like answer teams."

All that said, and the sugar high now perhaps waning, Sister Catherine doesn't think that the crux of the problem, or the heart of her criticism, lies in the discernment process itself. She suggests that perhaps it's endemic to the church—to the church that functions as an institution. There's a way in which the church hasn't discerned its own place in the universe story for now, in this moment. It angers her that they worry about flagging attendance, and strategize how to get more people back into the pews: "I think you tend to have a group of people within any institutional church saying, *Our business is attracting people* . . . Okay, for what? So you've attracted five hundred people. Now what are you going to do? Is the joy of your life (or of God's) to keep five hundred people walking in your door every Sunday? I mean, for what? Sometimes we forget just why we come together in faith communities; just 'getting the numbers' becomes an end in itself. When that happens, our talk about providing spiritual nurture, solace, education, worship gets lost in the context of the church as a business—big business." Perhaps, wonders Sister Catherine, "people aren't coming to church for very good reasons." Perhaps the church isn't responding to the genuine current needs of the world. Maybe the church, in order to respond to its own call, shouldn't be shaped the way it is now—with steeples, and pews, and altars, "qualified" priests, and Sunday services. Maybe it's about land preservation, retreats, and environmental education programs for eight-year-olds.

It's a radical position, one that someone like my father, who treasures precisely the steadfast and long tradition of the church, would have trouble agreeing with. But if you listen closely, it's really not all that radical—it's just articulated radically. In truth, it's a triumph of articulation. As Sister Catherine herself said at the beginning of our conversation, *it's wonderful how words can mean what you need them to mean.* Sister Catherine's ideas are deeply rooted in history—*her* version of it. "We didn't just kind of arrive on the planet fifty-five years ago, or twenty years ago, or ninety years ago. We arrived with DNA, and the DNA we came with carries the entire chain of all creative evolution, clear back to the fireball. And the hydrogen in our bodies was created about 13.7 billion years ago. These are not brand-new hydrogen molecules. They've been on earth for a very long time and they just happen to be occupying space in Sister Catherine Grace for this hundred years or so, but then, that's it, and they'll go back to the earth or somewhere else in the universe to be used again." Her position is informed by that gobbledy-gook Bible, specifically, the imitation of Christ's acts on earth—"I think it's revealing how we skip from Christ's birth to death to reincarnation. We're talking about an incarnate person, after all, and we're going to skip his *life?*"—and the idea that creation is eternal, divine revelation. Most of all, her argument is deeply rooted in the Judeo-Christian ethic of brotherly love: "The whole universe is relationship-, or community-, oriented. Quarks don't occur alone, they only occur in groups. I certainly appreciate my time alone. I'm an introvert, so being alone is the way I renew my energy. However, the real growth, the real connection, the real influence, and the real challenge of community is that who we are as a whole is much more than the sum of our parts. That's just the way it is."

Two of the more indigestible components of the idea of religious calling are the premise of an audible God and the fraught practice of people judging the validity, the legitimacy, of another person's calling, whatever you hear, in effect, trumping what someone else in good faith has heard or perceived.

For better and worse, in a modern, democratic, post-Enlightenment society, we tend to give everyone's perception a kind of blanket legitimacy. We eschew the privileging of one perception over another—at least on principle. This is a gross generalization, but recognizable as a brand of Americanism—self-determination, laissez-faire relativism. And as long as we keep to the realm of non-criminal or undangerous perceptions, the notion of a hierarchy of *perception* makes us distinctly uncomfortable.

But the ordained ministry is a job within an institution. It is middle management. Hierarchy is built into the system, as it would be with any job in an institution. One person's perception of what he or she is meant to be doing within the structure of an institution is always going to be subject to someone else's jurisdiction—from line workers on up to CEOs. This is not a realm where a person's self-perception is allowed pure play. In America, we like to think that one can become anything with enough perseverance, grit, or entrepreneurial gumption. But as anyone who aspires to be president, or a multimillionaire, a Nobel laureate, or an NBA MVP knows, there are hoops to be jumped through first—some of them are flaming.

As for the subject of audibility, in the Judeo-Christian tradition, God was audible to mankind at two moments in history. First, when he delivered the Torah to Moses on Mount Sinai. The Torah became the "living word," an idea that includes God's word, or audibility, surviving there in perpetuity. That is to say, God spoke once but continues to be heard through the pages of his testament. The second major instance of God's audibility happened with his incarnation through Jesus Christ. And as Christianity worships not the written word of God but his figure—through devotion and "imitation"—Christ is the perpetuity of God.

Religion in this specific context both collapses and constructs linear time. History lives through legacy and lineage. The present is the space of our business here on earth, and the future is the world (or kingdom) to come.

Linear time also lives in this idea of the constant presence of God's audibility. Perhaps the single most comprehensible conception of calling takes its root in the Jewish idea of the covenant: "a divine call persisting through all ages and encompassing all lands, *a continuous activity of the spirit* which has ever summoned for itself new heralds and heroes to testify to truth, justice and sublime faith, with an unparalleled scorn for death, and to work for their dissemination by words and deeds and by their whole life."[27]

The single calling precludes the notion and the necessity for successive, individual callings. In essence, a Jew is born with a calling, and his task in life is to suss out how to activate, realize, or manifest that calling. The burden is there. The responsibility already lies on each individual's shoulders. The failure to realize it potentially confronts all.

This begins to speak to an important formal difference between a priest and a rabbi. Acceptance into rabbinical school, and thus into the ordination process, is not based on a determination of calling but rather a determination of ability. The ability under consideration for an applicant to the rabbinate is principally scholastic—the ability to teach, to be a leader in scholarship, to assimilate and interpret Jewish law, and the attendant abilities to lead a community and administrate. This system in its most generic sense is quite a bit closer to the basic American ideal of being able to become whatever you want. If you study hard and are able to demonstrate religiosity and moral integrity, you are effectively permitted to pursue your vocation. This is all fine and well, but forces us to remember that a rabbi is in effect closer to a teacher and circuit court judge (theologically speaking) than he or she is to a priest—that is, one entrusted through sacrament to a holy mission. More important, it returns us to the idea that vocational discernment notwithstanding, every Jew is a priest and already entrusted with a holy mission.

Christians are brought into this original calling through the sacrament of baptism. Baptism is a renewal of the covenant—something that must be recovered after the breach of "original sin."

The "eternal" call is in the creation story; and then there are little calls along the way to help you figure out how you fit into creation.

This is a difficult notion for rationalists as well as for those who work daily with the idea of calling and its application to discerning priests. My father, for example, used to explain that he was perfectly *disposed* to believe in the presence of intelligent life in outer space, little green men, flying saucers, and abductions—hostile or friendly. It was just a matter of getting the flying saucer to land in his backyard. As soon as he'd seen it for himself, he'd be happy to believe in it. "Heck," he'd say, "I *hope* a flying saucer lands in my backyard. That would be so cool." When people involved in the discernment process face the *prophetic* component of their task, they are not looking for quantifiable or outwardly visible signs, but rather something that reflects faith, the belief in the invisible. To some extent, they are looking for that overwhelming sense of calm that represents finding the right answer—they are just doing it on someone else's behalf.

That said, when the Reverend Anne Richards talks about the role that calling plays in the discernment process, she specifies that "a decision is not ever made on the basis of hearing a call or not. Because everyone imagines all kinds of things—not even imagines, just *feels* all kinds of things. Nobody can ask God, or X ray the mind of God. So what you look at is what surrounds the *sense* that you're hearing a call—what points to its authenticity or its lack of authenticity."

"Man must become habitually mindful," wrote the historian A. O. Lovejoy in *The Great Chain of Being*, "of the limitations of his mental powers, must be content with that 'relative and practical understanding' which is the only organ of knowledge that he possesses."[28]

In the diocese of New York, the discernment is not about the legitimacy of the call itself, but rather "what surrounds" the sense of call. It is left entirely in the hands of the aspirant to prove that he or she is interpreting his or her own motivations correctly. Furthermore, he or she is charged with clearly representing those motivations in a way that will evoke a response from a congregation—a way of allowing someone in the pews to listen to this person and find something to relate to.

Among the possible misconceived motivations stands prominent *redemption*. I've come to learn that redemption is a predominant, though somewhat buried, theme in the topic of religious vocation. It is very easy, for example, in the wake of the pedophilia crisis in the Catholic Church, to assume that the men who committed these crimes were drawn to the priesthood because it would afford them total access to small children—as if perversion necessarily preceded vocation. It is more realistic, however, to consider the possibility that fervently religious men who perceived uncontrollable desires in themselves hoped to cure themselves by entering a purer life. They also hoped that by sacrificing themselves to the constraints of a celibate and selfless existence, they would receive atonement for those urges. Perhaps they even thought that God would protect them from their urges in exchange for their attempt to devote their lives to him. "By becoming a priest," wrote Thomas à Kempis, "you have not diminished your burden, but have taken on a stricter discipline, and are now obliged to strive for greater perfection and holiness." He continues, "When clad in sacred vestments the priest takes the place of Christ and humbly and suppliantly intercedes before God for himself and for all people."[29]

The activist Catholic lay group the Voice of the Faithful, formed in the wake of the pedophile priest scandal, held a conference during the summer of 2002 at the Hynes Convention Center in Boston. I attended, curious to know what, if any, connection might be drawn between religious vocation and this real-life crisis. I also went because the incredible enthusiasm, moral conviction, and tidal wave growth of this group struck me somehow as momentous—and I wanted to experience it.

In one of the afternoon panel discussions about the effect of the scandal on the clergy, a veteran priest, Reverend Robert Bullock of Our Lady of Sorrows in Sharon, Massachusetts, took the podium and told the gathered crowd about a summer retreat he had attended as a young seminarian in the late 1950s. In a soft Boston-inflected growl, Father Bullock remembered that there "was an extraordinary young seminarian there, a few years younger than I was. He was so charismatic, so gifted, he was *so completely a priest* that we all admired him—and we were all secretly a little jealous." This man was so unmistakably gifted with a vocation, explained Bullock, that he made the others question if they were truly meant to be there. The gifted seminarian was Paul R. Shanley—one of the most notorious protagonists of the Boston diocese sex-abuse scandal. And the sucking in of air in the overcrowded conference room was audible when Bullock revealed his name. This was someone who we'd all come to associate with the most criminal element of the priesthood—and here he was being described in such admiring terms. It's not an irreconcilable notion; it's simply a very complicated idea to digest. Father Bullock's point was not that Shanley was a wolf in sheep's clothing—which he was—but that he was also incredibly charismatic. The abiding question is whether that charisma came from a gift or an illness.

Whether or not Shanley would have been accepted at all into the Catholic priesthood if he'd applied after the 1981 addition of psychological screening to the application process is probably impossible to predict. And these specific issues are certainly not my father's. But I think that every aspirant to the priesthood of a religious order must at one point question whether their fantasy is to find penance for past mistakes in a religious vocation. Or is the hope, instead, to curb or mitigate unhappy forces in the present? Does this personal sacrifice (literally, "making sacred") to the challenges of ordained ministry constitute an unconditional offering, or is it a bid for self-improvement? At some level, the ritual of ordination at once acknowledges a degree of purity—which includes absolution for past sins—and puts a priest on a "holier" plane, perhaps giving the illusion that God will now protect you from yourself.

"How can we tell the difference between the word of God and mere human words?"[30] wondered Irenaeus, the bishop of Lyon at the dawn of the third century. It was a critical question for Irenaeus, to whom the task had basically fallen of editing the books of the New Testament—determining what would be canon and what would be apocrypha. The historian Elaine Pagels, who tells Irenaeus's story in her recent book *Beyond Belief,* chimes in: "How are visions received, and which are divinely inspired? Practically speaking, who is to judge? This central—and perplexing—question is what Christians since ancient times have called the problem of discerning spirits: how to tell which apparent inspirations come from God, which from the power of evil, and which from an overheated imagination." She continues, "Although most people at the time—Jews, pagans, and Christians alike—assumed that the divine reveals itself in dreams, many people then, as now, recognized that dreams may also express only wishes and hopes, and that some may lead to fatal delusions."[31]

In the Old Testament Jeremiah defended himself against accusations of false prophecy by saying that the Lord had come to him and said: "I am against them that prophesy lying dreams . . . and cause my people to err by their lies, and by their wontonness; yet I sent them not, nor commanded them" (Jeremiah 23:32). Or more to the point: "The prophet that hath a dream, let him tell a dream; and he that hath my word, let him speak my word faithfully" (Jeremiah 23:28).

Irenaeus, determined to consolidate an astonishing diversity of beliefs and practices in order to strengthen the ranks of persecuted Christians, tended to dismiss outright any revelation that didn't conform to tradition. Tradition, for Irenaeus, followed the spirit of Matthew, Luke, Mark, and John—the gospels—and any revelations that deviated were for him not the word of God but of Satan. *Tradition* was his tool of discernment.

A stunning proposition for discerning God's word from dreams comes down to us from the Gnostic gospel of Mary Magdalene, discovered in Egypt in 1896. In the surviving opening fragments of the ancient document, the risen Jesus appears to Mary and she immediately asks him *how* visions occur. "How does one who sees the vision see it—through the soul, or through the spirit?" He answers, "One does not see through the soul, nor through the spirit, but the mind which is between the two: that is what sees the vision."[32]

Here Jesus offers *the mind* as a principal tool in discernment.

But when Mary goes on to repeat what Irenaeus would call the "unorthodox" teachings Jesus revealed to her, the rest of the disciples object. Peter argues, "Say what you will about what she has said, I, at least, do not believe that the Savior said this, for certainly these teachings are strange ideas." In defense of Mary, Levi replies: "Peter, you have always been hot tempered. Now I see you contending against the woman as our enemies do. But if the Savior made her worthy, who are you, indeed, to reject her? Surely the Savior knows her very well. That is why he loved her more than us. Rather, let us be ashamed, and . . . preach the gospel."[33]

So while one faction defends a revelation based on its content, the author of the gospel of Mary Magdalene suggests that a revelation's merit can be simply based on *who* receives it. Discernment is *circumstantial*.

Meanwhile, the philosopher Justin of Caesarea (100–165), an older contemporary of Irenaeus, spent many years seeking "truth," and concluded his search when he met an old man who explained that the Hebrew prophets "alone both saw and proclaimed the truth . . . being filled with the holy spirit. They did not use [logical] demonstration in their writings, since they were witnesses to truth *beyond* such demonstration."[34]

The early Christians wrestled with the question of how to discern God's will and intentions, only to arrive at conclusions that eschew empirical knowledge—as to some extent we must when trafficking in the unknowable, when the foundational tenet of the philosophy we're contemplating is faith, "the ability," according to Paul, "to imagine the invisible." The fact that the Old Testament prophets and Christian church fathers fretted about the difficulty of verifying the word of God is consoling. Today, when you ask the church outright how one might go about running a background check for divine call—how to make absolutely sure that a candidate is or isn't called by God to the priesthood—the answer is forthright and unapologetic: You don't. "No one can X-ray the mind of God."

If only it were that cut-and-dried. Although the Episcopal Church doesn't claim a direct line to God's will, it is also not in the business—as the church fathers were—of confirming prophets and consolidating Christianity into one catholic, or universal, religion. The task at hand—discerning a call to the priesthood—is a smaller one, whose qualifications combine mystical summons with more worldly, quantifiable talents. The priest is not a prophet, but a pastor, a "servant leader" in the lexicon of contemporary Christianity. In mainstream Protestantism, the priest isn't responsible for divine revelation or prophecy. He or she is responsible for bearing the word of God as it has already been canonized. Priests are not even part of the apostolic succession from Peter; bishops are, and priests partake in *their* grace through the sacrament of ordination.

So what is this divine call that makes or breaks priests? What is its relationship to the quantifiable qualifications of community service and leadership—the standards for which are increasingly clear-cut as organizations are held increasingly accountable for their employees? And how does spirituality, an unquantifiable qualification that doesn't rely on divine call, come into play? The answer is at once ancient and in constant development.

If we were to go back a moment "to the source," to when the divine revealed itself in dreams, we might wonder: do people dream about becoming a priest? It's certainly not a well-paid or celebrity life. It's not the kind of life that little girls fall asleep wishing for their future, or that little boys cross their hearts and make spit pacts with their buddies—"One day I'll be a priest!" Once upon a time it was a person's lot in life. Second sons in Emily Brontë novels—the ones who weren't going to inherit the family fortune (because in those days it still hadn't occurred to anyone to share?)—became Anglican priests. Now, as we shall see, the desire to become a priest must be strong enough to withstand not only the prospect of a humble lifestyle, but also a tremendously difficult screening process, as well as a long and expensive preparation, indicating that, yes indeed, people do dream hard about becoming priests—or else no one would come out the other side.

The intellectual, wrote Richard Hofstadter, "in some sense lives for ideas—which means that he has a sense of dedication to the life of the mind which is very much like a religious commitment. This is not surprising," he continues, "for in a very important way the role of the intellectual is inherited from the office of the cleric: it implies a special sense of the ultimate value in the existence of the act of comprehension. Socrates, when he said that the unexamined life is not worth living, struck the essence of it."[35]

Many of us live according to these Socratic modes without necessarily identifying them as such. And more important, we happily live *without* the impression that we're either intellectuals or not—and that whether we are or not comports any particular "role." Very likely, we all simply think in the manner that comes most naturally to us—grateful for the ability to accomplish mental tasks, happy to be able to contribute to dinner party conversation, and perhaps occasionally welcoming a new cerebral challenge with the notion that rising to a cerebral challenge will exercise the brain muscles and forestall eventual atrophy—"to defeat the shrinkage of age," as Virginia Woolf once put it.

There is a moment (of indeterminate length) of utter chaos, of flying a trapeze without a net, in between the state of being convinced of the correctness of your idea and entertaining the plausibility of another, new idea. For you must let go of one idea before embracing its alternative. This is the tumult of thinking—and such chaos, most would agree, is a very limited pleasure. Chaos is primordial ooze, chaos is Armageddon, chaos is the Tower of Babel—chaos is the whole picture as opposed to the microcosm. We prefer our disorientation to be controlled and circumspect. We prefer a street fair, a boisterous night on the town, a roller-coaster ride, the bottom of the ninth in a tied World Series game.

If you worship at the altar of reason, the idea that there may be some "higher truth" beyond your own mental faculties is distressing. It's swinging without a net. But all you have to do is look at the newspaper or scan a history book to be reminded that reason has at best a tenuous hold over civilization. This is not to say that reason and conviction are at all mutually exclusive from things such as truth and faith. For the majority of us, all these operations work in tandem. Intellectuals have convictions (otherwise they would drown in relativism). Religious make tireless use of reason in order to describe the holy presence in worldly terms. Fundamentalists use reason in order to position their faith—and then sit tight. The rest of us read books, make life decisions, vote, and contribute to dinner party conversations without ever deconstructing and identifying our own individual theory of knowledge.

Yet reason has a glass ceiling. Reason can be deceptively reassuring. The reasonable argument is as good or correct as its logic is coherent. An idea arrived at through reasoning is in a sense built from the bottom up. To evaluate the legitimacy of an idea, you work backward from the idea through its argumentation to make sure that all the pieces are in place. You can see that the top of this model is the idea itself—the glass ceiling. The idea is an artificial or man-made construction. Ideas are tools, writes Louis Menand in *The Metaphysical Club*, "like forks and knives and microchips—that people devise to cope with the world in which they find themselves." Menand goes on to explain that ideas are social: "They do not develop according to some inner logic of their own, but are entirely dependent, like germs on their human carriers and the environment . . . ideas are provisional responses to particular and unreproducible circumstances, their survival depends not on their immutability but on their adaptability."[36]

The idea of calling may not actually be as well constructed as is, say, the Darwinian idea of evolution. But it is an idea by virtue of its historical existence and adaptability through the ages. The path of the idea of calling is based more on its longevity than on its rationale. It moves freely, without inhibition, between reason and something "higher."

There are two possible conclusions that my father can draw from the response to his application. He could determine that the church, as an entirely man-made (and not necessarily God-endorsed) enterprise, has rejected him for a series of entirely worldly reasons: age discrimination, financial discrimination (in the sense that they can't afford to invest in a minister so close to mandatory retirement), discrimination because his ideas are too cerebral or too intellectual and not "accessible," or because he has a "different way of being and doing in the world"—and the church that preaches inclusion doesn't necessarily practice it at the middle-management level. Or my father could let go of one trapeze to reach out for the next—the answer kind of floating in a liminal space. This is all about divine calling—about what God wants for him. And is that a question that man can answer?

PART THREE

The Process

There was never anything by the wit of man

so well devised, or so sure established,

which in continuance of time

hath not been corrupted.

—Church of England Prayer Book, 1549

*G*rasping my father's sense of call requires first grasping his religiosity. Unlike someone who meets him today and who gets to know him as a religious man—who can take his faith as a given—I have to acquaint myself with his faith. It's a progression, not a given. Probably in order not to alienate us, my father kept his own religious progression away from us. Once it was firmly a part of his life, he began letting it creep into our interactions. If he hadn't then upped the ante so dramatically by wanting to become a priest, we probably would have simply come to accept the differences between his style of life and ours as just that—differences.

There is a disjoint between the ineffable Christianity of our father and our experience of him as a practicing Christian. At the most basic level, the person who regularly attends church believes in the inherent value of attending church. This is the only thing about which an onlooker can be sure, if going to church is the only way spirituality is expressed. A person who talks openly about his beliefs reveals a spirituality that extends beyond church attendance. And the person who practices his religion in some fashion outside of church indicates an even broader commitment to religion or faith. I am talking about demonstrable faith, which, for someone like me, an outsider, is faith that can be witnessed.

For many years my father's only demonstrable expression of faith has been attending church and participating in the church community as a lay reader and choir member. Since his second marriage, in 1992, my father has regularly gone to church on Sunday morning. If my visit happened to coincide with a Sunday, I very occasionally have opted to tag along. But until my father revealed his project to pursue ordination, we didn't discuss religion, and I didn't witness anything that I might have recognized as a Christian lifestyle in his home environment.

If you get beyond the discernment process, and are accepted into the priesthood—after three years of seminary and one year serving as a deacon—then you have an ordination ceremony, during which the bishop confers to you the sacrament of holy orders. The ceremony is included in the Book of Common Prayer, a copy of which my father sent me soon after I embarked upon this project. The ordination liturgy includes an "examination," made up of nine questions the bishop poses to the "ordinand." This examination essentially defines the vows of priesthood. The first question is "My brother [or sister], do you believe that you are truly called by God and his Church to this priesthood?" To which the ordinand responds, "I do believe I am so called." Another question asks, "Will you do your best to pattern your life [and that of your family, or household, or community} in accordance with the teachings of Christ, so that you may be a wholesome example to your people?" And right after that: "Will you persevere in prayer, both in public and in private, asking God's grace both for yourself and for others, offering all your labors to God, through the mediation of Jesus Christ and in the sanctification of the Holy Spirit?"

The setting of a prayerful, wholesome example is one of the priest's foremost obligations. It distinguishes the priest as an "island of holiness," a reflection of the wholesome and moral example that the church is to set*—the heart of my father's commitment both to the church and to the priesthood. He wants to provide a moral and religious example so that others (who are floundering as he once floundered) might have something to follow.

Throughout the screening process, a candidate is evaluated on

---

*The nonspecific clause is, it should be said, the loophole through which most forms of discrimination also slither.

how they practice their faith—their spirituality. Do they say grace? Do they go to church? Do they pray at night before going to bed? Do they teach their children to say prayers? Do they go to midnight mass on Christmas Eve? Do they keep Lent? And so forth. This aspect of the screening process is a constant across mainline denominations. Chancellor Schorsch of the Jewish Theological Seminary explains, for example, that the two central qualifications for rabbinical school are intellectual preparation and religious observance—"to what degree the individual has begun to internalize religious observance."

It seems an entirely self-evident qualification. A religious leader should have a strong personal practice. This was perhaps the reason why I had difficulty understanding my father's motives or qualifications for religious leadership. Despite the fact that he went to church every Sunday, I had never really gotten the impression that my father's household was a paragon of religious observance. Sentiment, ardor, ethics—yes. Observance—no.

And then they started saying grace. Or rather, they started saying grace *even* in front of me. Once I was invited to participate, it was clear that in one form or another, and with some real degree of regularity, blessing over food has been said in my father's house ever since the children were old enough to appreciate such a gesture. When I say that blessing *began* being said, what I mean to say is that it was being said with such ritual regularity—the religious practice had become so internalized—that it was no longer comfortable to skip even if there was "company."

The fact that I didn't witness grace for a hunk of time, which extended just barely into my initial research, meant that I didn't know my father's family said it. Which meant that when I reflected on the question of my father's commitment to religious observance, I came up in a panic. What if he's only a good Christian on Sunday? I thought. That doesn't possibly count.

Though, in actuality, there's no reason why it shouldn't count. A man setting out on the road to the priesthood is going to look different from a man who has already arrived there. The "examination" that is part of the ordination ceremony doesn't, in point of fact, take place until long after the initial screening of discernment. I was confusing the expected preparation of an ordinand with the expected will of an applicant to *become* formed for the priesthood. A seminary graduate, who has been preparing with their bishop for several years and has even interned in a parish, will know how to act like a priest both in public and private spheres. Whereas an applicant, we must assume, is learning—more precisely, aspires to learn.

One expert I talked to, a consultant at the diocesan level on discernment, argues fiercely against this tendency to evaluate applicants according to preconceived expectations of what a priest should look like. And yet there is in place an operative model of "the perfect candidate" to ordained ministry. According to the Reverend Jamie L'Enfant, who serves on the Commission on Ministry in the Diocese of Western North Carolina, the perfect candidate is someone who already seems a priest (in appearance and self-presentation), has an impressive roster of church-related experience behind them, speaks a clear Eucharistic theology, and has the support of his or her immediate community. But, L'Enfant explains, "basing the ordination process solely on this model is severely limiting because it assumes that formation precedes ordination." We must broaden our understanding, she writes, "to allow for growth and development within and after the ordination process. We need only turn to the Bible to find a cast of characters shockingly lacking in spiritual maturity or vocational clarity who were, nevertheless, chosen by God for God's work. Moses was a murderer and tongue-tied sheep farmer, Jacob a scheming trickster, David a boy shepherd, Peter a self-protecting disciple who denied Jesus three times."[1]

Saying grace is praying—that hasn't escaped my notice. The Hasidic rabbi Abraham Joshua Heschel described the art of prayer as "the momentary disregard of our personal concerns, the absence of self-centered thoughts. Feeling becomes prayer in the moment in which we forget ourselves and become aware of God." In praying over meals, he says, "the thought of personal need is absent, and the

thought of divine grace alone is present in his mind. Thus, in beseech-
ing Him for bread, there is *one* instant, at least, in which our mind is
directed neither to our hunger nor to food, but to His mercy."[2]

One of my father's historic tirades on the subject of his Catholic
upbringing is against prayer as a contract: you ask for things from
God and promise other things in exchange. It's a perversion of the
meaning of prayer, he'll tell you. Simone Weil described prayer as
inclining the self toward God, turning your face up, opening yourself
to his grace. The contemporary Israeli thinker Isaiah Leibovitz
wrote: "'Why does prayer and at times the prayer of the righteous,
upright and innocent go unanswered?' And the response is: *There is
no prayer which goes unanswered!* . . . Since prayer is only the expression of the worshiper's goal to serve God, the very act of prayer is
the attainment of the goal."[3]

Grace was skipped once upon a time on my account—my
father's family unit instinctively kept praying to themselves. It was a
form of intimacy that they wouldn't have imposed on me, a guest
for better or worse. My father has explained to me, "We've been
saying grace about ten years, but we generally ignored it when you
guys were around in order to avoid discomfiting you." He continued, "I have no trouble recognizing that it is hard to give thanks
when our daily thoughts are focused on a level of such tiny
details—all of which comes alive when we wish to address Infinity."
So now, I wonder why he didn't want to risk discomfiting us "guys"
if there was a possibility that our mundane little thoughts would
come alive.

At my father's dinner table everyone has a chance to participate.
The prayers are very explicit and formal-sounding to my untrained
ear. "Bless, O Lord, *thy* gifts to our use and us to *thy* service; for
Christ's sake. *Amen.*" Inevitably, my father will say *"for Chrisssake!"* as
if someone had just cut him off on the freeway, making Nic laugh,
and I'll smile shyly, too. That was a joke, I know. I'm essentially an
interloper, but the "spirit" as my father would say, "is right."

Saying grace does throw me off. Nothing about ritual in the

home feels natural to me. (Call it "family tradition" instead and I won't bat an eyelash.) I don't understand how you can be there in the midst of preparations—half the food is on the table, the pickle plate has long been demolished, something gravylike is searing on the range, no one's managed to find napkins yet, there's a telemarketer blathering on through the answering machine, and my little sister, Katyana, really, really, really doesn't want orange juice to drink—and the beginning of dinner is declared. We all stop, join hands, and pray to some apparently external element: God. Everything about the dinner up to that point has seemed to belong exclusively to us, to the people cooking and the people waiting to eat. We've found the ingredients, mixed them, applied alchemy to make them edible—this is all about us. But we stop and we thank God. And at a certain level, even for me, it's good that we call a halt to all this *us* and stand back. It's good for our character, our sense of proportion, and capacity for concentration. It's good for our digestion. It's good to remember that we have things we can count on but that we're not *entitled* to them. I get to hold hands with my little sister (who is invariably sneaking peeks at me, her prodigal big sister, rather than praying) and my little brother, who otherwise at this point in his maturation would "rather not hold hands." If I stay more than four days, the rotation lands on me and I have to come up with something to say. I try to remember some Hebrew, fudge some sounds, throw in a couple of Sanskrit words picked up in yoga class, and hope that nobody notices I ended with a *"shel Shabbat"* for the Sabbath, even though it's Wednesday.

"All bishops are mad," Thomas Merton is reported to have said to Guy Davenport[4] one day in the late sixties, walking the Kentucky woods near his Trappist monastery. There are no end of apocryphal tales about Merton—many of which begin with him saying something wise or outrageous, breaking his vow of silence (he was a particularly outspoken Trappist). Another tale dating to the 1960s recounts him dismissing a young Trappist novice from the monastery with the explanation "This is not for you. You're too smart. This is for Kansas farm boys who don't know what else to do."* One might speculate that Merton had wished for some such similar cautionary discernment when he first came to the Trappists, or that he was enacting on the newcomer his own vision for a reformed church. Mostly it's an interesting anecdote, in that it reveals Merton performing an act of discernment in direct contradiction to the act of the monastery fathers who had already accepted the novice into the order, suggesting at the outset the plasticity of the discernment process.

"Discernment," the practice designed by Saint Ignatius of Loyola to cultivate prayer and spiritual meditation, to bring the practitioner into mystic communion with the Lord, is the divining of spirits and the casting out of devils. Merton once described Ignatius's *Spiritual Exercises* as "very pedestrian and practical—their chief purpose being to enable all the busy Jesuits to get their minds off their work and back to God with a minimum of wasted time."[5]

Any number of years ago in the course of some conversation or another, I can remember my father boasting about the screening process the Episcopal Church puts its would-be priests through. No, they didn't just take anybody, they carefully screened against pedophiles, criminals, and wing nuts, he might have said, painting with broad strokes. It was a point of pride, representing a church that looked after its flock by providing it with pastors of a certain quality, selected with an attention that paid respectful tribute to the precious nature of the charge. The conversation comes back to me now. It took place around the same time that my father was first exploring his own vocation with Father Chuck.

Reverend Douglas Brown is prior of the Holy Cross Monastery (a Benedictine Episcopal monastic order) in upstate New York, and an expert in discernment. He told me that the first step toward

---

*This anecdote is totally apocryphal. It was passed down to me thirdhand. It nonetheless has a tone and temperament totally consistent with Merton's style.

recognizing a calling to the priesthood always happens more or less in the following way. A person sort of starts to think that maybe he or she might like perhaps to be a priest—but it's sort of an absurd idea. Who am I to want to be a priest? they might wonder. Why would I want to do that? And so they try to shake the feeling off.

Becoming a priest is a big deal, a life change, a sea shift. It's not the same thing as deciding you might like to try to get a job in theater administration, for example. What's more, it might seem a little arrogant—"I am such a holy person that I am suited to lead others in holiness." That just sounds funny. "Illusions of grandeur," said one Catholic priest, describing his parents' reaction to his entering seminary.[6] But the idea might well settle and stick in a person's mind, and the person might find him- or herself trying it out on someone—maybe even as a joke, just to see what effect it has. "Just to see whether people swallow their forks, or scream," adds Brown. It's the same way someone who thinks they want to be a poet might casually share a poem they "just kind of wrote," hoping that the reader will respond, "Wow, this is a really good poem. You should be a poet." And sometimes the person who dares to say they might want to be a priest gets the unexpected response "Of course you should be a priest, you'd be wonderful!" Other people describe the alternative experience of being told by someone that they should be a priest and, upon hearing the words, realizing, "Yes, that's what this feeling is; I want to be a priest!" like when someone suggests an interpretation of a troubling dream you've had and the interpretation at once just feels right. In one way or the other, the idea has its first utterance, its first embryonic expression, and then there it is, out there in the world.

The only way to "become" a poet is to write poems; at a certain point the writing of poems becomes an inextricable part of one's identity. The Reverend David Lee Carlson of Saint Augustine's Church in Croton-on-Hudson, New York, explains that a person's calling to the priesthood evolves through a similar kind of "ripple effect." The first hesitant utterance aloud, "I might like to be a priest," is like a pebble dropping in a pond. "Language starts to come around," he says. More and more people "become included in this individual calling, and it starts rippling out into the broader community until the point where—if you get there—you are being ordained for the church." Your calling belongs to the whole pond.

If you get there. In between that first tentative utterance and the sacrament of ordination lies "the Process," a trial by fire so arduous that it doesn't seem as if it could have anything at all to do with that lovely pond in Reverend Carlson's image. Most Episcopal Church members won't know that the discernment process leading to the priesthood is such a beast that it merits a capital letter. But people who have been through it and people who administrate it or participate somehow do know. One recent seminary graduate I met was genuinely startled that I was even familiar with the moniker—it's a familiarity evidently reserved for a kind of inner circle, like the rules of a fraternity hazing.

Which isn't at all to say that the requirements of the discernment process are a guarded secret; quite the opposite. The standardized series of requirements, forty-five separate steps, are public and detailed in "Title III—Ministry" of *The Constitutions and Canons of the Episcopal Church*. The canons are the rules of the church, reviewed and amended on an ongoing basis at the triannual general convention, a governing congress of clergy and laity. The "standard" steps outlined in Title III are then customized (interpreted) to suit the local needs of each given diocese. The size and makeup of the different dioceses vary enormously—as do their interpretations of Title III. It is a standard requirement, for example, that a psychological evaluation be conducted on candidates for priesthood. How the exam is administered, who administers it, which examination procedure is used, who pays for it, and who has access to the results are all issues that are determined locally. Approximately 72 percent of all dioceses maintain a set of printed guidelines in the bishop's office, which anyone interested in pursuing ordination has access to. The existence of published guidelines goes a long way toward emphasizing that the Process is standardized—the same rules will apply to all applicants. The information is not privileged, nor is it, however, instinctive. It's a code and a process, candidates are subject to review, and the desire of an individual is anything but the last word.

The Right Reverend Robert H. Johnson is bishop of the Episcopal diocese of Western North Carolina—a gorgeous, tangled rural district with its diocesan offices in a split-level stone hunting lodge, hidden down a dirt road in Black Mountain, and its cathedral on a main street in tony Asheville. It is considered a small diocese, comprising only seventy-two congregations and seventeen thousand members, too small to even have its own set of local canons. Bishop Johnson is a handsome, sandpapery fifty-something, with the illusory gauntness and large bones of a taller man than he actually is. The day we met (in the hunting lodge) he was sporting a brilliant magenta silk shirt (which impressed me as terribly flashy until I learned it is part of a bishop's standard vestments) and a cleric's white collar, and if I'm not mistaken, a large silver and turquoise belt buckle—or maybe it was a string tie. He's contagiously friendly, with a ready big-toothed smile, and a way of redirecting the conversation toward meaty digressions. He talks the way you'd hope a holy man from Black Mountain might talk—"So the discernment process started early on after the initial Christians started proclaiming the good news that God's gone and forgiven us through the person of Jesus Christ"—and he prayed over me and blessed me before sending me back off into the North Carolina hinterland. I believe him when he assures me that the Process works, "it's a good process"—I believe him because his confidence is convincing. But still (because it's easy to get lost in the formal language of the church canons) I ask, "How does it work?"

"Each diocese has its own process," he explains, "that has some similarities to other dioceses and some differences—that's just the way it evolved. A person has to be in a congregation for at least a year. Then if you feel that gnawing in your heart, that sense in your spirit that God is trying to take something, then you go and talk to your priest about that. If your priest feels like you're ready for this discernment committee, then he'll set up your discernment. Men and women—some of whom know you, some of whom don't, a good mixture—help discern whether you would make a good priest in the church. You share your spiritual journey with the people on the committee. It's not a grilling, so to speak, it's just an invitational process—a get to know each other. And usually after six months of regular meetings the committee makes a report."

He says that how often the committee meets during that time varies, but that it should be at least once a month. Then, he continues, "the candidate has to write their spiritual autobiography, and they share that. It's all a very open, honest kind of process. And the committee is supposed to share out of their hearts and spirits, so it's not just one person getting grilled all the time.

"I tell parish committees that their job isn't always to say yes. It's also to say no or maybe or 'Wait, and come back later.' I tell clergy that, too.

"So after that the parish committees *rate* the person—that's a term we use. 'This person has wonderful gifts, but she's very immature; three years of seminary should take care of that'—they might say that sort of thing, and so forth. I get the report and meet with the person and then if everything appears in order between me and the person and this committee, then I recommend that they go on to the diocesan Commission on Ministry, which has a similar process, but these are people they don't know, who are more representative of the whole church instead of just the local church.

"The parish committee has to approve them, their priest has to approve them, and then the diocesan Commission on Ministry and the Standing Committee together have to approve them before I will put them in seminary. The seminary has the chance to get a total picture of the person, their spiritual material. And at the end of it all, they take the general examination."

I ask him whether the members of the Standing Committee or the Commission on Ministry have any special training in discernment.

"No," he answers, "they're just good Christian people who are proactive in their churches, who have the sensitivity to look beyond the obvious, to try to get to know people—man, woman, clergy. We try to be as good a cross section as we can be, and stay in line with the differences. They meet with the person for a whole weekend twice a year, spending social time with them—mealtime with them, beer and wine time as well as dialogue time, one on one, or in small discussion groups. The questions we talk about are usually around how our faith speaks to different issues—about poverty, the war effort, how people interpret the Bible, fundamentalism, scripture. They're fun weekends, because there are no right or wrong answers. Just trying to get to know the people, so they can make a decision: Should this person pursue? Does this person have those gifts? And if they recognize them, then I get to talk to the person and figure out where they go to seminary."

The emphasis on the community is a constant throughout the ordination process—whoever you talk to. Evaluation by the laity is considered integral to discernment. The "Supporting Material for Vocations Committees" in the diocese of Ohio explains it this way: "Through the Holy Spirit, people with the gifts and qualities of leadership are identified for ordained ministry with that vocation affirmed and authenticated by the Church. Early Christians saw themselves as having the responsibility of identifying and appointing leaders. Out of their experience of community, they could readily identify the servants best suited for the trust of leading the Church in its life and mission. This approach to leadership is indigenous to Christianity." The "early Christians" referred to here are third- and fourth-century Catholics, who compelled popes and bishops into their seats by popular election. The importance of the congregation's role in selecting its own leadership was revisited during the Reformation—at which point it was the Protestants who argued that the community's role had become too diluted and that ministry made sense only when it related to an actual congregation: a call to service of God *and* the church.

In early Protestantism the power and authority of a minister was considered divine—he spoke and acted in the name of God—but the authority itself was bestowed by the congregation. It was the people who granted the minister his divine authority, so that somehow before the minister assumed the position whereby he represented the divine, the people channeled the divine in order to elect the minister. Herein we find the origins of the Process as it is conducted today—with tremendous emphasis put on being judged and selected by a jury of peers.

My father's discernment was suspended relatively early in the process, and he completed only a fraction of the steps that normally constitute a full screening. He first sought guidance and formal sponsorship from a priest (Chuck Ransom), then he filed a paper application with the diocese that included his spiritual biography. A vocations committee was formed by the bishop's office to respond to his application. Every diocese has its own system for forming this first stage of peer review—some committees are culled from your own congregation, others might include fellow applicants. In my father's case, his vocations committee was made up of a priest and two laypeople from a neighboring congregation. Ideally the vocations committee will meet with a candidate a number of times from several months to a year. The Ohio guidelines instruct committees to convene over a three-to-four-month period, with the "expectation" that they will meet with the applicant at least four times. There is no "exception clause" appended to that standard, saying something like, "Unless the applicant seems entirely clearly obviously wrong for the ordained ministry . . . in which case suspend early and save yourselves." This was the nonexistent clause apparently attached to my father's application because he was granted only two and a half meetings in total and some e-mail exchange before this committee passed a negative decision on his application. Now, my father did make a terrible early impression by arriving late to his third meeting—which, if a pattern, is considered a red flag for "authority issues." But the precise point of an extended screening process with repeat visits is to establish that which is a pattern and that which is a genuinely good excuse. Sociopathy or chronic tardiness notwithstanding, my father's discernment process as it was would, by every definition and throughout the church, be construed to be *irregular*.

I ask Bishop Johnson what he would say to someone who came to him, wanting to go on in the process even if he or she hadn't been supported by the parish committee.

"I send them back to the parish, because I'm so committed to the understanding of the call that comes out of the body of Christ—out of the church—that the candidate has to be connected with the whole parish, not just with the bishop. When I've met people from other dioceses who didn't go through this process, I find that they don't really understand what a community of faith is all about. They see themselves as solo performers. There's no such thing as being clergy by yourself. You need your brothers and sisters. All Christians need each other."

According to a 1996 internal review of the modern ordination process, "Title III—Ministry" of the Episcopal canons in theory summarizes a system whereby "a congregational process in the local parish gives way to a Presbyterian process in the Commission on Ministry and (often) Standing Committee, to an academic and communal process in seminary, all of them overlapping and recurring several times, with occasional contacts with an Episcopal personage."[7]

Unpacked, that description means that a candidate first gains the support of his or her congregation, or in some cases a body that represents the local congregation. In the diocese of Ohio, where my father entered the process, for example, the initial screening isn't within a person's own congregation but with members of neighboring parishes—a vocations committee whose makeup is intended to represent the average congregation of the region. In New York, the vocations committee is made up of members from an individual's own congregation. The advantage of that system is that the group knows the candidate and has seen him or her already operating in the church environment. The disadvantage, explains the Reverend Anne Richards, formerly of the diocesan staff in New York, is that the group knows the candidate, is inclined to support their own, and thus tends to lack some objectivity.

The "Presbyterian process" refers to meetings that a candidate will have with a council of "elders," or "presbyters," represented by the diocesan Commission on Ministry and the diocesan Standing Committee. Those committees are made up of clergy and lay-people. Their terms of office and the mode of their selection are determined by the local canons or guidelines of each individual diocese. In the majority of dioceses, bishops appoint the members of the Commission on Ministry,* and nominate candidates for election to the Standing Committee.† Both groups play an important role in the Process. The Commission on Ministry is canonically charged with supporting the bishop in selecting and screening candidates for holy orders; and the Standing Committee is charged with approving candidates who present themselves for holy orders.

Embedded in this stage of the process are a series of exams and background checks. Applicants are required to provide school records (a B.A. with sufficient emphasis on liberal arts), and submit to thorough medical, psychological (personality, cognitive, intelligence), and psychiatric evaluations.‡ "We probably turn down half the people who apply on psychological grounds," says Richards. "That doesn't mean they're crazy (some of them are) but it means they are simply not appropriate for the ordained ministry." All

---

*According to the 1996 Stafford-Falkowski survey, in dioceses that responded, the bishop appoints the Commission on Ministry in 101 dioceses, compared to 14 dioceses where the commission is elected by diocesan convention and 28 where the commission is partially elected and partially appointed and 14 where the bishop appoints and another body confirms.

†As dictated by the canons of the Episcopal Church, Title I, on the formation of the Standing Committee.

‡The financial burden of paying for these medical and psychological exams, several thousand dollars, is the sole responsibility of the applicant.

information provided in their application is checked: "I've known people who seem like they're natural to the ordained ministry— smart, attractive, well-spoken—who have faked their transcripts!" The paperwork component generally includes personal essays as well. Everyone submits a spiritual autobiography, and some dioceses ask for other writing, such as a "leadership history." In New York, candidates are required to fill out a seventy-five-page personal his- tory questionnaire—to "hasten the process." It's very personal— "leaves no area of the person's life uncovered," says Richards.

The psychological exams that are now a standardized part of the application process—not only in the Episcopal Church, but in the Catholic Church* and for rabbinical school as well—test foremost for debilitating psychological conditions, and then for what can best be described as stability of self. In other words, clergy not only are in community leadership roles and counseling positions, but are the worldly center of people's spiritual life. Parishioners project a whole variety of unrealistic impulses onto their priest or rabbi, often, for example, mistaking them for God, expecting superhuman abilities and not allowing for human infallibility. "The people in my congre- gation think I'm like the Blessed Virgin Mary!" exclaims one priest. "And it's a very sophisticated congregation. But I'm idealized there because of the collar. There are a whole lot of projections that just get *whooshed* onto you." The greatest mistake that a clergyperson can make (consciously or unconsciously) would be to buy into those projections, setting the stage both for abuse of power and for a self- destructive sense of responsibility. Which is why one of the central qualifications for clergy and aspiring clergy is an incorruptible sense of self, a solid ego.

The academic and communal process in seminary is a somewhat more straightforward (or at least immediately comprehensible) part of formation. A candidate attends seminary, goes to classes, is instructed,

---

*Since 1981, the American Roman Catholic Church includes psychological eval- uation as part of its discernment process.

evaluated, promoted, and graduated. Along the way, candidates are immersed in a Christian lifestyle and a community of their peers—considered in itself an integral aspect of formation for the priesthood.

"Occasional contacts with an episcopal personage" means that to varying extents a candidate will have an ongoing relationship with either the bishop who is supporting them or with a canon on the bishop's staff. This extends from the first formal acceptance of a candidate into the process to training and support, ongoing evaluation, and eventually the conferring of holy orders. Bishop Cate Waynick of Indianapolis, for example, meets personally twice a month with her postulants—the candidates in her diocese who are in seminary. This would be considered "frequent contact," and she has developed this system in part because the majority of her postulants attend the large Christian Theological Seminary (Disciples of Christ) whose campus abuts the building where the diocese of Indianapolis has its offices. Because her postulants are not studying in a strictly Episcopalian environment, she meets with them often to tutor them in canon law and the Book of Common Prayer. In order to finish their formation, they will still have to complete at least a year's worth of course work at an Episcopal school. In other dioceses, a seminarian might have contact with his or her bishop as infrequently as four times a year—the minimum contact required by canon law. This contact with the bishop during seminary usually takes the form of letters (Ember Day letters) that the seminarians submit reporting on their spiritual and formational progress.

These interactions, taken together, recurring at different stages throughout formation, make up an extended screening process. No candidate is guaranteed ordination,* and any significant change of

---

*Several lawsuits in public court over the last decade have demonstrated that acceptance into the ordination process does not constitute a guarantee of eventual ordination. It is also notably the case that a master of divinity degree does not confer any guarantee of acceptance into the ordination process—nor indeed is it necessarily even taken into special consideration.

circumstance or humor along the way can lead to a reversal of fortune. Once a candidate has successfully navigated the Process, however it operates in his or her local diocese, the candidate is ordained a "transitional deacon" for six months to a year—a further, practical preparation—after which he or she is conferred the holy orders of the priesthood.*

There are, naturally, a variety of approaches to the transitional diaconate. Some bishops ordain their postulants during the last year of seminary, so that the fulfillment of their practical formation (the apprenticeship in a parish) coincides with graduation from seminary. More commonly, bishops schedule the transitional diaconate for the year after graduation. And some bishops require an internship year under an active priest earlier in the process—during the discernment, or "screening," period, or even during seminary—in addition to a year spent as a transitional deacon. Most seminarians spend their summer vacations either training in hospital chaplaincy work (CPE) or apprenticing in a parish.

The vast array of interpretations of the Title III canons for discernment is genuinely impressive. Consider that the forty-five separate requirements described by the canons and embodied in the general description above are each subject to distinct formulation within every one of the over one hundred Episcopal dioceses.

Incoming bishops are likely to review and modify anew the process according to their own interests, experiences, or convictions. That means guidelines in one diocese are not necessarily consistent from year to year when there are changes in the bishop's staff. And every diocesan Commission on Ministry, charged with advising the bishop on discernment, is going to bring that many more interpretations of canon law into the equation.

The role of the Commission on Ministry is perhaps the most sig-

---

*Current proposed revisions will likely eliminate the transitional diaconate as a mandatory step over the next few years. See the next section for a more complete discussion of proposed revisions.

nificant modern incarnation of the notion that a call to the priest-hood must come from the people, from "the congregation." The commission's mandate is broadly expressed. It assists the bishop with the implementation of Title III, which includes not only the raising up, recruiting, and discerning of priests, bishops, and dea-cons, but also the support of active clergy (in terms of salary, bene-fits, and continuing education) and the development of the "Ministry of all baptized persons"—a large group, to say the least. There are two and a half million Episcopalians in America, eight thousand active clergy, and approximately another six thousand retired clergy.

One of the commission's primary tasks is to work with the bishop to determine the needs for ordained and lay professionals at a local level. The fact that each diocese has a carefully determined idea of what its needs are in terms of ordained clergy is critical to the understanding of how the Process works. Once ordained, a priest serves the whole American Episcopal Church, yet every individual applicant applies to a distinct demographic, with distinct local con-cerns. A rural diocese, for example, may need priests with a demon-strable capacity to understand and attend to the pitfalls of an agricultural economy (and the attendant focus on acts of God in nature), while an urban diocese may determine that it desperately needs young bilingual priests who can provide immediate and ener-getic outreach to teenagers. The commission's input is necessarily a democratic approach to the understanding of local needs. While a bishop of a large suburban diocese might be looking for priests with a special knack for enticing busy professionals, a lay member of the commission may be perfectly positioned, there in the heart of the community, to point out that the diocese really needs more people specially qualified to counsel for substance abuse. And as each mem-ber of the commission is going to bring his or her special interests to bear on the dialogue, so, too, will the bishop bring a personal per-spective to the discernment process.

How decisive a role the Commission on Ministry plays in the dis-cernment process varies according to the bishop's temperament. In many dioceses the commission takes over the process from the bishop. The bishop comes in at the end to evaluate, approve (or disapprove), and promote and ordain—to "rubber stamp." In other dioceses the commission is auxiliary, working in dynamic tandem with the bishop. And in still others, the commission has a discrete role in the screening process, makes a recommendation, and then stands back. Of course, every bishop has different concerns, areas of interest or ability, pet projects, ambitions, and—depending on the size of his or her diocese and staff—different administrative loads. Some bishops might take a special interest in recruiting new priests; others might focus on developing congregations. If a bishop trusts the system already in place, he or she may not get too involved. I asked Bishop Bob Johnson if he ever reversed a recommendation made by his Standing Committee, and he said that he seldom did. "The process is good," he answered. "It's a good process and so it weeds out people."

These diocesan committees—the Commission on Ministry, the Standing Committee—and local parish committees constitute the big unknown factor in the process. People in a diocese have a good idea of what their bishop is like, because he or she is an extraordinarily public figure, whereas the members of the different parish and diocesan committees are an assembly of people and clergy from "the private sector." Unknown people are charged with the powerful duty of "weeding out" people. Supporters of my father's application, who were disappointed by the verdict handed down by his vocations committee, made comments such as "He didn't even get a chance to talk to the bishop!"—suggesting that if only he'd gotten past the palace guards, he would have gotten the chance to work with someone who had the "competence" to recognize his gifts, and suggesting, more importantly, a lack of confidence in the ability of the vocations committee to make a fair decision.

And yet, in the architecture of the Episcopal Church, these unknown people are not guards to the bishop's palace. If they are guarding anything, it's the church itself, the community at large.

Bishop Waynick of Indianapolis referred to a scene in Robert Duvall's 1997 movie *The Apostle* about an evangelical minister in the throes of a personal crisis. He's on the run and he arrives in a tiny backwater town, where he finds an abandoned church that he decides he wants to resurrect. He locates the former pastor, who's in retirement, and says to him, "The Lord sent me here. The Lord told me to come here." And the old black pastor sits back in his chair and says, "Well now, if the Lord's been talking to you, the Lord'll also be talking to me."

"That's just perfect!" exclaims Bishop Waynick. "Because it's not about setting yourself up in business. It's about wanting to help the communion, the community, answer faithfully the call that God issues to everybody. But the discernment of vocation is a community project; it's not simply a matter of a person having the conviction that God has called him or her to do something in particular. We can figure out where our hearts are, and we can come to a realization that we want to serve God, but in terms of at least the Episcopal Church, the discernment of how that call might work within the church and within the ministries of the church belongs to the church."

If you, like Bishops Waynick and Johnson, have faith in your parishioners—if you are a good Christian who believes that your fellows are to the best of their ability acting as good Christians—then you wouldn't question the conclusions reached by the vocations committee, or the Commission on Ministry, or the Standing Committee.

The authors of the 1996 internal review of the ordination process (charged with surveying the Process throughout the church) reached a less confident and less reassuring conclusion. "Dioceses need to give much careful thought," they wrote, "to the overall effects of requiring almost limitless self-exposure of aspirants to committee after committee of people they do not know and have only abstract reasons to trust. The 'process' often becomes a post-graduate education in passive aggression." What's worse, they noted, was that the results of their survey "show scarcely any awareness of this possibility."[8]

The Reverend David Lee Carlson, who in New York is on both the Commission on Ministry (as an appointee) and the Standing Committee (elected), defies the notion that passive aggression enters the equation. He explains, "The Commission on Ministry and the discernment conferences are a profoundly humbling experience, and also profoundly affirming." Specifically, he says, "It's such a precious conversation in terms of the person who has arrived at this point, and I remember being at that point, too, and I remember how incredibly vulnerable you are." Like my other interlocutors, Reverend Carlson also reminds me that calling belongs to the "corporate body—the body of Christ, the church." Frankly, after spending time with Father Carlson, he doesn't seem one bit an exemplar of latent passive aggression (at least where people coming to the priesthood is concerned); quite the opposite. And I secretly wish that my father had had Carlson on his vocations committee, because I imagine that I would trust any judgment he might arrive at. But one doesn't often get to choose who stands in judgment on one, does one?

Before we met in person, David Lee Carlson and I exchanged e-mails, and that led me to examine the Web site of Saint Augustine's Episcopal Church in Croton-on-Hudson (a medium-sized bedroom community about forty-five minutes north of New York City), where Carlson is rector. The Web site features a loony picture of him, hovering in full white vestments against a feathery digital background—his hair is rumpled and puffy and he wears the pleased expression of a drunken peasant in a Dutch Renaissance painting.

When I arrived at the church, I found the main entrance bolted shut with a Gothic forbidding in keeping with the general aesthetic of the small tree-ringed church—a look that belies the contrasting proletarian aesthetic of the neighborhood it sits in. I pushed through the fortified wooden door of a secondary entrance and found myself in a pretty, sun-dappled recreation room with a tall ceiling and mullioned windows, where about seven seniors in tracksuits seemed to be preparing for some kind of exercise class. I asked where I might find Father Carlson and was directed next door, to a somewhat wobbly clapboard house, the first floor of which is the church's second-hand charity store (the requisite musty smell of old clothes over-powers a person upon entering); the second floor is where the administrative offices are: a pristine secretary's office, a small room with a large table and whiteboard for lessons, and the rector's office. A photocopy machine is wedged into the cramped hallway. Carlson's office is filled to overflowing with books, framed pictures, lovely dark-wood antiques, and a clamorous grandfather clock ("Big Ben").

In person Carlson was quite unlike the picture I had found of him on Saint Augustine's Web site. He is a self-possessed, handsome man in his early forties, with big, warm brown eyes and a charmingly self-deprecating sense of humor. He has an easy laugh and a smooth open manner that makes you feel instantly at ease. He is, in short, nothing like George Herbert, or Jonathan Edwards, Cardinal Bernard Law, or even Bing Crosby—he is nothing like the images I had in my mind of what a priest might be like, and yet he is undeniably a priest.

He told me that as a "cradle Episcopalian" he is a "rare duck" among Episcopal priests. Many converts to the Episcopal Church are the ones who feel (as in my father's case) the strong sense of grati-tude and devotion that bring them to the desire to serve it in a deeper way. The majority of Episcopal priests were not in fact brought up in the Episcopal tradition. Carlson was eleven years old when he first approached his rector about being a priest, and his rec-tor was extremely respectful, and sat him down and told him about what a hard life a priest's life is. Though Carlson had one major detour in his itinerary (a stint in drama school), he says now that he can't imagine doing anything else. "It seems to be where I've been headed my whole life."

He talks of his own faith in terms of an ongoing exploration. "I think a faith that's being questioned is alive, and the older I get, the longer I am a practicing Christian and a priest, the more questions I seem to have." His memory of his own discernment process, which he went through in the same diocese where he now serves, is still vivid in his mind ("I was a wreck!") and he brings that memory to bear on his work discerning others. "It is so hard to say no to someone," he tells me, "because every person who comes to us wants it very badly and they all deeply believe that this is right for them. Who are we to say no? But this," he reminds me, "is our process and it's our construct and all we can do is seek to serve it well."

Reverend Carlson says that his work at the discernment conferences, as a member of the Commission on Ministry and the Standing Committee, and as a spiritual director for the last ten years, is guided foremost by the Baptismal Covenant of the Episcopal Church—"to respect the dignity and freedom of every human being." That promise in effect guides all aspects of his work as a priest. By the time he meets a candidate at a discernment session, he explains, "they've already been through psychological evaluations, physical evaluations, and preliminary interviews, as well as some sort of parish discernment group. They've already experienced quite a lot of vulnerability, and it's important," he says, "to have a sense of what comes with them when they walk in that door. To be in that position, discerning whether I think—and then as a group, we think—this person should proceed in the process, it's awesome and profoundly humbling. But I always have a sense that in the breadth of personalities and even backgrounds that we represent as a commission, everyone is on that page." If there is any bias at all, he believes, it's toward positive affirmation. "We want them to go forward. I think that's where we all begin from—from openness." He describes the work of discernment as being guided by the Holy Spirit, "a spiritual exercise." "Even though 'the Process' is a human construct," he explains, "as is the church, for that matter—a construct around our organization and the way we live our faith—God breaks through it and uses it and directs us."

What actually happens at these diocesan discernment meetings—typically the final step before a candidate is recommended to a bishop (that is, accepted formally into the process) and sent on to seminary? Anne Richards described the experience as very intense: a two-day conference with six aspirants and twenty-five interviewers. Each aspirant is interviewed by small groups of three or four, and the groups rotate among themselves for two days. Carlson's version is less intimidating: "We have small group interviews with the aspirants (because they're aspiring), and then over lunch we all chat casually. They are always on, poor lambs! They're on the whole time and we're listening and asking questions. We have plenary discussion beforehand, where we're told, maybe, how to approach a particular aspirant, or what particular area might still need working on. And we also talk together, trying to help each other out in upcoming sessions. There are a number of these small group discussions throughout the day, and then we usually have a service of Holy Communion, and then the candidates leave. When we begin to discuss our conclusions, we give ourselves an open-ended amount of time. Then we vote on each person and either recommend them or not to go on. Our report goes to the bishop, who evaluates it, and agrees with our recommendation or not—that's the bishop's prerogative."

Carlson is (remarkably) the first person I had talked with up to that point who is involved in the Process and who makes a direct connection between discernment and God. I press him on the subject, trying to get him to explain how "God breaks through" the obviously grueling examination he's just described. A great deal of it, he answers, has to do with not going into a meeting with an aspirant with preconceived notions. Instead of referring to the "little checklist" we all have in our heads when we meet someone new, he says, "we're trying to make Christ the center of our lives, so that each new presence is an acknowledgment of Christ's incarnation in our lives—each of us has God in us. This fact changes our decision making, all of it, and our relationships. When I meet someone in this process and hear their incredible story of God in their lives, drawing them along, leading them, healing them, challenging them, and calling them—it's amazing. It's about listening. Not listening for God's voice to thunder in and say, *David, ask this question!* But sometimes I am amazed by the questions that I do ask. A lot of the time, I

realize that I'm asking good questions because I'm listening well—
I'm not listening with an agenda. I love hearing people's stories. It's
awesome—in the sense that you have to realize, Okay, I hear you and
I hear God. That's true for every person whether they're approved
by the commission or not."

Returning to the theme of the corporate calling, Carlson says the
best question in the discernment materials is the one that asks,
"Does the church need this person to be a priest?" Notably, the question isn't "Does this person need to be a priest?" The objective of the
meeting is to make a decision on behalf of the church's best interests, not the aspirant's. It's easy to see the rationale then behind
rejecting a person who seems motivated by personal interests. One
priest explained to me, for example, that a lot of people enter the
process looking for an identity in the priesthood—because they
haven't been able to find one on their own. Another aspirant might
have the purest intentions and a healthy spirituality, but such a limited background that he or she wouldn't be able to serve the church's
broad interests. Still another aspirant may not have the academic
skills or financial resources to get through seminary. Anne Richards
says that this part is mostly common sense. "A fifty-eight-year-old
guy comes in, he's got thirteen dependents, and his wife's dying of
cancer. It doesn't really look like he's being called to go to seminary,
which costs thirty thousand dollars a year!" Even my father's case
could have been subject to this kind of criteria. After three years of
seminary, he would be sixty-three years old, and have less than nine
years of service before the mandatory retirement at seventy-two.
(He wasn't, however, sent away because of his age).* These are all
examples of obvious, tangible answers to the question "Does the

---

*Which isn't to say that age isn't a big issue in some dioceses. I was told of one
diocese that basically will not accept anyone over forty into the process. As a religious organization that reserves the right to hire on the basis of creed, the Episcopal
Church is not subject to provisions made under the Equal Opportunity Employ-
ment Act, including provisions against age discrimination.

church need this person to be a priest?" Often those kinds of applicants don't even get to the point in the process where Reverend Carlson would meet them. The way that question is going to be posed
and answered in the context of Carlson's work is significantly more
ephemeral.

In fact, he finds that it's the "no" votes that more often than not
come out of vague sensations. "Sometimes," he says, "it's that very
sense of vagueness that causes us to think, I don't know about this.
I'm not getting a clear impression. We can debate a single 'no' vote
for hours." Interpersonal chemistry obviously comes into this facet
of an examination judged by impressions and sensations. Carlson
thinks that this is the very reason why the diversity of the commission is so important—lay and ordained people, people from different
racial and socioeconomic backgrounds. "There will be personality
conflicts," he says, "conflict in the sense that an aspirant will come
along and maybe someone will say, 'I don't get this person at all.' So
we say, 'Okay, you vote no. The rest of us are going to vote yes.' As a
group we're all so committed. I can't emphasize enough what the
sense of privilege around this work is. After all, this is a person's life
we're discussing, and we're part of a very important change of direction, or fulfillment of direction, in their life. As a body, we have so
much power today over their tomorrow. People come in and they
are just so tightly wound. They're seeking our approval, and they're
so tense."

Getting past that tension is the most important stage in the discernment meeting. Carlson described one aspirant who came in and
when the question "Why ordination?" was put to her, she dissolved
into tears. After that dam burst, he explains, we were able to start the
discussion. Rather than judging her reaction negatively—as someone, perhaps, who couldn't handle a difficult situation—Carlson
says, "It was fantastic; it was real; it was authentic." He claims that
he gets suspicious of people who "seem to have pat answers for
every question. When someone comes in and they have it all
wrapped up in nice little answers, I just want to say, What hurts

you?" Not because, he qualifies, he wants everyone to sit there and sob, but he wants to know about people's struggles, about the moments they've doubted their faith and how they've moved through that. "Not only because it's more interesting, but because it reveals more about a person's journey and their beliefs and how they're going to articulate that as a leader."

I got contradictory information on the subject of "pat answers." One priest said flat out, "There are buzzwords they're listening for." And another said, "Anything that's canned or appropriated never sounds true. The only way to go through this process is to be yourself." One priest who came up through Bishop Johnson's diocese and now works on the Commission on Ministry there writes that the discernment process absurdly tries to ascertain "beyond a reasonable doubt" that someone is called to the priesthood based on evidence which "usually consists of a polished, well-articulated eucharistic theology and a list of lay involvements in the parish." When I asked the priest who made the comment about buzzwords for examples, she said, "*Call* is a big one . . . and *sacramental presence*." *Eucharist* is another.*

The contradictory opinions about specific language suggests that there are in fact certain concepts that they are listening for, but a candidate is well advised to present them in a way that doesn't seem rehearsed.

Meanwhile, Carlson's anecdote about the weeping aspirant points to another, related subject that seems less controversial: emotions and behavior. The idea that God's call can be read through behavior or emotional expression is predominant. One discernment training manual suggests that some "signs" to watch for during a discernment session are peacefulness, joy, a "temporary experience of

---

*Offering the sacrament of Holy Communion, the Eucharist, can be done only by a priest or a bishop. It is virtually the only function that cannot be performed by a lay minister or deacon—which means that the most logical answer to the question "Why ordination" is "Because I long to lead the Eucharist."

disorientation followed by calm and serenity," tears ("that are comforting and tranquilizing rather than disturbing and fatiguing"), a
sudden sense of clarity—"strands of experience that seemed unrelated begin to converge and fit together"—and persistence.[9] The
cataloguing of acceptable emotional experiences is weirdly a more
egalitarian practice than looking for buzzwords. That is because language changes over time and varies enormously by region and
according to socioeconomic background.

In his 1746 *Treatise on Religious Affections,* Jonathan Edwards outlined the common pattern that conversion narratives followed in his
day—demonstrating that the watch for familiar signs is an antique
aspect of discernment.* "I know very well how they proceed," he
writes,

> for I have had frequent opportunities of observing their conduct.
> Very often their experience at first appears like a confused chaos,
> but then those parts are selected which bear the nearest resem-
> blance to such particular steps as are insisted on; and these are
> dwelt upon in their thoughts, and spoken of from time to time,
> till they grow more and more conspicuous in their view, and
> other parts which are neglected grow more and more obscure.
> Thus what they have experienced is insensibly strained, so as to
> bring it to an exact conformity to the scheme already established
> in their minds.

In other words, religious experience tends to shape itself according to a
known model. People evaluating the religious experience for authenticity will look at least initially for elements of a familiar pattern.

On the same theme, but interpreted in wildly different ways
from one region to the next, is the expectation that applicants will
have had a visionary experience. One priest in her calling narrative

---

*Though the Puritan minister Jonathan Edwards would not have used the word
discernment to describe his process of authenticating conversion testimonials.

identified her "yearning and desire to celebrate" the Eucharist by describing a vision she had of hands around the eucharistic chalice. Bishop Waynick says that she first felt called as a child. There was no such thing as a woman priest back then, so she abandoned the idea. Years later, totally immersed in church lay activities and a mother of three, she "got to a point" where she just couldn't sleep through the night. And then one night, in a fit of insomniacal frustration, she got out of bed, pulled a book at random off the shelf, and opened it at random. It was the *Imitation of Christ* by Thomas à Kempis, and the passage her finger fell on read something like "it doesn't matter how much you're doing if it isn't what you want to do." Bishop Johnson felt God's presence physically embrace him one cathartic, tearful evening ("More than catharsis," he says, "it was a kind of born-again experience") after he was already in seminary. Already on his chosen path, he just sort of heard God say, "Bob, you're in the right place. Stay with it. Stick to it. You're doing the right thing." In New York, I'm told, they're going to pay extra close attention to the results of the psychological exam for an applicant who comes in spouting stories about visions and visitations.*

The common denominator of all three modes—buzzwords, behavioral clues, and visions—is that religious experience is intensely intimate. It's hard to find the words and the ways to convey it. Language fails. At the very least it disappoints. The biggest challenge, hands down, put to an applicant to ordained ministry is that of finding some way to describe his or her religious experience that other people can understand.

---

*Another representative of the New York discernment process elaborated that "if I was sitting with someone who was talking about the possibility that they had a call to the priesthood and they used language like *God tapped me on the shoulder* and so on—and that was primarily how they articulated themselves—I wouldn't outright dismiss that they had a vocation, but I would be more on the negative side. Because that description sounds like they are not taking responsibility. It's too passive."

Bishop Johnson's ordination guidelines suggest that the fundamental questions to be answered in the early stages of discerning a call are "Is this person living out his/her baptized ministry in ways that build up the life of the parish and community? Has this person demonstrated leadership abilities and/or the desire to serve others in particular, effective ways? Is this person's spiritual and personal life balanced and reasonably whole?"

Anne Richards suggests a similar set of initial questions: "What kind of person is this? Is this a person who's other-directed? Is this a person who can hear a lot of ambiguity? Does this person have a sense of humor? Is this person really smart? A good communicator? A natural leader? Does this person believe in God?"

After attending a Priesthood Discernment Conference offered by the diocese of Ohio, my father says, he felt "satisfied that his talents lay in the priesthood—in liturgy and empathy, with a specialty in preaching." Based on the exploratory questions suggested to me by Reverend Johnson and Reverend Richards, my father's call seems perfectly well defined—at very least, by his actions alone ("By their fruits ye shall know them"). As a lay reader, a former Sunday school teacher, choir member, substitute organist, his leadership and contributions over the years to the strength of the church community are unassailable. His love of theology and scripture and his ardent desire to serve as a priest are palpable. But a passion for liturgy, a capacity for empathy, and a knack for preaching only suggest a calling, they don't prove it "beyond a reasonable doubt."

In other words, the background checks, the personal history essays, the psychological exams, the physical exams, the applicancy fees, and evidence of a healthy spiritual life, taken together, represent the evaluation of a person's qualification to ordained ministry, whereas the testimony of divine internal call represents the theology of ministry—the theology that binds a minister to the tradition of the Christian mission.

There are conceivably other means by which an applicant's commitment to the Christian mission and link to the historical tradition could be evaluated. But that's not the "construct" (as David Carlson would phrase it) that the church uses. And in this axis between qualification and calling we locate the core of the Process. "It is," says Bishop Waynick smoothly, "part observation, part intuition, and part decision making; it's a way of knowing." The bishop's office takes care of making sure a candidate's qualifications are in order. The corporate body, the church, recognizes the call. The word used for this recognition is *discernment*—not discernment in the lexical sense of distinguishing a cat from a bat, but discernment in the Ignatian sense of weeding out the false gods and devils, and identifying the authentic movement of the Holy Spirit.

My father belongs to the Episcopal Church, USA. The American branch of the worldwide Anglican Church, or Church of England, is a historic and traditional mainline Protestant denomination that is considered "center-right" in the tug between orthodox and liberal sects. The first Anglican church in America was built in 1607 by settlers of Jamestown, Virginia. For a period, following a legislative declaration in 1619, all Virginians were declared to be members of the Church of England. After the Revolutionary War, England pulled Anglican bishops out of America, and in 1789 the Protestant Episcopal Church in the United States (later renamed the Episcopal Church) was established. It's not a large church today, boasting only around two and a half million members. For the sake of comparison: the American Roman Catholic Church has 60 million members; among the various denominations of the Baptist Church there are 30 million members; and the Mormon Church of Jesus Christ of Latter-day Saints has 5 million members. The Pentecostal churches, the Presbyterian Church, and the Lutheran churches are all significantly larger Protestant sects.

There are approximately 6 million Muslims in America, and 4 million Jews.[10]

The Episcopal Church isn't large like a Cadillac, but it's been with us since Jamestown and grown up along with America, from the vision of the Founding Fathers on, reflecting American values, pluralism, and ideals of democracy. My father characterizes the Episcopal Church as a "straddler," and in American religious history, the Episcopal Church's trajectory is indeed frequently characterized as the "middle ground." That middle ground was largely the sure but gradual transformation of an Old World English church into an entirely American enterprise.

In the beginning it was a matter of geography—the sparsely populated settlements, so far from England's patronage, invented and made do with their own form of governance, necessarily conforming more to the individual personalities of prominent figures than to Anglican precepts. From the first, the early Virginia settlers found themselves jerry-rigging, or ignoring church altogether—despite the fact that many saw their settlement in America as a holy mission. Their purported bishop was off in England; their first minister (a vicar from Heathfield) died within a year along with many of the first colonists. The earnest efforts of his successors were upstaged by the ferocious governor, Thomas Dale, sent by England to bring order. Dale mandated twice-daily worship and executed heretics. Hardly the "good news" that would inspire discipleship. Later, the Episcopalians suffered along with (and even more than) all denominations a dramatic depopulation, and transformed themselves (prudently) during the populist Great Awakening, adopting some aspects of revivalism and evangelicalism in order to survive. In embracing its independence from England after the American Revolution, the Protestant Episcopal Church formulated its own Book of Common Prayer. The preface to the first (1789) edition acknowledges a debt to the Church of England for its "first foundation" and "nursing care and protection," and explains that Anglican doctrine provides for alterations in the interest of tending "to the preservation of peace and unity in the Church; the procuring of reverence, and the exciting of piety and devotion in the worship of God." The founders go on to say in recognizably "American" ideological terms:

> But when in the course of Divine Providence, these American States became independent with respect to civil government, their ecclesiastical independence was necessarily included; and the different religious denominations of Christians in these States were left at full and equal liberty to model and organize their respective Churches, and forms of worship, and discipline, in such manner as they might judge most convenient for their future prosperity; consistently with the constitution and laws of their country.

Today, the Episcopal Church is organized into just over one hundred separate dioceses—a geographical designation—each under the administration of a bishop and made up of congregations. Congregations are either parishes or missions. Parishes are self-governing and self-sustaining churches, led by a vestry, or board of parishioners. Missions are churches run, financed, and staffed by the bishop's office. At the national level, the governance of the Episcopal Church is legislated by two bodies, the House of Deputies and the House of Bishops, which meet every three years. The House of Deputies numbers over nine hundred members, made up of four laypeople and four clerics from each diocese. The House of Bishops has approximately three hundred members, who meet twice annually. There is an elected presiding bishop, currently the Most Reverend Frank T. Griswold, who serves as chief pastor and primate of the church. The organization and legislation of the church is outlined in *The Constitutions and Canons of the Episcopal Church,* subject to revision and approval by the acts of the general convention. The Book of Common Prayer, however, is the central document of the Episcopal Church. Last updated in 1979, it outlines the religious practices—the liturgy—and the articles of faith.

"We are really a people of the book," one church official told me, "the prayer book."

The orders of ministry and the forms of ordination are traditionally what distinguish the Catholics from the Episcopalians and the Episcopalians from other Protestant denominations.[11] There are three orders of clerics in the Episcopal Church: deacons, priests, and bishops. Ordination is successive. To become a priest, you first have to be ordained a deacon; to become a bishop, you first have to be ordained a priest. The church also recognizes monastic orders, monks and nuns who live in communities and take vows of chastity, poverty, and obedience.

Q: What is the ministry of a priest of presbyter?

A: The ministry of a priest is to represent Christ and his Church, particularly as a pastor to the people; to share with the bishop in the overseeing of the Church; to proclaim the Gospel; to administer the sacraments; and to bless and declare pardon in the name of God.

—The Episcopal Catechism

The classic image of a Christian priest, according to the Catholic theologian Richard P. McBrien, "is really a fusion of several different roles: disciple, apostle, presbyter-bishop, and presider at the Eucharist."[12] Each of those roles represents a kind of ongoing codification of the life and acts of Jesus and his followers. But that's hardly a job description. The Reverend Hannah Anderson answers the question "What does a priest do?" with the following description of her work: "I pray, attend meetings, spend time with parishioners, study scripture, prepare sermons, design workshops, offer my services as a consultant to other parishes, visit people who are ill in the hospital, teach, celebrate midweekly Eucharist, baptize, marry, and bury people." Having digested that diverse list of activities, she concludes, "A priest is not so much a job as a vocation. It's a way of being in the world."

Brother Douglas Brown, prior of Holy Cross Monastery on the banks of the Hudson River in upstate New York, explains that "there are different ways of exercising the priestly ministry. What is common to all priests is their sacramental function. They celebrate the Eucharist. A parish priest would be connected to a church where they would have an altar. But the day-to-day expression of their priestly life is one of teaching, for example, or healing."

The work of a priest is earthbound and temporal—it will shift and change emphasis and character according to the specific needs of the time. The ministry of administering a parish, as unspiritual as it may seem, is obviously critical in an American system where, for example, a religious organization is a nonprofit, with special tax status, allowing for fund-raising, requiring fiscal transparency, and necessitating paperwork. A parish hires people, pays salary and pension, makes purchases, holds insurance policies, pays rent or mortgages or bank loans. In a broader sense, although we don't tend to think of bureaucracy as a great leveling device, it is. And American Protestant churches evolved under the umbrella of American society, striving accordingly for ongoing equanimity and responsibility in its governance. Today, Protestant churches are large institutions in every sense of the word. Two centuries ago, parishes were village based, and priests were formed through tutelage under their local rector. That formation was called "reading divinity." Then too, the work of priests took on any number of designations, but that had more to do with a formation that was as various as there were priests begetting new priests in their image. This vocation, the priesthood, this "way of being in the world," is constantly redefining itself.

In 1985, fifteen years after the Episcopal Church had implemented its present canonical guidelines for ordained ministry, Margaret Fletcher Clark prepared an internal review of the priesthood, entitled *We Need People Who: An Exploration of Criteria for Ordained Ministries in the Episcopal Church.* In order to illustrate the variety of roles a priest might fill in a community, she compiled a list of ten different priestly prototypes—or "dream priests," as she called them. Among the prototypes are priests who administrate, heal, preach and teach, take to the streets, live model lives, build communities, worship and accompany their congregation in spiritual life and development, and are witness to an "infectious love of God, not so much by action as by presence." Although one of these models alone might broadly describe the way any single priest fulfills their ministry according to their talents, the duties of ordained ministry encompass all of these abilities in varying degree.

Add, then, to these prototypes a prototype built on the memory that every individual brought up in a religious home has of the single priest that meant "church" to them. After 1974 in the Episcopal Church, add "female" to your priestly prototypes.

"The true Masters," said Saint Francis, "are those who set an example to their neighbors in good works and kindness. For a man is learned in so far as he works for others; he is wise in so far as he loves God and his neighbors; and he is a good preacher in so far as he knows how to do good works faithfully and humbly."[13]

One cold early-spring day last year, Reverend Carlson was driving me around Croton-on-Hudson. He suddenly slowed the car down to seven miles an hour in order to wave enthusiastically to a young man on the sidewalk. "I just baptized his little girl," he explained to me, "and I married him a year ago. That's why I love what I do, because I get to share the biggest moments in people's lives. It's an incredible privilege."

> One day a young fugitive, trying to hide himself from the enemy, entered a small village. The people were kind to him and offered him a place to stay. But when the soldiers who sought the fugitive asked where he was hiding, everyone became very fearful. The soldiers threatened to burn the village and kill every man in it unless the young man was handed over to them before dawn. The people went to the minister and asked him what to do. The minister, torn between handing over the boy to the enemy and

having his people killed, withdrew to his room and read his Bible, hoping to find an answer before dawn. After many hours, in the early morning his eyes fell on these words: "It is better that one man dies than that the whole people be lost."

Then the minister closed the Bible, called the soldiers and told them where the boy was hidden. And after the soldiers led the fugitive away to be killed, there was a feast in the village because the minister had saved the lives of the people. But the minister did not celebrate. Overcome with a deep sadness, he remained in his room. That night an angel came to him, and asked, "What have you done?" He said: "I handed over the fugitive to the enemy." Then the angel said: "But don't you know that you have handed over the Messiah?" "How could I know?" the minister replied anxiously. Then the angel said: "If, instead of reading your Bible, you had visited this young man just once and looked into his eyes, you would have known."[14]

Theologian Henri Nouwen offered this parable as an object lesson to ministers: look up from your Bible and *see* whom you're ministering to. It is an especially powerful illustration of what happens when the clergy grows out of touch with the people it's serving—of a premodern clergy that serves God before the people. The Bible in this parable is the minister's red herring. The word of God divorced from the people of God becomes an abstraction—a rulebook or an answer book rather than a guide. Vatican II and the Episcopal revised Book of Common Prayer, along with the birth of a variety of new Reformation-style Protestant denominations, had as their primary scope the returning of the clergy to the people and bringing sanctity to daily life. The new model for the clergy thereafter became a "servant leader," a noncategorical designation that allowed for flux. A minister might serve God and lead the people in one instance, or might be led by the people to serve God in another, or might simply serve the people in another. Predominantly, the minister's work today embodies the balancing of all those obligations.

The parable provides an equally valuable comment on discernment—*see* the person for who he his, not solely his circumstances, and not solely in terms of the Bible as an abstraction. Perhaps we can add to this the mandate not to see someone solely in terms of the standardized definition of divine calling handed down by a Commission on Ministry. In fact a lot of room is built into most discernment processes to consider an aspirant on his own terms. Most dioceses have picnics and retreats where aspirants and their families mingle with members of the Commission on Ministry, giving those involved in discerning ample opportunity to look their candidate in the eyes.

One can go too far in this direction, too. When someone charged with discernment radically privileges his or her ability to read a person, then both the need for and ability to explain *why* flies out the window. "He didn't *feel* like a priest to me," offers one vocations committee member, explaining why she rejected a candidate to the priest who had supported that candidate. That explanation expresses really the most Victorian kind of prerogative. Out in the secular, litigious American environment, one could never sustain such an argument. ("The applicant didn't *feel* like a Michigan State Law School student, so we rejected her." "That employee didn't *feel* like management material, that's why we never promoted her.") But religious organizations are exempt from laws governing equal opportunity, which is appropriate to their mission and structure. And although many religious organizations establish internal provisions for equal opportunity, the capacity for self-monitoring isn't automatically going to extend to such a tricky arena as the discernment of religious calling—which for genuine lack of an answer book depends in no small part on intuition. *Intuition* is "the spiritual perception or immediate knowledge, ascribed to angelic and spiritual beings, for whom vision and knowledge are identical."

On the left bank of the Hudson River in West Park, New York, sits Holy Cross Monastery, an Episcopal Benedictine order founded in 1884. Since 1902 the monastery has occupied this arcadian hillside, hidden from the main road by a long grassy slope and an extravagant tree garden. Visitors leave their cars in a pebble parking lot in the middle of the pines, halfway down the winding dirt path that leads to an undeniably beautiful, though eccentric, tripartite complex: one part Hudson Valley mansion, one part Romanesque church (complete with cloister), and one part swanky French New Wave dormitory. Holy Cross is a popular retreat center, and the modern wing is the guesthouse. The ten resident monks live and work in the mansion, where the main library and dining hall are also located. The monks and their guests celebrate daily Communion, maintain a vow of silence after dinner and into the night, and four times a day gather to celebrate the daily "offices"—a chanted prayer service that includes scripture reading.

To my enormous disappointment, that midsummer day I visited all the monks were wearing Bermuda shorts and sandals with sports socks. (They didn't don their flowing white robes until it was time for the startlingly beautiful afternoon vespers service.) That initial aesthetic blow was my only disappointment. Holy Cross's prior, Brother Douglas Brown, O.H.C., is one of the most well regarded spiritual guides in New York. He counsels and teaches at the General Theological Seminary in Manhattan, and has served as a special consultant to the diocesan Standing Committee and Commission on Ministry on the subject of "discerning spiritual maturity in priesthood aspirants."

His description of "call" is predictably complex, and starts with recognizing your worldview. He says that the worldviews of believers typically fall into four general categories, and when he leads discernment retreats and workshops, the first task is figuring out which one describes you.

The *deistic* model believes: "There is a God. God put all this in motion, but basically we're on our own to do the best we can according to the best lights we can come up with." Brown believes that this is more or less the model of American society.

The *fundamentalist* view of reality sees God as the only agent of reality. "Here," says Brown, "God micromanages. God finds me the parking spot on Forty-seventh Street. God wants me to be a priest. God tells me who to marry. We're just along for the ride." Adding understatement to that description, Brown suggests, "It's a fairly passive and fatalistic understanding."

He coined the term *the answer book model* in order to describe the notion that God has a book somewhere with all the right answers. Douglas Brown is supposed to be a priest. Minna Proctor is supposed be a writer. "And all you have to do is figure out what the right answers are, and do them."

The last model is *situational*—what Brown describes as a more interactive vision of reality, "where God is involved but there are other agents, namely us. As I formulate what I believe and make my choices, I have to consider my concrete world and the people I'm actually dealing with—not the way I wish it were—and then try to make the best choices I can in that situation."

Most call language, he explains, falls into the answer book category. People say, "I have a call. The call is not from me. The call is from outside me and I'm responding to it. Which makes me secondary." Since God is the agent of the call, Brown admits that this model is closest to the biblical model of the conversion of Saint Paul on the road to Damascus: "Where he's struck down, struck blind, picked up, led, literally blind, into the city." That's the most frequent way the word *call* is used. But, says Brown, "I think that's woefully simplistic and not the experience most people have. A call has as much possibility of beginning from within me as from without." A person doesn't stand around waiting for someone to come along and say, "I think you should be a priest."

"It begins with my beginning to imagine my being in the world as a priest." What grows from that, explains Brown, is yearning, longing, desire—as well as fear and anxiety—because as soon as you bring that desire to an office, to the church, then the whole community becomes an active participant. That's when it gets "really tricky."

Tricky because, according to Brown, "All of us carry around an ideal—all sorts of ideals that we rarely examine. They're just there, amalgamations of images from childhood, young adulthood, etcetera. If I ask, 'What is a priest?' you refer to your ideal," because your ideal is based on an experience or collection of experiences and is therefore concrete; it has "a particular kind of personality." Brown explains that we test people and ourselves against that ideal. "When my ideal of a priest and your ideal of a priest are very different," he asks, "how do we find the language to communicate and discern together whether or not I have a vocation to the priesthood?" The solution? "You have to unpack the ideals and recognize that my ideal of a priest may not exhaust the possibilities of what God thinks is a priest, or what other members of the church think is a priest."

He's not sure that this unpacking gets done in the course of a regular discernment process. When he talks to the Commission on Ministry members, he tells them that he can't do it for them, but that they should remain aware of the possibility that they are operating with unexamined ideals, and using them to judge other people. "We're told by Jesus, and the Bible in general, that judging other people is a dangerous project and should be done with discretion and delicacy. I make the suggestion that they are operating within unfriendly ideals and that part of their call as members of the commission, performing their ministry, is to take a look at what their ideals in fact are. Are they too broad or too narrow?"

Since Douglas Brown has been a monk for twenty-seven years and before that he was a parish priest, I feel as if I can confess something to him. I confess that I am utterly confused, and frustrated by the idea of this listening process, which is supposed to hear what God wants, and simultaneously hear what an applicant wants. It seems bipolar at best, and yet the upshot is presented as a decision that's being handed down from God.

After several long sighs, Brown explains, "The language certainly implies that the process arrives at a decision or choice that linguistically represents itself as God's will. But we don't have direct access to God's will, so the determination of what is God's will is always tentative, provisional. So . . . ," he says, gazing deep into his coffee mug, as if the rest of his sentence might be swimming around in that tiny tepid puddle. "Vocation begins as an intuition and then grows with experience and has its manifestation in the vow. Certainly in the language of vocation, we talk about this vocation as if it exists out there in the world as an independent thing—it's the only way we have of talking about it. But in the actual ordination service, the bishop does not ask the candidate, 'Does God call you to be a priest?' The bishop says, 'Do you believe you are called?' In other words, I can be convinced to the point where I'm willing to put my life on the line—but, can I say this is God's will? I can't."

At the very end of the process, when I was finally ordained, the Bishop asked me, "Hannah, do you identify more with the crucified or the risen Lord?" I looked at him and said, "The crucified. I don't know if I've experienced the risen Lord." His face went ashen, and he suddenly looked profoundly concerned. I think it was only then, after the eight years I'd gone through to arrive at ordination, that he realized how much suffering I had really endured.

The Episcopalians tend to speak of "gifts" ("There are diversities of gifts, but the same Spirit") and the Catholics of "charisms"—gifts of grace. Either term is suited to describe a certain unquantifiable quality that seems at once to encompass openness, vivacity, serenity, and intelligence. When Karen Armstrong was a young girl about to join a convent, she had the impression that the nuns in their long skirts walked without touching the ground. Their lightness of step seemed to represent enlightenment, an enlightenment that came from being spiritually grounded. I haven't seen any hovering—the nun who lives in the ancient rectory on the hill behind my house smiles radiantly when she greets me on my afternoon walk, but she shuffles in her rubber galoshes as we all do in rainy winter weather. I did meet people in the course of my research who seemed to glow especially, who had a certain ineffable grace, perhaps no one more recognizably so than Reverend Hannah Anderson, who now works in the diocese of New York as a canon of congregational development—the same woman who after eight years in the Process admitted that she could only relate to the crucified Christ.

Reverend Anderson is a tidy fiftyish, with a minister's silver blond bob, and compact features dancing across a sweet open face. There's a greasy spot shining on her forehead between her eyebrows, because our scheduled meeting falls during Holy Week and she's just been blessed and unguented by New York bishop suffragan Cathy Roskam (who is herself easily one of the most beloved figures in the church). On this Tuesday of Holy Week all the priests from throughout the diocese come to the Cathedral of Saint John the Divine in Manhattan to attend mass, receive a blessing, and to collect their year's supply of holy oil from a large glass vat set up in one of the altar niches. Reverend Anderson fills two pretty little tincture bottles (they seem too tiny to hold a year's supply of anything) and tucks them away into a secret pocket deep inside her vestments. Anderson stops several times to greet people on the short walk between the cathedral and the diocesan offices. The offices are a string of little gabled structures abutting the cathedral—and like so much New York City architecture, including the cathedral itself, an entirely improbable style for that unlovely stretch of Amsterdam Avenue. This is her second official day on the new bishop's staff, and though everyone seems to know who she is by sight, she hasn't been formally introduced to anyone. Promises to get together, plan this, and discuss that fly through the corridor, as she opens doors somewhat at random trying to find a quiet place for us to talk—she still doesn't have an office. We take over an empty function room—tall arched ceiling, pale cobbled glass windows, stacks and stacks of folding chairs—without realizing that we've barricaded access to the water fountain and coffeemaker.

I had originally been referred to Reverend Anderson not because she'd had a difficult experience in the ordination process, but because as a former Quaker, she's considered by her peers to be an expert in discernment. The Quaker meeting, which includes no sacraments, scripture, ritual, or priests, is a practice based in listening. Silence is regenerative, it's the space within which to disentangle the myriad voices and influences of daily life, and to locate thus a certain kind of inner truth. Life is a sacred journey, and everyone is constantly engaged in the itinerary of that journey—not passively but with intention and with attention to each step. God will guide you, but you have to be listening.

According to the very popular Quaker writer Parker J. Palmer, the old Quaker saying "Let your life speak" means not telling your life "what you intend to do with it," but listening for "what it intends to do with you." Vocation, explains Palmer, "does not come from willfulness. It comes from listening. I must listen to my life and try to understand what it is truly about—quite apart from what I would like it to be about—or my life will never represent anything real in the world, no matter how earnest my intentions."[15]

There is a custom in the Quaker community whereby when one person is faced with a difficult decision or choice, he or she convenes a "clearness committee," which is a small group of friends who neither judge you nor give you advice, but ask you probing questions that will lead you to a decision in harmony with your inner truth.

Inner truth is one of those locutions that sends up instant red flags for a writer. Writers are trained to avoid such elegant-sounding phrases that seem to mean something but resolve in total ambiguity. In fact, *inner truth* stands for *the right answer,* and discovering it with a clearness committee has nothing squashy or even supernatural about it. Your committee keeps you honest, makes you answer questions that maybe you were avoiding because the answers might jeopardize the decision you secretly (or subconsciously) already made, or threaten what you hope will be the outcome. Palmer describes a clearness committee session he convened to determine whether or not he should accept a job as a college president. When asked point-blank what he'd like best about being president, he could initially come up only with things that he *wouldn't* like. He finally stumbled upon something he'd like: having his picture in the paper with the word *president* under it. As one member of the committee quite reasonably pointed out, "Parker, isn't there some easier way to get your picture in the paper?"[16]

A clearness committee has certain real advantages over therapy (which is more long-term, less concerned with day-to-day decisions, and in which feedback isn't itself a necessary factor) or hashing something out with friends or family (who are distracted with their own problems and influenced by whatever crazy dynamics between you and them are already in place). A clearness committee makes a pact to concentrate on one person and one person's question. Dynamics are left at the door, as are distractions, and careful, considered feedback is of the essence. A practice of silence before and after speaking means that people don't speak in haste or recklessly, and that every answer is given due consideration. This system attracted the attention of other sects, and a number of Episcopalian discernment processes are modeled more or less after the Quakers'.

For this reason Quakers are considered "experts in discernment," and someone like Hannah Anderson, who was a Quaker elder and retreat leader before converting to the Episcopal Church, might be a point of reference on the subject of discernment. In fact it is her Quaker background that she believes recommended her for her current position (a canonry on the bishop's staff is a high position, especially for a self-described "new kid on the block in the diocese"), and also qualifies her for the work. A newly created position, the canon of congregational development focuses in part on congregations in crisis. In one capacity, Anderson and her colleagues will be serving poor parishes on a "congregational support plan," which means she'll minister (under the auspices of the bishop) to a thriving parish that doesn't have the funds to pay for its own full-time priest. In a second capacity, she'll be working as a mediator in conflict management, something that she has already been doing on a consultant basis. She'll work with churches that have come to an impasse in a conflict within the vestry, for example, or between the vestry and their rector, or the vestry and the congregation. She explains that in such situations she enters as an objective presence, able to listen to all sides of a situation, and set ground rules for communication and behavior to enable the battling parties to begin hearing each other's side more clearly.

Before becoming a priest, Anderson worked with learning disabled and bilingual children, and she thinks that this experience also plays a part in her current work. "I'm doing now what I did then, which is to walk into a situation, discern what's going on, and to diagnose and strategize, to find people's strengths and their modalities of learning, and then go with it."

I ask her what she means by the word *discernment,* and she answers: "To figure out where God's Spirit is moving. God's Spirit is almost always present—though sometimes I've wondered where. You ask, where is the energy, where is the movement, where is the life, where is the love? It's a process of listening and asking questions."

And though Reverend Anderson seems perfectly placed now, sitting at a table in this cluttered function room—smiling like a child in front of a large cake as she anticipates her immediate future, and concentrating like the consummate professional she is on our conversation—the road to get here was nothing short of devastating. It was Jobian. "My theme was wandering in the wilderness and learning to receive God's manna in very small increments—enough to get through, enough to know that God was leading me on some sort of pilgrimage into a promised land that I may or may not recognize. I had to learn how to be true in the wilderness."

In the mid-eighties, Hannah Anderson was happily married with two small children, she was Quaker elder and leader, and suddenly she started getting the urge to go to seminary. She ended up at Lancaster Theological Seminary taking a few classes, dabbling in Hebrew and the Bible on an exploratory basis. A friend she'd made at the seminary coaxed her along on an intensive four-day Episcopal retreat called Persio, and it was on this retreat that she took Holy Communion for the first time in her life. "And I didn't get struck down by lightning," she assures me, "even though I wasn't baptized. But something else happened to me. I received this sacrament and just burst into tears. I had grown up believing that sacraments and ritual were empty things—so this experience really threw me into a quandary. I talked to the priest on the retreat, who suggested that I get into spiritual direction right away. The seminary dean listened to my story and set me up with the priest at the local Episcopal church, Father Pete. He was wonderful. It was just a real intensity suddenly breaking into my life. He saw immediately that I had a call to ordained ministry."

That might sound strange: a Quaker elder who hasn't even been baptized has a call to ordained ministry in the Episcopal church—although, as I said, Reverend Anderson does sort of glow. Indeed, her first steps into the Episcopal Church had an element of fairy dust about them. She was sort of ushered through conversion straight into the discernment process. The church had, relatively speaking, only just started ordaining women, so they were recruiting: an enthusiastic attempt to redress the imbalance. Anderson, a family woman in her early thirties, with church leadership experience and a genuine eucharistic vision, was a dream candidate. And it was all wonderful, and too fast. When Father Pete told Anderson after her first month of attending early services at Saint John's Episcopal that she had a call to ordained ministry, she dissolved in laughter. After all, she'd been brought up in a tradition that didn't even have ordained priests. At that point she was still going to her ten o'clock Quaker meeting after mass at Saint John's, and wrestling with the idea of conversion.

I asked Reverend Anderson what it felt like to be told she had a call. How did she know what it meant? She said that she didn't know; she just started watching Father Pete. "That was the only way I could understand what a priest was. He was my role model. I knew already what a leadership role might be, but the role of priest was very different. I sat in the pews and watched."

In truth, the decision to enter the Episcopal Church wasn't so much a decision as a drive: "There was an incredible urgency when I was on the cusp of leaving Quakerism. The intensity was so alive in me—I've rarely experienced that—something was trying to break loose but I didn't know quite what. . . . I often talk about the spiritual life as a river flowing, and there are times when the water is dammed up for whatever reason, and then it breaks loose and you realize that the Spirit is moving in you."

Six months later, she reports, on her way to Ohio, where she was the keynote speaker for the yearly meeting with Barnesville Friends, she heard a voice. "It was an internal, but very clear voice: *It's time. Are you ready?* And I knew what it was about." She arrived at the conference, delivered the keynote address, and then told her sponsors that she wouldn't be staying for the rest of the conference, because she was going to go home and leave the Quaker denomination to join the Episcopal Church.

"Some people were hurt by my declaration, stunned, some people even called me a traitor. But I'd heard that call, so I came home and set up a Sunday for baptism. I was baptized along with a twelve-year-old girl and an infant baby. It was glorious. Then Father Pete said, 'Now I think you need to go into the discernment process.'" This was only nine months after she'd taken her first Communion from an Episcopal priest.

The discernment process that Anderson experienced in the diocese of Central Pennsylvania was actually somewhat unusual, and probably deserves attention in terms of better and worse screening methods. Once she had support from her priest, she entered a discernment group. This group of people, all trying to discern their call, would meet monthly over the course of a year with the canon to the ordinary. During that time they would have workshops in liturgy and teaching, they would give one another feedback and evaluations, and at the end of the year decide together who had a call to the priesthood—mutual evaluation. The next step was an internship under a parish priest. When that was over, and if it went well, the bishop would send the candidate on to seminary.

Except that Anderson at that point called a stop to the whirlwind. She told her bishop, "My external process is ahead of my internal process and I want another full year of doing nothing but sitting in the pew and watching, reading, and growing." After all, she'd been an Episcopalian for only two years at the time.

I asked why she thought everyone was pushing so hard for her to become a priest—so hard that she had to ask them to slow down. "I think they knew I had abilities that really could be used in the ministry. I care deeply about people, I have children, I was living in a family, I am a woman. They were actively recruiting women who were in a position to take the risk of going to seminary"—which means relocating—and for that she had the all-necessary financial support of her husband.

It was once she entered seminary at Sewanee, Tennessee—the University of the South—that the massive changes she'd brought about in her internal life began to have an impact on everything else. Her family had relocated with her to Tennessee, and at the end of Anderson's first semester, her husband had a major heart attack. She arranged to continue in seminary part-time, which stretched the whole process out, and she lost the bond she had formed with her original class. Even without the sickness, seminary was an intense, challenging experience. The floodgates of this new life had just opened up, and Anderson experienced her priorities and energies shifting along with the pressures on her. In addition to the seminary syllabus, she also was responsible, as a postulant in the diocese of Central Pennsylvania, for six canonical exams that she had to travel back to Pennsylvania to sit. (These exams were in addition to the big general ordination exams, held during the last semester of seminary.) The examining chaplains who she had to meet with at the diocesan level exercised what she considered to be an abusive level of intimidation that was a stark contrast to the encouragement she'd been experiencing up to this point.

With all the new intellectual material that seminary introduces concentrated into a student's life, Anderson describes the period as one in which you would like to be able to completely break apart, flail around, experiment, and rebuild yourself. But that's exactly what you can't do, she says, because if you don't live up to the expectations being placed on you, you can be "dropped like a hot potato." When the changes and new priorities started revealing themselves in private life, her marriage suffered irrevocably. When she contacted her bishop to tell him that she was separating from her husband, she was shocked at his response. He didn't think he could continue to support her in the process, explaining, "You can't have the sacrament of ordination if you don't hold together the sacrament of marriage."

"My life was falling apart. I had two kids. I was going to lose my home, a nineteen-year marriage, all the financial backing of that relationship. And this was his response? Hardly pastoral." But she didn't despair; she reflected. She began to establish a disjoint between her relationship with God and her relationship with the bishop. "I think I came to understand that the institutional church and the people who function in the church are vulnerable and frail and we're all just human, we're just normal people who somehow hope to be guided by the grace of God and we all have our blind spots and we all have different strengths and weaknesses." Her bishop, she realized, had been formed to think in terms of sacramental theology. His objection to her divorce was almost legalistic, and so she had to respond legalistically. After six months, she returned to the bishop and argued that she had been married in a Quaker ceremony, where there was no mention of Christ and certainly no sacrament. It couldn't be considered through the same lens as the sacrament of ordination. "I didn't come into the sacramental tradition and get baptized until I was thirty-three," she told him, "and that turned my soul upside down." By finding a way to understand her bishop's position, she found a way to give him a good reason for letting her continue—albeit reluctantly—in the process.

But Anderson was no longer the revered ideal candidate—rather, she had become a sort of exception to the rules. After she left seminary and was ordained a transitional deacon, a position typically held for a year before receiving ordination to the priesthood, the bishop wouldn't allow her a full-time parish ministry like the other deacons. Because of the divorce, he said, she was "too controversial."

Once she was ordained a priest, still a "divorced woman and single parent," he wouldn't grant her a parish ministry and instead sent her to be chaplain at Hershey Medical Center, where she worked in oncology and with patients suffering from Lou Gehrig's disease— almost all terminal cases. This was an appointment that she loved initially, despite the rigors of working with so much crisis and loss. On the weekends she was allowed to serve as a *deacon* (not a priest) in a "yoked congregation"—where an inner-city parish forms a partnership with a suburban parish to share clergy—under a reactionary priest who was still resisting the idea of women in the priesthood at all. This meant she had to be in downtown Harrisburg for the early service, then race to the suburbs (with ten minutes' traveling time) for their first service, then race back to Harrisburg for the late service, and back again to the suburbs—her children in tow. Priests aren't promised an easy life—postulants are usually regaled with real war stories about how hard things can get—and Anderson was no exception. But her children (being dragged back and forth) didn't have any opportunity to form relationships within this Christian community that was consuming their mother alive, and they decided to go back to Tennessee to live with their father.

After losing custody of her children, she finally felt overwhelmed. She was surrounded by too much loss, and she begged her bishop for relief and at long last he assigned her a stable parish ministry.

I asked her whether she thought she'd been subjected to a higher standard of wholesomeness as a woman, and she said that she absolutely had been. "I don't think a bishop ever would have said he couldn't place a recently divorced man in a parish priesthood." Women priests are still not entirely accepted by parishioners, so they have to go further to prove themselves worthy. It's interesting because although she was actively recruited as a woman candidate, she was among the first generation of women priests, and much of the terrain was still unbroken. At seminary she found herself surrounded by the white male students the system continued to favor, many of them Southerners, and she had the impression that they just breezed through their classes and then moved directly on to cathedral staff—church leadership track. She asked herself, if she had a major crisis in her life, would she go to one of those guys? "No, my soul would gravitate toward somebody who had known suffering and loss."

"I made a deal with God," she tells me. "It's the one deal I ever made: God, if you ever need me to be a mentor for another woman going through this process, I will do that." She says that soon after she was placed in her first church, she was appointed to the diocesan Standing Committee, where she could mentor people going through the process, and where she could advocate on their behalf against the levels of intimidation and abuse that she'd experienced. So she got to fulfill her one deal with God.

Reverend Anderson describes a recent conversation with her son, now grown and off at university. "Mom," he asked, "tell me why anyone would want or need to go to church. It's just a joke. People who go to church pretend they're perfect, but they really live just like the rest of us during the week. They're hypocrites. Tell me one good thing about church."

Anderson is good at listening, and that's what she did instead of talking. She said she listened to "a young man whose life had been shaped and somewhat shattered by his mother's choice of vocation as priest, who'd seen the underbelly of the institutional church as I endured the ordination process that lasted ten years and placed incredible stresses on family life. I listened to a young man whose voice represents a generation who wonders like he does what such a broken institution such as the church has to offer them."

I asked her whether she thought she had been tested—not just to prove her worthiness as a woman, but in a larger sense, to prove her call. She said that there were certainly times when she felt like she was being tested, and that's what attracted her to the biblical example of the Israelites. But more than that, she says, "I came to understand that I was being shaped and formed into a particular kind of priest. And I didn't know why probably until I got to Hershey Medical, where I was chaplain to people who were dying and experiencing loss all over the place. I began to understand what I had been through and how God used those experiences to place me as a hospital chaplain. I had the capacity to be with people experiencing that level of loss. . . . Ministry is about being broken open at some level. As servant leaders," she concludes, quoting Henri Nouwen, "we are called, we are blessed, we are broken, and we are fed to the world."

In their ancient incarnation, priests were never considered emissaries of the people to God, but rather servants (ministrants) of God. This was because the people themselves had no role in electing priests. The priesthood was considered a grace (or gift) extended by God, which means that priests—touched by divine selection—were essentially more holy. *Holy,* explains religious historian Karen Armstrong, originally meant "otherness," "different" and "separate"— *kaddosh* in Hebrew—but has come to mean "higher or morally superior."[17] The root of the word *clergy* (*cleros*) also means "set apart," and designates a group within the baptized, identified and separated out for service. Even twentieth-century Judaism talks about the priesthood as a unit separated out from the rest. In 1928, Reform leader Kaufmann Kohler wrote,

> Only the fundamental idea, that Israel as the "first-born" among the nations has been elected as a priest-people, must remain our imperishable truth, a truth to which the centuries of history bear

witness by showing that it has given its lifeblood as a ransom for humanity, and is ever bringing new sacrifices for its cause. Only because it has kept itself distinct as a priest-people among the nations could it carry out its great task in history; and only if it remains conscious of its priestly calling, and therefore maintains itself as the people of God, can it fulfill its mission. Not until the end of time, when all of God's children will have entered the kingdom of God, may Israel, the high-priest among nations, renounce his priesthood.[18]

In the Christian empire, the set-apart clergy began to rise above the laity in the fourth century when Constantine made Christianity the state religion, which meant clerics were ranked among civil servants and won commensurate privilege. The priesthood "exceeds a kingdom," wrote John Chrysostom, protesting monarchical control over the church, "as much as the spirit differs from the flesh."[19] A Neoplatonic trend in theology (that is, classification) during the Middle Ages further emphasized the separation between clergy and laity, attaching to the different groups a Roman gradation of higher and lower beings, respectively. It was during this period that the pope ascended to the top rungs of a ladder wending heavenward. In a much less clearly delineated form, this notion of a priesthood balanced somewhere between different and superior continues into the present day.

Whether or not you believe that priests occupy a higher link on some great chain of being, you might think that they're supposed to. Or you might think that you're supposed to think that they do. Or you might think that *they* think they do.

My father is one of the most charismatic people I've ever met. But if by virtue of his religious ambition, he is extending heavenward, he is also shackled to this world by all sorts of plain old human qualities. Which is fine as far as the Episcopal Church is concerned. Their priests are charged with the difficult task of behaving and communicating a wholesome and prayerful Christian vision—but the last thing this stately, practical, earthbound church wants or expects in its service is a legion of superhumans floating heavenward like so many helium balloons. They want you to come with some knocks and they want you to be able to talk about them.

You can't go very long in a discussion of vocation before someone brings up *The Wounded Healer*. Henri J. M. Nouwen's influential 1972 monograph defined how this generation of church leaders understands the ministry of pastoring, and remains the "first text" in contemporary pastoral theology. Even people who haven't read the book refer to it. For *wounded healer* is an ever-so-slightly self-evident catchphrase that perfectly suggests its own argument, an argument that defines what's come to be a rather consolidated portrait of the ideal late-twentieth-century minister. Self-evident because the phrase itself describes someone who heals from personal experience—rather than, we can assume, from goodwill, instinct, professional training, or book learning.

The central thesis of *The Wounded Healer* is that the minister should "make his own wounds available as a source of healing." This is not so much a declaration of the metaphysical role of the minister as it is an indication of and gesture to the mood of the times in which Nouwen was writing, the late 1960s, early 1970s—defining years indeed for contemporary America. The average age of Episcopal priests today is sixty, which means that most of the church's leadership base was either ordained or formed during those turbulent years—the same period to which my father assigns his regrets, the same period he refers to in terms of epidemic moral decline. And in fact, the group whose attentions Nouwen focuses on are not the healers so much as the wounded—that is to say, those who the wounded healer sets out to heal: the young adults, college students, the sixties generation, the flower children, the youth revolution—the future of the church. Who, in point of fact, by their exodus represented the future potential demise of the church.

In Nouwen's analysis, the tumult of that period came out of the

young people, or "nuclear man"* as he labeled them, having lost
faith in their institutions (or the people running the institutions),
including the institution of history, as well as church and government. In different ways, these institutions derive their influence from
a promise for the future: you study history to apply its lessons to the
present and future; government operates explicitly off an ongoing
campaign for improvement; the church promises redemption, the
immortality of the soul, and a worthy, more serene now. So the
greatest loss, ironically, was that of hope.

The somewhat eccentric moniker *nuclear man* (comprising the
group commonly known now as the baby boomers) is a reference
to the advanced technology that has produced weapons of mass
destruction and a glut of other, similarly dehumanizing "conve-
niences." "Nuclear man," wrote Nouwen, "is painfully aware that
the same powers that enable man to create new life styles carry the
potential for self-destruction." Technology has brought us past sub-
sistence, past comfort, into a dynamic of constant boredom and the
perpetual threat of annihilation. We don't want for anything—
food, clothing, shelter, nuts, berries, clean meat—which means that
everything becomes a matter of choice, and our days are devoted to
figuring out how to fill them. By the same token, we've become
irrevocably dependent on the scientific advancements that have
raised our standard of living to such remarkable levels (modern
medicine, heat, hot water, telecommunications), and we are also
utterly vulnerable to them (nuclear bombs, biochemical warfare,
computer viruses)—and of course we also fundamentally distrust
anything of man's own creation that wields such power. This strange
combination of concerns has, in Nouwen's formulation, shaped a
man who is historically dislocated and ideologically fragmented,

---

*Writing on the cusp of the feminist revolution, Nouwen explicitly apologizes
in a note for his "male-dominated" language and says that he hopes "women read-
ers will have patience with my attempt for liberation, and will be able to recognize
themselves even in the many 'man's' and 'he's.'"

and—keenly aware of his own mortality—thus he is disinterested in immortality.

These symptoms overlap with one another, and feed into the sort of generic character of a period in our social history that we're well familiar with: a period of protest, upset, sweeping dreams, attrition, apathy. In effect, the revolutionary fervor that lingered after the civil rights movement into the antiwar protests was typically unfocused—the first growing pains, perhaps, of mass disenfranchisement. My mother reports that the campus of Oberlin College in the late sixties was exciting on one hand, because at a social level you felt that something might really come out of the youth revolution, and totally frustrating on the other, because the students labeled everything "irrelevant" and believed that everything was "irrelevant." Nobel laureate Czeslaw Milosz, teaching in Berkeley during the sixties and seventies was convinced that the social uprising was really a march against the squares ("the truth is the proclaimed aims of the students have little to do with the dynamics of the movement. . . . What one should preach here is a bit of pity and compassion for 'squares' ").[20]

Nouwen describes this as "historical dislocation" and "ideological fragmentation," which caused free-floating anxiety. Man's most basic creative impulse—to art, science, and propagation—stems from a desire for immortality. When immortality as an operative concept is debunked, creativity goes astray. Nouwen described fluttering, displaced creativity as "convulsiveness"—a fascinating symptom of creative despair or disconsolation. Acutely aware of mortality and bereft of any sense of legacy—or for that matter, any hope for redemption—this generation is necessarily unhinged from tradition. Again here, *tradition* is not a hatchet of fundamentalism, but rather a link in the chain that ties man back to his roots, to a meaningful history, and forward to the future.

Therefore nuclear man, according to Nouwen, is fully concentrated on the present, he is a "prisoner of the now," because he is trapped in a moment where "the future has become an option." This leads to solipsism.

Solipsism is the defining characteristic of my father's experience of cultural decline in the sixties and seventies—individualism in the extreme, leaving society without any "common expectations of moral behavior." Henri Nouwen characterized nuclear man as subject to inwardness, fatherlessness, and convulsiveness. The "fatherlessness" of the sixties and seventies generation was a willed orphaning, a flat rejection of authority. Having shed reverence for institutions, tradition, authority, and *symbols* of authority, nuclear man was "fatherless." Children didn't see themselves as a continuation of their parents' earthly trajectory. The drive to self-determination that had defined American value systems took on a new hue—or perversion.

Individuals create themselves. Anything handed down, such as tradition, is at least suspect if not criminal. Faith will obviously falter under these conditions. If anything, faith becomes purely a personal matter—"an attitude which grows from within," according to Nouwen, divorced from tradition. He wistfully notes that "we could have anticipated this situation ever since we started saying that man is free to choose his own future, his own work, his own wife."

The downside of bold absolute-self-individuation is that instead of the father, youth becomes "captive to itself," captive, that is, to a far less wizened master. In this new paradigm, everything is self-referential and utterly ahistorical. The weird double twist is that in Christianity, the symbol of the father represents not only tradition (history) but also future (heaven). Without the future father, youth culture gets mired in the present, in the status quo. (The status quo—*yawn.*)

The here-and-now is emotionally devastating. The idea of a future world seems a far-fetched development of this awful one, and without any real sense of future, the idea of immortality is thwarted. Immortality is the central impulse driving creativity—to produce, invent, or propagate. Consequently nuclear man is depressed, apathetic, and idle. Ideology becomes fragmented when through the mass media nuclear man is "confronted with the most paradoxical human experiences": doctors can save a life with a heart *transplant,* while thousands of people die every day from lack of food. Interestingly, the modern capacity for diversity comes, in Nouwen's view, from the fact that no one believes that anything means much.

In order to pass through this meaningless black hole—in order to "reach a moment, a point or a center, in which the distinction between life and death can be transcended and in which a deep connection with all of nature, as well as with all of history can be experienced"[21]—young people escape, in Nouwen's analysis, with mysticism (through drugs or meditation) or revolution. But there is, according to Nouwen, a "third way" of escape: Christianity. Yes, personal, interior revolution is utterly consistent with a generation that feels cut off from its neighbors. Through the revolution of Christianity, the "illusory quality" of society can be rebuilt, an improved sum total of its parts rather than a tired and corrupted version of its sum total.

Nuclear man is frustrated and angry and has no access to a saving creative impulse (because that went out the window after historical dislocation) and is thus subject to undirected violence, or suicidal withdrawal. Unconstructed miserable. Nouwen cites two French teenagers who burned themselves to death in example of this "convulsiveness." With the more perfect focus of retrospect, and the illustrative zeal of a novelist, Philip Roth in *American Pastoral* cites the self-immolation of the Buddhist monks protesting the war in Vietnam—seen on the evening news. In Roth's portrait, we not only have the bewildering convulsiveness of nuclear youth—in the pampered daughter Merry who becomes a terrorist and blows people up to protest the war—but we have in her father the deterioration of the American dream (as it once was) and a dying generation trying (convulsively) to understand where it went. This is Roth's "American berserk." In 1978, 916 people drank cyanide-laced Kool-Aid and then lay down to die in concentric circles around their charismatic leader, Jim Jones. Was that convulsiveness, or a bid for transcendence?

Here Nouwen's prescription for the wounded healer comes into play. Tomorrow's Christian leader will reach nuclear man, instructs Nouwen, by being a clear articulator of his own inner experience, by being a man of compassion, and by being a contemplative critic. Because nuclear man is inward looking (solipsistic), the minister needs to be able to lead through the inner experience by dint of example. He needs to be able to give expression to his own religious experience: "The first and most basic task of the Christian leader in the future will be to lead his people out of the land of confusion into the land of hope. Therefore he must first have the courage to be an explorer of the new territory in himself and to articulate his discoveries as a service."[22]

This vision of remedy through the sharing of personal experience, it should be noted, was already a vibrant part of the culture in this period. The written word (with the plastic arts on its heels) underwent a not unrelated seismic shift (which can be described in terms of technique but also reflects a new privileging of the individual over the institution). "Throughout the twentieth century," wrote Tom Wolfe in 1973, "literary people had grown used to a very stable and apparently eternal status structure." The "upper class" in this structure, Wolfe goes on to say, "had exclusive entry to the soul of man, the profound emotions, the eternal mysteries, and so forth and so on. . . ." According to Wolfe, the real-life demise of the class system had left novelists without plots. Indeed, the novels of Henry James or Edith Wharton, for example, relied on class struggle for their central drama. Wharton's *House of Mirth* heroine, Lily Bart, tragically commits suicide after a precipitous fall from society. Without a society to fall from, midcentury writers turned to the "novel of ideas"—which increasingly failed to reflect the soul of man, eternal mysteries, "and so forth." Moreover, by the 1960s, eternal mysteries and the soul of man had—as we've seen—themselves suffered massive discrediting. The concept that the novel has "a spiritual function of providing a mythic consciousness" and that the novelist held a "sacred office" was at odds with a society rejecting mythic consciousness.

The artistic antidote to these social disparities had a prototype in New Journalism—nonfiction prose writing that used the dramatic techniques of the novel—of which Tom Wolfe was, of course, the vanguard. New Journalism embraced realism: it was, like nuclear man, entrenched in the here-and-now. It conveyed realism to an unprecedented degree through the medium of personal experience and anecdote: the reporter wasn't an objective eye, but a subjective participant. This brings us full circle, back to the wounded healer. The people in the pews want to look up and see themselves somehow in the face of the man in the pulpit.

Not only does such a man need to communicate identifiable life experience, but he needs to express compassion far more than he needs to express the authority that past generations of ministers boasted. Nouwen called for a new brand of leadership that eschewed traditional trappings of leadership. Compassion was the cornerstone of Nouwen's vision. Compassionate leadership is about neither sympathy nor pity, but comes from a genuine recognition of our neighbor as a fellow. "Through compassion it is possible to recognize that the craving for love that men feel resides also in our own hearts, that the cruelty that the world knows all too well is also rooted in our own impulse. Through compassion, we also sense our hope for forgiveness in our friend's eyes and our hatred in their bitter mouths."[23] Compassionate leadership relies on a minister's capacity to articulate his own experience, and simultaneously to remain detached enough from the world to demonstrate Christianity as a safe path apart—what Nouwen calls being a "contemplative critic." In other words, this new Christian leader has to be able to take from his experience of the here-and-now but not be mired in it.

"The paradox of Christian leadership," wrote Nouwen, "is that the way out is the way in, that only by entering into communion with human suffering can relief be found."[24]

Nouwen recognized the generational gap (or clash) that exacerbated the abyss between the traditional, organized church and contemporary society. This was quite a different clash from the intellectual one that pitted religion against modernity a century earlier. And it was a startling shift from the religious growth that characterized the immediate postwar period. This was an emotional divide, the fruit of evolved modernity—anonymity, corporate commercial-based culture, technology divorced from humanity, the nuclear threat of obliteration—and the church's failure to address the threat of society as opposed to the threat of mortality. In traditional narrative terms, the church was born out of a conflict between man and nature. Man went a long way toward controlling nature with technology and medicine—"scarcity no longer motivates his life"—and so he was left with a new conflict: man against man.

It would be a mistake to talk about what the church expects from its clergy without taking Nouwen into account, and it's interesting to compare Nouwen's diagnosis of spiritual malaise with my father's experience and the fateful seventies. My father's great disappointment is in himself, in his inability to act according to his own moral standards—he accepted society's vague and trendy negation of social behavior in the place of an enduring vision. He left church and family behind without having something else in their place to go to. It's also pertinent to examine how enduring Nouwen's thesis is thirty years later, especially because it *has* endured. When we seek to define what a priest is in the third millennium, the practical answer will include a variety of functions, interpersonal skills, and emotional brilliance.

Today there is a lively band of young priests in the Episcopal Church who gather under the name the *NeXt Generation*. They are clergy and active laity who were born between 1961 and 1981, and who will define the future of the church. Not surprisingly, the first item on the NeXt Generation agenda is simply getting more young people into the ranks of ordained clergy. In 1997, there were only

296 Episcopal clergy (priests and deacons) under thirty-five, less than 3.5 percent of over eight thousand ordained ministers.[25]

The explanation for these figures is simple. For years—largely under the influence of Nouwen's prescriptions—the Episcopal Church systematically turned away young applicants to the priesthood. The reason for that is simple, too. Young applicants lack maturity. A priest must inspire confidence—a rosy-cheeked youth doesn't *look* like a person who can sympathize or even understand life's great complexities; doesn't fit the bill of "wounded healer." Applicants in their twenties were sent away to "get some life experience." Many of them went away and never came back, and the church suddenly found itself with an aging clergy, and a foreseeable deficit in the future. It's *also* well worth noting that the church contemporaneously found itself with an aging constituency, and a more critical foreseeable deficit in the pews. Reverend Christopher Martin, a Generation X priest, wonders if the situation isn't the manifest expression of the "Anglican Death Wish."[26]

Perhaps Henri Nouwen's inspired analysis of how to minister to "today's youth" was starting to date itself. Certainly, a possible explanation for the lack of interest among young people for the church was that mature clergy didn't know how to attract young people. Reverend Richard Kew, a veteran priest and director of the Anglican Forum for the Future, explains that since the opening of the Episcopal priesthood to women, "we have successfully built a rapidly aging clergy force, who despite its greater comprehensiveness is mostly equipped to maintain the church it received—and then to retire within a decade or two." He goes on to predict that after "having spent more than twenty years traveling the length and breadth of North American Anglicanism . . . most of us presently in leadership cannot even conceive, let alone build, the sort of church that will speak and live with the power and grace of Christ in the emerging world."[27]

Two correctives have been put in place over the last few years, both of which will have a significant impact on the future of the ordained ministry in the Episcopal Church. The first correction came from the top down in the form of new recruitment efforts by active clergy, reinvigorated college chaplaincies, and an injunction to more seriously consider the applications of young people in the ordination process to the priesthood. Stop sending people away to get life experience; let them get experience through their work in the church. One young priest described her experience going through the ordination process *before* this corrective was instituted: "I dutifully followed and honored the Byzantine channels of the 1990s ordination process, so clearly geared to people at midlife. . . . I tried to understand the perspective of interviewers who seemed more concerned about making sure I invoked Baby-Boomer buzzwords like 'wounded healer' and 'vulnerability' than about my love for Christ and the church. I tried to take cues from the much more numerous midlife seminarians who kept dropping remarks about postulants who were too young to know anything because, after all, they had never suffered."[28] The subtext here is, of course, that this priest tried to conform to a dated vision of ministry, knowing all the while that this wasn't her vision of the future of the church.

The second corrective, launched by the NeXt Generation group themselves, is to embrace evangelicalism into the high church—to rid outreach of the stigma of revival tents, Pentecostalism, taking up serpents—and use it to bring people back into the pews. The so-called Information Age laid new tools (public relations) at the disposal of these young priests, and they propose to use them.

By evangelism, the NeXt Generation does not mean proselytizing or soapboxes. They mean outreach in the same way that poetry advocates mean outreach when they plaster our subway cars with verse. Instead of poets, the Reverend Jonathon Jensen compares the project (ironically) to alien abduction.

Citing a 1999 Gallup Poll that put the number of people who believe they've been abducted by aliens at over 4 million, Jensen compares that number to two and a half million Episcopalians in the United States and asks the obvious question "What are the aliens doing right that we Episcopalians are not doing?" He points out that the aliens have better visibility than Episcopalians, they're all over the mass media, they go where the people are, and even though they seldom speak and have no "magic method" or "Gnostic marketing tactic," they manage to "get their message across." He notes that the aliens come to us. "An interested person doesn't have to go looking at the end of a hidden street or search for meeting times or go for a background check. I have never," he continues, "heard of an alien saying, 'Anyone we would want to come, already knows where we are.'" Aliens are totally egalitarian, and abduct from a full cross-section of the American population. "They really are for all people."

Jensen goes on to note that alien abduction "marks and changes people" for life, and that abductees aren't afraid to "tell their story as truth to a multicultural society even if it's embarrassing or if another already believes something else." Abductees search out communities of people who've shared their same experience and they don't care about an institution's bells or whistles. They don't care about bells or whistles because they have clarity of vision; "they didn't make it across the Milky Way by arguing about who should be in or out." Jensen concludes, "Aliens know why people join them. Do we?"

As entertainingly preposterous as Reverend Jensen's analogy is, it's difficult not to see his point and also appreciate his delivery itself as a big part of the point. Within the polemics of the NeXt Generation we can apprehend an intriguing conflict, a reorganization of the meaning of tradition in terms of the church. Although the Episcopal ritual and liturgy remain steadfast at the heart of this religious experience, the traditional organization of ministry stands to be upended, with a significant shift toward (modified) progress.

The generation that Nouwen wrote about was fatherless, convulsive, and inward. It needed, in his estimation, a leadership that was compassionate, articulate about personal experiences, and a contemplative critic of the world around him. One of the truly revolutionary aspects of Nouwen's project was that it not only admitted that the church needed to attend to its time, but sought to understand those times. He seized the moment with steely resolve. The obvious question a generation later is: are we still in that moment?

The sixties generation was "fatherless" in an Oedipal sense. The father represented the institutions and traditions that had betrayed them—progress devolved into self-immolation (Hiroshima and Nagasaki, the Cold War), corrupt government systems (McCarthy, Nixon, Kent State, Vietnam), and to some extent, the values specific to first- and second-generation immigrants (assimilation, cultural homogenization). The father was rejected—thrown over, killed off—symbol of a larger disenfranchisement.

Today's young adults are fatherless in a less *symbolic* sense. The children of divorce, nonconventional families, relaxed and shifting moral codes, many of us were actually fatherless. We're a markedly self-sufficient generation—despite the early billing of "slackers." Out of necessity, we are scrappy, we've invented the terms of our own survival—though we move cautiously, testing the ground constantly for black ice. We might crave father figures, look with more interest upon heroes, mentors, and role models—but we do so with certain apprehension and self-protective distance. We're all too aware of human fallibility and tend to quickly locate weakness in potential leaders. With each blow to the institutional and governmental model—from Nixon, to Iran Contra, to Monica Lewinsky, to Enron, to the Catholic pedophilia scandal—we take failure and fallibility increasingly in stride. We have modified, *diminished* expectations, which, in a perverse way, we value in and of themselves. Our vision prizes realism and is cynical about progress (in the sense that we like it but don't hope it will improve anything). We put too much emphasis on the media, but are loath to take responsibility for it. We work, cumulatively speaking, many more hours of the week to keep home and body together—we allow ourselves to be subjected to absurd financial structures (insurance, health care, education, credit cards), but we haven't as a group cultivated any ability to identify and challenge the absurd. We can't identify and challenge the absurd because we don't have any strong ideals to contrast it against. We have modified, diminished expectations. No one will disappoint us.

We have a much more ample capacity for tolerance of difference and tend, nonetheless, to view individualism as a liability (that's our conservative face). We're starved for innovation, timid about conflict (residues of divorce, or backlash from the greedy 1980s?). We look for protection and salvation (if salvation is our concern) in ourselves. Self-individuation is no longer an abstraction, but an essential, inextricable component of our identity. I think we would accept a hero, or even a mere role model—but can't find one.

One night on the telephone, my father tells me tentatively, "You know, with all the preaching and reading that I do, some people already think of me as a priest. They say that."

At the time of this conversation, I'd been compulsively turning over an idea in my head—the idea that the priesthood was the closest thing that a person could get to a promotion in the world of religion. When you love something, you learn as much as you can about it, you practice it diligently, you get good at it. The natural next step is to want to get better. When you've mastered something, you become a maestro. A maestro is a teacher. A priest is sort of a teacher, in terms of levels, if only because, like becoming a teacher of something you love, becoming a priest means that you've attained a certain kind of accreditation—formal acknowledgment of your study and commitment and ability. I've wondered if there isn't an inherent problem to this religious system whereby the primary formal acknowledgment of mastery is ordination. And the way to express how profoundly committed you are to the church is to seek ordination.

It turns out that not only does the Episcopal Church share this concern of mine, but they've been industriously working on ways to rectify it. The first canon in Title III, on ministry, is called "The Ministry of all the baptized." It reads, "Each Diocese shall make provisions for the development and affirmation of the ministry of all baptized persons in the Church and in the world." Increasingly, the church is trying to emphasize that no matter how a person expresses their religion, whatever ministry they feel called to should be considered to be of the greatest value and should be actively affirmed. If a person is called to be the musical director of the choir, or called to volunteer in a homeless shelter, or called to be a schoolteacher—all of those endeavors are equally as valued by the church as is ordained ministry.

The ordination material provided by the diocese of Ohio specifically addresses this situation. "There continues to be considerable concern," read the guidelines, "that ordination not be seen as a validation of lay ministry or an elevation to a higher order. Many gifted, capable, motivated and committed people have a difficult time believing they are, as lay people, what God has called them to be: authoritative sources of life and ministry in the Body of Christ." Part of the problem that the church faces in trying to convince people of this is that (short of endlessly repeating it) they haven't figured out how to affirm everybody.

"That's not what I believe," my father specifies. "I don't already think of myself as one. But other people do."

"Well," I answer, "if you believe in ordination as a sacrament at all, then of course you don't agree with them."

"Of course not. Ordination brings you into apostolic succession. The laying on of hands."

I decided to put my idea to him: "Maybe when they say that they think of you as a priest, they're trying to find some way of expressing that they think you're a good Christian. But they can't find any other way to say it."

Silence, and then he says, "That would be fine, to be a good Christian."

"You know, Daddy, as a Jew I already am a priest. God called us all to be priest-people. Even though I can't get anyone to tell me what exactly that means. But I am a priest."

"Yes you are!" he says delightedly.

Then his voice drops to an uncommon whisper. "You're so lucky."

PART FOUR

Polemics

The abdication of Belief
Makes Behavior Small
Better an ignis fatuus
Than no illume at all.

—EMILY DICKINSON

On the top of Mount Purgatory at the gates to Eden, the earthly paradise, Virgil, the guide, abandons Dante, the pilgrim. In the afterlife of Dante Alighieri's medieval poem the *Divine Comedy*, Virgil is a "virtuous pagan"—born before Christ, he is fated to spend eternity in the limbo outside hell alongside figures from the Old Testament and unbaptized newborns. Though he has led Dante down into the deepest nether region and back up the Mountain of Purgatory, at the gate to paradise he must take his leave. Virgil's parting words:

> The temporal and eternal fires, my son,
>> you have now seen, and you have reached a part
>> where I discern no further on my own.
> I've led you here by strength of mind, and art;
>> take your own pleasure for your leader now.
>> you've left the steep and narrow ways behind.
> Behold the sun which gleams upon your brow,
>> behold the grass, the flowers, and the young trees
>> which this land, of its own, brings forth to grow.
> While we await the glad and lovely eyes
>> whose weeping made me come to you, you may
>> sit here or walk among them, as you please.
> No longer wait for what I do or say.
>> your judgment now is free and whole and true;
>> to fail to follow its will would be to stray.
> Lord of yourself I crown and mitre you.*

Purgatory 27:124–42. Translated by Anthony Esoleu (New York: Modern Library, 2003).

Virgil takes Dante through purgatory, instructing him on art and philosophy, walking him literally through the process of purging, or shedding earthly sin, but cannot follow him into the land of salvation. When he goes, he ordains Dante, making him lord of himself, marking that Dante has passed through purgatory and become not only purer but also a *better* version of himself.

Dante's Virgil is a remarkable character in devotional literature. As the tragic hero of the *Divine Comedy*, Virgil represents the drama of a pre-Christian world: unredeemed man trying to live according to an ethical structure built exclusively upon reason. He is condemned to limbo because that ethical system failed. He describes his fate: "There with the little ones, / the innocent who felt the bite of death / before they were redeemed from human sin, / I dwell, and there I dwell with others who / were never robed in the three holy virtues, / but followed faultlessly the four they knew" (7:31–37).

The four cardinal virtues that pre-Christian man *knew*, because he could arrive at them through reason, were prudence, justice, fortitude, and temperance. The three holy virtues, instead, are faith, hope, and charity. Despite the fact that he doesn't own these three virtues, Virgil is not intellectually at odds with Christianity, or even resentful of his fate. In fact, in Dante's portrait, Virgil demonstrates such strength of character and reason that he is able to bring soothing perspective to the injustice of his own plight: "Be satisfied with '*So it is,*' Oh Man, / for if you could have known the whole design, / Mary would not have had to bear a son." We had to have ignorance and sin, in other words, in order to win salvation.

I love Virgil, because he is wisdom and art. I love him because Dante loves him for those same qualities and with his grand poem does everything humanly possible to redeem him—everything, that is, short of saving his soul.

Exploring the story of Christianity, as I have been doing, I feel like a virtuous pagan: flush with the virtues of reason, and a spectator to the theological virtues. The architecture of my life is predominantly secular, fundamentally rational. Yet, of the three—faith, hope, and charity—faith is the only virtue truly alien to my emotional experience.

Faith—the undoing of mankind—what Eve lacked when she was seduced by the serpent to taste the forbidden fruit of knowledge. Faith, the first conflict between free will and love, blind obedience to the invisible. Faith is perhaps our most complicated emotion and certainly our most elusive kind of knowledge. Midway through the journey of my life, I've wondered whether faith is not so very complicated that it requires a lifetime of instruction. I've wondered whether it's *attainable*, and I've wondered whether I even have the intellectual and emotional tools to fully understand it. If I don't—is that the consequence of my secular upbringing, or is it a communal bewilderment? Is it mankind's essential plight not to fully understand faith?

I am in any case acutely aware of not having been indoctrinated into a religious practice that is an expression of faith. And I suspect—from afar—that such religious practice gives organizing structure to the complexity of the emotion of faith. I say that I was never indoctrinated, and yet I have throughout my adult life identified myself as a secular Jew. At times I've felt this identification strongly, and cherished it—without necessarily being capable of, or interested in, analyzing that feeling. Being a virtuous pagan is one thing—being a secular Jew is quite another, with an entirely different set of responsibilities.

The term *secular Jew* is a fraught one—especially in the American Jewish experience. As historian Arthur Hertzberg details in his book *The Jews in America*, the Jews who immigrated to America, mostly from Europe, at the beginning of the twentieth century—with a record arrival of two hundred thousand in 1906—were disenfranchised not only by European anti-Semitism but by European Jewry. There was an express effort among the immigrants to distance themselves from the Judaism of their fathers. American Judaism has consequently had its own very individual evolution. A large sector of that evolution embraced a kind of secular or ethnic Judaism, and is often defined in terms of a history of assimilation. "Jewishness in

America," writes Hertzberg, "was thus fashioned, de facto, not as religion but as an ethnic community. America's Jews would define themselves by fighting their enemies and clinging to each other."[1]

Remarkably, you can track a kind of common moral ground among American Jews that has withstood the constant, expanding assimilation. There has been, for example, a "commitment to the welfare state"—great individual prosperity notwithstanding. Hertzberg calls that commitment a "reecho of the prophetic commandment to 'do justice and love mercy,' and to protect the weak, 'for you were once slaves in the land of Egypt.' "[2] My own family, on my mother's side, was heavily involved with the Workers' Circle movement in Philadelphia—a basically socialist organization that sought to consolidate Judaism as a community. My grandparents were raised in nonpracticing households. My grandfather never went to temple or participated in Jewish holidays until he entered retirement—this was first a consequence of his upbringing, and second a matter of time. He was a tireless worker, provider for his family, and pursuer (to scant avail) of the American dream. At sixty-five, he was starting Jewishness from scratch. Hertzberg writes that this was a common plight:

> Jews who cared about being Jewish knew, if only in their bones, that they had to turn to religion—and most did not know how to begin. They were not heirs to a religious past. Their ancestors who had come to America had brought little learning in Bible and Talmud, and they had imparted less still to their descendants. Mainstream Judaism in America, at its most religious, had emphasized the tangible rituals, the practices, and not the learning that had been accumulated for three millennia. Thus, a community which was uniquely "American"—that is, pragmatic and not intellectual or spiritual, even in religion—knew only that it ought to become "more observant."

There is a strange paradox at the heart of this breed of Judaism as social activism and ethnic identification that is part of my legacy.

According to a 1983 study by the sociologist Jonathan Woocher, two out of three Jewish activist leaders believed that the Jews were God's Chosen People. Such a belief is a fundamentally religious idea, and is also theoretically at odds with the democratic, pluralistic ethic that these same Jews espoused. These were not "religious" Jews.*

At a certain point in my mid-twenties, when my father was (in my mind) merely the family theologian (and not an aspiring priest), I asked him if he could help me understand what made me *feel* Jewish. I had an impression of myself as adhering to a personal ethical and political system that struck me as Jewish—but this didn't make any sense. I hadn't been taught these principles as religious principles and I felt that I'd arrived at many of those principles on my own. Specifically because I'd invented my own moral code, I wondered how I could possibly be sure it was a *good* one. Experience and instinct were my only judges—but that all seemed ludicrously relativistic. I thought that if I was so very convinced of the correctness of each of my various moral positions, this meant I couldn't have invented them. For if I'd invented them, then I couldn't rely on their correctness. Because correctness, goodness, had to be a value independent of my own fabrication, of my brain—otherwise it wasn't *essentially* good. Unless, of course, I was prepared to posit my brain as essentially good—which I wasn't.

"It is because the will has no power to bring about salvation," wrote Simone Weil, "that the idea of secular morality is an absurdity. What is called morality only depends on the will in what is so to

---

*Jewish leader Mordecai Kaplan (1881–1984) explained that *God* is the term we use for the sum of our highest ideals, and that there can be no "Chosen People," in such a system. "A religion is the organized quest of a people for salvation, for helping those who live by the civilization of that people to achieve their destiny as human beings. In the course of that quest, the people discover religious truth and abiding values. These truths and values, like all others, are universal. They are not the monopoly of the group that discovers them. They may be discovered by other groups as well. Religions are distinct from one another not so much ideationally as existentially" (Hertzberg, 57).

speak its most muscular aspect. Religion on the contrary corresponds to desire and it is desire that saves."[3]

Where did all these values (not all necessarily "American" values) come from? I approached my father because I was wondering if they'd somehow been coded into my upbringing; they certainly had not been explicitly conveyed. How peculiar would that be, I thought, amassing values through code! My hypothesis of the moment was that they were actually Jewish values, which I decided meant that I should be able to locate them in the scriptures—right? Or could something be Jewish without coming from the scriptures, and if so, what made it Jewish? Was I an ardent defender of the underdog because "we were once slaves in Egypt"—without really knowing in my heart that we were once slaves in Egypt?

My father is a sophisticated abstract thinker. He's always interesting, but he's also perfectly content with non-answers. That day on the telephone, I came away with something like a non-answer. First, we discussed—on my father's prompting—the reordering of the Old Testament books in the New Testament. Picking up on my suggestion of codified values, my father wondered if there weren't in fact some sort of extractable code in the distinction between the two Bibles. It was a sort of juggling of numbers, and chapters, that quickly devolved into something that seemed to me like a set theory of theology. It was easily as abstruse as my father's brand of music theory (which uses mathematical analysis to explain aesthetic functions), or Kabbalah study. Sensing I wasn't buying the set-theory explanation of morality, he took recourse in his trusty "Entirely Fallacious Theory of Inherited Memory." Then he reminded me that when I was four, I had proposed a solution to the then-raging agricultural subsidies debate that consisted of collecting all the arable land and redistributing it in equal parcels to every American farmer. He concluded that this was an obvious example of nature over nurture. I was, as far as he was concerned, born communist.

So, by that same argument, I was born Jewish. Predetermination only temporarily satisfied my identity quandary, as I found myself before long falling frequently into bitter debate with a coworker over my conviction that Judaism was a racial quality. I was reckless with my terminology in these arguments because my coworker—my friend—was Jewish, too. But she wasn't born Jewish, she was born Catholic, and adopted and raised in a Conservative Jewish household. She is a committed practicing Jew, and extremely devout, yet she wasn't born Jewish. I had effectively been ignoring what it meant to be a practicing Jew—and inadvertently devaluing something precious to her by fixating on the single element of Judaism that didn't belong to her.

A secular Jew without a community, unafflicted by anti-Semitism, estranged on moral principles from the Israel project, and unwilling to define herself exclusively in terms of the tragedy of the Holocaust*—I was depending on an, at best, amorphous identity.

I asked my friend Rabbi Andy Bachman one day over a hamburger lunch if he could help me define secular Judaism. Rabbi Bachman, who is the director of Hillel at New York University, is a very good-looking and friendly man—so handsome and friendly that it's easy to forget how deadly serious he is. He stopped his hamburger midway to his mouth and fixed me with a forbidding glare, then sternly told me that Judaism is a religion. "Jews," he said, "believe in God. They believe in doing good, the law of the word, and that children are a blessing."

Andy allowed that I could be a secular Jew if I wanted, but from his perspective it was almost a hollow identity—an identity that was nothing more than an identity. Jewish identity is bound to religious

---

*Evocation of the Holocaust and the support of Israel have long been secular modes of community building among American Jews. I am not a Zionist—as I am not a nationalist ("Holiness is a religious category," wrote Isaiah Leibovitz in his book *Judaism, the Jews, and the Land of Israel*, "and it cannot be applied to any political or social purposes, not even the Zionist State," Hertzberg, 233). I do believe in mourning the dead and grieving a tragic history. I don't believe, however, that the communal memory of the Holocaust can or should be the sole sustaining element of a Jewish identity.

values. "Period." Even though Andy's answer effectively negates my entire matrilineal-socialist-secular-Jew vision of myself, his conviction is eloquent.

Rabbi Bachman wasn't brought up in a religious household either—his father was Jewish and his mother Lutheran. His first "Jewish" memory is of his dad and uncle clobbering two drunken thugs at a White Sox game in Chicago. The thugs had been taunting them, calling them *kikes*. As they decamped from the scene, four-year-old Andy asked his father, "What's a kike?" The answer, "It's a Jew. It's what you are."

"It's so silly, it's almost like a TV show," he says. "It's the ultimate statement of a post–World War II assimilated American Jewish male who fought in the war—*No one's gonna call my son a kike.*" Now in his family, through his work with college students at Hillel, and in his local community, Andy tries to create a Judaism that's nurturing, informed, and uniting—not just defensive. Judaism is built on small units: the family, the school, the quorum of ten required to make up a prayer minyan.

"To acquire history," wrote Leo Baeck, father of Reform Judaism, "to possess history, is the task of every people. When a people discovers within itself an idea, a determining, genuine thought, when it then clings to it, the time of its great history commences. Little peoples too, more than great peoples have gained great history; world history commenced with them."[4]

Dr. Ismar Schorsch of the Jewish Theological Seminary in New York says that at his best, the rabbi "represents an ideal of Judaism. And in that sense, the rabbi is an island of holiness in a secular world." What distinguishes the rabbi from the priest is that this ideal of holiness is strictly achievable. There's nothing holy or divine separating the Jew from the ideal. That's the democracy of rabbinic Judaism.*

---

*In practice, it isn't easy to get into rabbinical school either. There are psychological and physical exams to sit, personal essays to write; rabbinical school requires a very strong academic preparation and Hebrew language, as well as a demonstration

I ask Dr. Schorsch if there's any such thing as a secular Jew. "Oh, there's a lot of secular Jews walking around," he replies. "Largely ethnic Jews. Their bond to Judaism is nonreligious in character. They identify with the Jewish people, or with Jewish history, or the Holocaust, maybe with Israel. Those are all forms in which secular Judaism expresses itself." And I'm relieved for a moment as I listen— then crushed. "It works for a generation or two," he says lightly. "The major weakness is that it's very hard to transmit secular Judaism from one generation to the next because there is no ritual. Without ritual you don't have any vessels. It's possible to transmit the religious culture of Judaism, because it comes with so many rituals. The rituals contain the values, the attitudes that make up the religious side of Judaism."

Codified values transmitted across generations by means of ritual: tradition is the lifeblood of religion. This is especially true in the Diaspora—where tradition as a simple shape of life and habits, as family and local culture, dissipates easily into the larger social culture. In 1979, Rabbi Eliezer Menachem Shach wrote, "What explains the fact that we have remained one people, even though we were scattered to the four corners of the earth? We have not disappeared among the people, but rather we have guarded our uniqueness. How did we do this? What kept us separate from them? Only our holy Torah. . . . We do not have to pay any attention to territories, to how much land might remain in our hands, but only to the true source of our existence."[5]

And again we see the importance of the connection my father made with tradition as rooted in the eternal. Tracing his own roots through humanity—twenty-six life spans back to Jesus—he distinguished the relative nanosecond that was his family's rootless, scattered immigrant experience, his father's perpetual "homesickness,"

---

of deep religiosity and commitment to Judaism. Rabbinical school—a full graduate-level curriculum, with one year required in Israel—constitutes the formation for the rabbinate; you are ordained a rabbi upon graduation.

from the time that is the human experience and all that is built upon it. Religion responds to that terrifying notion that we are just a speck of dust, a flash of light in all of history by constantly integrating us back into the corporate body of all humankind.

Such a concept, of course, does get twisted in an individualistic environment, so that we come to understand religion as professing the immortality of the individual soul—a tit-for-tat challenge to death.

This is a very similar construction to the idea of immortality through artistic legacy, the apex of man's creative impulse. Dante, Virgil, Shakespeare, Milton, Caravaggio are our immortals. "A beautiful thing involves no good except itself, in its totality, as it appears to us," wrote Simone Weil. "It is because beauty has no end in view that it constitutes the only finality here below. For here below there are no ends. All the things that we take for ends are means."[6] Weil's "beauty," however, was not found in the dark transparencies of a Caravaggio painting, but in the "action of gravity on the fugitive folds of the sea waves, or on the almost eternal folds of the mountains."[7] The art of man is beautiful, according to Weil, only when he has been "infused with the light of God." And that kind of beauty is harder to measure.

Where legacy is concerned, artistic pursuits seem like total hubris on one hand—the celebration of one person's life or achievements over life itself. On the other hand, the creative impulse itself is a form of *imitatio Dei,* the imitation of God the creator. "The rights of individuals are absolute," writes Hertzberg, "for every individual is created in the divine image. Each has his or her particular virtue and capacity for service. The proper response to life is piety and reverence, not only before God but before other people." We are part of this world, made in the divine image, and in that sense, we are all infused with divine light. Not individual units but a continuity of person, not rootless but bound in time.

This kind of faith, explains Garry Wills, is "a 'synchronic' faith, one in which eternity is continually intersecting—literally, cutting across—time. We are created *now*, at every now. Christ comes now; the Incarnation is now. The great judgment is now. 'The accomplishment of everything impends' (1 Peter 4:7). That is the good news Jesus came to bring. Believing it is what makes me a Catholic."[8]

If faith has shapes, an emotional architecture, then this shape of continuity is one that even I can begin to apprehend. And with that, my father's own journey becomes suddenly less disparate. He's gone "back" to Christ, and he's also gone back in time to Christ, and beyond Christ to the primordial ooze, recognizing all of us in a trajectory that extends backward and infinitely forward—not a Queens boy or a country boy, but a member of the giant movement of life through time: faith as perpetuity. His return to the church is not a distancing from me, his churchless daughter, but rather a return to time eternal, which I am entirely part of.

It is fortunately a complex argument—and one that I won't pursue further. As Dante said when he reached the Garden of Eden, "My Reader, if I had a longer space / I would keep singing" (*Purgatory* 33:136). Or perhaps more appropriately, as Virgil said, *Non discerno più*—"You have reached a part / where I discern no further on my own." I am, after all, only a virtuous pagan here.

Faith therefore hopes also for this life, but be it noted, by virtue of the absurd, not by virtue of human understanding, otherwise it is only practical wisdom, not faith. Faith is therefore what the Greeks call the divine madness. This is not merely a witty remark but a thought which can be clearly developed.

—KIERKEGAARD

This generation of mine (the NeXt Generation, Generation X, the slackers, the godless, the thirty-somethings) grew up under an advanced form of sociology known as "demographics," or "markets."

When "they" want to target "us," they play songs from the early years of MTV, or push our nostalgia buttons through allusions to *Three's Company, The Brady Bunch, Laverne & Shirley*—our mutual culture of television. My memory may be fading, but I don't believe that the Brady Bunch ever went to church. Which isn't to say that my entire cultural identity is bound up in the Brady Bunch (I'm not *that* easy), but religion isn't part of our lingua franca. Religion is local, it's personal—part of the fabric of a common life, woven of individual experience, the threads intertwining but separate.

"We 'intellectuals' in America," wrote William James, "must all work to keep our precious birthright of individualism, and freedom from these institutions [church, army, aristocracy, royalty]. Every great institution is perforce a means of corruption—whatever good it may also do. Only in the free personal relation is full ideality to be found."[9]

Tocqueville observed,

> The American clergy stands aloof from secular affairs. . . . In America religion is a distinct sphere, in which the priest is sovereign, but out of which he takes care never to go. Within its limits he is master of the mind; beyond them he leaves men to themselves and surrenders them to the independence and instability that belong to their nature and their age. I have seen no country in which Christianity is clothed with fewer forms, figures, and observances than in the United States, or where it presents more distinct, simple, and general notions to the mind.[10]

The godless among us define the terms by which religion will be discussed in our culture. Secularism is the default position of authority.* Religious fundamentalists are very aware of this, and assume it's a position to be vanquished. Marvin Olasky, the author of *Compassionate*

---

*In 1935, the scholar H. Richard Niebuhr was sufficiently plagued by this conflict to edit a book along with Wilhelm Pauck and Francis P. Miller tellingly entitled *The Church Against the World,* in which they argued that American Christianity had

Conservatism, complains that the *"hostile"* separation of church and state is a perversion of what the Founding Fathers had in mind. He doesn't believe that there is anything about separating church and state in the establishment clause of the First Amendment, that the phrase itself comes from Thomas Jefferson's personal correspondence (which is true), and that "the founding fathers would be aghast at court rulings that make our part of the world safe for moral anarchy"[11] (which is a very misleading conclusion).

Frustrated members of the moral minority are aware of our secular mandate—and frustrated by it. The drafters of the Bush administration's faith-based initiative know that the challenge their politics face is not a matter of policy but of rhetoric and that the terms of the polemics are driven deeply in our emotional intelligence—whereas we, the people of the secular, don't often think about any of this. The issue is so very rarely open to debate. We are a secular country and everything *has to* fit under the umbrella of this rubric. When we do reconsider such questions—in the context of a conflict over school prayer or the words of the Pledge of Allegiance—the debate itself is a matter of principle: the right to believe whatever you want without being subjected to the beliefs of others, especially by those others who bear the authority of the state. This is a funny kind of entitlement since in some respects the state is the least influential of public entities—and MTV is the most influential.

Brainwashing is the stuff of movie plots (fantasy) and cult (desperation). American democracy grew out of basic Christian values and we are fortunate that over the years those values have accommodated and continue to accommodate vast diversity. The *really* secular governments of our time, the antireligion governments, were Hitler's Germany, Stalin's Soviet empire, Chairman Mao's Republic of China—the specter of those same regimes led us once upon a time to put the word "God" into our Pledge of Allegiance.

---

become too entangled with political and economic culture to assert any real positive and/or alternative influence on society.

In a roundtable discussion on religion and politics, the writer Barbara Ehrenreich complained that as an "out atheist," she feels marginalized because, she points out, "I can't think of any 'out atheist' who has won any significant political office—in fact, I think it would be almost impossible for an atheist to win such an office."[12] This is certainly an interesting point, but reflects more on a staid stereotype of what a leader should be like than it does on the part religion does or doesn't play in politics. Belonging to a church is PR shorthand for having a strong moral foundation and the capacity for compassion.* It's not that atheists don't have these qualities; it's just that atheists don't have any shorthand with which to put them on display. Most politicians wear their religion like a tie or hairstyle painstakingly selected by a campaign manager—and those who don't wear it tend to make us edgy, because we don't know how to evaluate their moral caliber. Which actually makes Ehrenreich's point more of a problem that the atheists have to fix, rather than a quality the religionists should learn to mitigate.

Assume we occupy a middle ground, dominated by secularists and populated by the faithful. How informed are we, the secularists, about this alternative world we debunk, ridicule, ironize, fetishize with such pious abandon? "All religion is fanaticism," said a magazine editor I work with. But what do we on the outside know specifically about doubt, yearning, faith, concord with the invisible, and the will to believe?

Turn to a market model for an example. Consumerism, the mature expression of capitalism, is a response to yearning. The system of supply and demand is the secular antidote to the pain of

---

*Bringing the point home, Ehrenreich goes on to say, "I would be interested in hearing some Christian say, 'My policies will flow from the values in the book of Matthew,' or some Jew say, 'My policies will flow from the Prophets.' I might vote for them on that basis. But that's not the kind of morality that people are finding in the Bible. Instead they seem primarily interested in the details of our sexual behavior. To me, this represents not just a trivialization of religion, but a trivialization of morality."

yearning. First: achieve the ability to manufacture longing—to inspire demand. If you can manufacture or create something, that means you control it. Then: compromise the helpless nature of yearning by positioning yearning as an obstacle to be overcome that *can* be overcome. Yearn for that which can be acquired: an object, a lifestyle. Acquire it; achieve it. In this way, yearning is demoted from an existential state of being to a temporary state of irritation. We have constructed a market model to redress yearning.

By "breeding out," in the Darwinian sense, our tolerance for yearning (so that yearning becomes vestigial), we also undercut fundamental tenets of theistic religion: longing, mystery, even faith to some extent. Mystery, too, as religious historian Karen Armstrong points out, is no longer revered but denigrated: "Since the Enlightenment, a 'mystery' has been seen as something that needs to be cleared up. It is frequently associated with muddled thinking. . . . A detective story is called a 'mystery' and it is of the essence of this genre that the problem be solved satisfactorily. . . . Even religious people came to regard 'mystery' as a bad word during the Enlightenment."[13]

But organized religion, theology, and scholarship are resilient, tenacious; they've been in constant evolution since their inception. It shouldn't surprise that the church will respond to the new world order the way it has to each of the old new world orders. There are more women and openly gay people on the pulpit, there is a patron saint of the Internet, the 2000 jubilee in Rome had flashy corporate sponsors, black church leaders are celebrating the blurring of denominational lines that perfectly accommodates modern American mobility, pluralism, and the entitlement to self-determination.

Has our current model inadvertently, or intentionally, created an environment that is particularly "hostile" to religion—not even its existence so much as its expression? If so, how has that hostility changed the way people experience their spirituality?

The way a religious person navigates his life, choices, and the terms by which his vocation will be realized has everything to do with the world around him. My father locates his period of confusion—the period in which he strayed from himself and the church—in terms of falling prey to popular culture, something he still has difficulty reconciling with the intellectual life of his mind, and with the rigor of his academic training. "I *found* myself," he said, "embarrassingly influenced by the environment, by the way things were going in the social world, and I found myself behaving the way radio and TV said I was expected to." This is a devastatingly passive vision of one's own past. None of us are hermetic little orbs of integrity, or even selfness; we're dynamic creatures, responding to and absorbing the better and worse things around us. One simple way of understanding my father's calling as he articulates it is that he wants to help increase the "better" quotient of the ratio.

What my father means when he says that "the church led" him to recognize he was wrong is that it gave him a position of perspective—in one sense by taking him out of the mainstream—and lending him an effective model for self-analysis. Our secular world has an architecture, one that's grown organically from the inside out. We have yet, however, to cultivate a mode of self-inquiry that would correlate to the modes offered by religious tradition. (I'll come to psychology presently.)

Israeli writer David Grossman comments in an introduction he wrote for the book of Exodus: "Even today, the Jewish people read in the Passover Haggadah that in every generation, each individual is bound to regard himself as if he personally had gone forth from Egypt. This is a direct summons to the people of Israel to examine the essential components of their identity."[14] And like the Jews who fled from Egypt, "If they have any spirit left they will realize that a miracle has befallen them, that they are privileged to have been given the chance to reinvent themselves, to be redeemed. If they dare, they can fashion a new identity for themselves. But to do so, they must fight the ponderous gravity of habit, anxiety, and doubt of their inner bondage."[15]

What habits, anxieties, and doubt inhabit the bondage of secularism? Secularism neither compels nor asks for self-examination—though, as we might note, over the last quarter century, the vagaries of secularism have bred a will to assert identity: racial, professional, lifestyle identity.

Can we suppose that secularism, like the church, has an evolutionary trajectory? If indeed we have generated an environment that is hostile to religion, and we did so in order to accomplish the separation of church and state that has played such a critical role in the development of a multicultural, tolerant, democratic society, then is that environment only a phase? Or is it, rather, a cornerstone?

In an interview, English novelist and ardent atheist Jim Crace reflects the hope of an "evolved" atheism with this claim:

> I'm not struggling at all. I have no doubt whatsoever that there is no God, there is no afterlife, and there is a scientific explanation for everything. But I would still say that I have a very highly developed, highly brewed sense of wonder, sense of fear of those things that traditionally religious people are wondrous about and fear. My fear is that if the great religions of the world atrophy—which they seem to be doing to some extent—then we cannot afford to have a world in which there is no mechanism for fear and wonder and awe and transcendence, simply because atheism did not bother with that in the past. If scientific logic were to have its way and everybody didn't believe in God any longer, then we have to have some other form of mysticism to take the place of a belief in God. Because that kind of transcendence, that kind of mysticism is our Trojan horse for glorifying the fact of existence, for wondering at the diversity of the natural world. We would not want to be without those things.[16]

Indisputably, one of the greatest secular commentators on religion was the pragmatist and psychologist William James. His 1902 *Varieties of Religious Experience* remains a primary point of reference for religious practitioners both spiritual and literal, as well as for nonbelievers (spiritual and literal). At once rational and broadminded, James examines and gives psychological credence to the religious urge as a human condition.

Psychology serves the need to turn inward, and the need to address fears. It treats narration in the same way that religion and art do, as parable—a story with a symbolic logic whose interpretation moves toward understanding. Freud formulated storytelling as a psychological system. James and Carl Jung transposed that system onto religious discourse. James extended the will to believe onto an almost sociological model for the human relationship with the divine, while Jung explored the nature of that will through an interpretation of its manifest symbols. Their work makes religion palatable, comprehensible, scientific, and philosophical while maintaining something of the elemental mystery. Psychology, too, has its own romance with the unknown, the dark crevices of the mind, and the inexplicable in human behavior. It takes pleasure in the contemplative, almost prayerlike examination of the self and interpretation of the stories we tell ourselves.

Once upon a time psychology and religion were foes—now they are teammates, fending off a common enemy. Over the last quarter century, scientific advances continue to rattle the foundation of religious belief, but have had an even more significant impact on the shape of psychology. We are moving away from narrative toward chemistry. The "talking cure" is now a quaint companion to the practice of psychopharmacology. Antidepressants in their myriad applications have now made of despair a superable obstacle. Suffering is a chemical imbalance. Suffering can be cured. By the same token, behavior now has a scientific explanation that largely replaces the psychological one.

"Sure, pills are only a Band-Aid," remarks one Prozac user, "but why suffer if you don't have to?" It's an excellent point, one that would be examined if there weren't in fact a stable of medicines to keep you from "suffering."

The victory over personality afflictions puts a value system into effect that is far more judgmental and absolute than the system implied by psychology. Psychology places emphasis on understanding that which is normal and that which is abnormal within the received circumstances of life. That which we can't fix, we can at least explain. Psychology in many ways set the stage for the increased tolerance of difference and individuality, which distinguishes our modern age. With neurochemistry the aim is not to understand but to correct. We accordingly adopt a new attitude to the shapes of personality. Mystics are not visionaries but epileptics. Moody melancholics are not romantic but depressed. Moodiness and melancholy are imbalances; they are bad, like shyness, like distraction and distractibility.

Distraction, something that in the wake of the invention of Ritalin we consider an affliction—particularly in our children—is the subject of an essay by Simone Weil. In "Reflections on the Right Use of School Studies with a View to the Love of God" Weil condones the *practicing* of attention, because the act of paying attention trains the mind for praying—which is total attention, concentration, meditation. Inattention is bad—but why? Is it because, as Weil suggests, our children have no access to God? Or is it because unless they learn to concentrate they will eventually be unable to do complicated math problems or read classic books involving extended ideological themes and complicated ideas? If the answer is the latter, then, as God rewards sin—his own *didactic* technique—we will accordingly develop machines to compensate for our inability to add; we will write books and films that accommodate our inability to follow long or complex notions; and we will finally eradicate the art of conversation. Will we thus eradicate our need to explain the universe? Will we change our ways, or will we become so painfully boring to one another that we long for death to escape the boredom just when genetic engineering begins to close in on physical immortality?

America is without a common church, but that doesn't mean America is without values. Our Constitution imparts an explicit value system. Our culture operates on implicit value systems. The tension between, or viability of, opposing value systems is one of our common values.

The role of the artist once upon a time was to identify, comment upon, the prevailing culture—to take the grand themes of society and turn them back upon the individual. Arthur Miller, Upton Sinclair, John Steinbeck, Norman Mailer are examples of writers who performed that artistic function. In the wake of the modernist annihilation of "God," these artists examined the societal structures that replaced God. In the late twentieth century, the role of the artist as an observer of society has been annihilated (perhaps self-annihilated). The artist has turned inward, mirroring the triumph of individualism—which is another of our common values. Introspection has diminished the function of art as a provider of perspective. In order to understand what our value system consists of—if indeed we care at all—we appeal to different barometers.

Reasonable man, Cartesian man, post-God man believes in the absolute of science. And so we might look to science in order to understand what we value today—look in particular to the astonishing advances in the world of medicine, and how and where research is funded.*

There has been much written about the politics of AIDS treatment—the disease that threatens gays, drug abusers, and the continent of Africa, all groups that hold little influence on the world scale of power dynamics. Breast cancer research lagged far behind research on colon and prostate cancer treatment until the early 1990s, when the women's movement finally solidified into a powerful lobby of money and influence, giving women real leverage to call for better research. The idea that we can measure society's priorities, and by extension society's values, by interpreting the amount of money invested in finding a cure to diseases that discriminate is neither radical nor ridiculous. It's methodological.

---

*The largest financial backer of research in the field of religion is the Lily Foundation—the "Prozac People."

On a broader scope, it's interesting to think about the shift in our approach to medicine that has led to the fact that we engage illness combatively: we "race" to the cure, we stamp out the disease, we even model healing visualization techniques on a Space Invaders game model. For conspiracy theorists and biological warfare researchers alike, it can now also be said that we *employ* illness combatively. It is not that suddenly we've begun trying to conquer disease rather than comfort those who are ill—we have suddenly gotten better at conquering disease. In the process we've discovered that there is less need to contemplate the contingency of life because we've grown more expert at controlling that contingency. According to this bellicose approach toward sickness, one stops trying to understand affliction and begins considering it exclusively as something to be defeated.

How does the eradication of moodiness, disease, and the hierarchy of treatment relate to religion? One of religion's predominant functions through history has been to explain affliction, to offer answers, comfort, and contemplative models with which to confront life's cruel contingencies. What is the book of Job if not a study in the nature of affliction? Why was it important for Rabbi Harold Kushner to address "when bad things happen to good people"? Affliction, like contingency, is part of a relationship to the divine. In the absence of the sense that science can cure or control affliction, affliction is part of the greater order indifferent to individual man. Weil, who delved deeply into the nature of affliction—she used its principles to justify Christ's superiority over mere martyrs—wrote: "Affliction hardens and discourages us because, like a red hot iron, it stamps the soul to its very depths with the scorn, the disgust, and even the self-hatred and sense of guilt and defilement that crime logically should produce but actually does not. Evil dwells in the heart of the criminal without being felt there. It is felt in the heart of the man who is afflicted and innocent."[17]

But science hasn't eradicated contingency; it's only taken it on, offered one approach to it. Until we're all self-regenerating, immortal entities living in environmentally perfect bubbles, we will not have conquered those factors that are indifferent to the individual. Nature is larger than us and indifferent to us. "The sea is not less beautiful in our eyes," wrote Weil, "because we know that some- times ships are wrecked by it. On the contrary, this adds to its beauty. If the sea altered the movements of its waves to spare a boat, it would be a creature gifted with discernment and choice and not this fluid, perfectly obedient to every external pressure. It is this perfect obedience that constitutes the sea's beauty."[18]

Whether the system is nature, science, plague, society, emo- tions, cosmology, or the divine, individuals are always navigating a larger, critically indifferent structure. It is that confrontation with the larger structure where religion in its pursuit of our meaning on earth, atheism in its rejection of religion, and secular models all overlap.

After a long period of research, I had gotten to a point where I thought that I understood the Process—at least as well as I could as an "outsider." I'd learned some of the key talking points—Eucharist, ministry, wounded healer, vocation. I had constructed a mental nar- rative (on my father's behalf) of how they applied to him. I knew what kind of red flags the church was looking out for. I learned, for example, that the fact he was late to one of his discernment meet- ings was probably interpreted as a "problem with authority." I knew that his age was a factor, and that his divorce and time away from the church weren't. I knew that he hadn't been discriminated against because he was too highly educated. By the same token, I realized that he was going to have to figure out how to personalize his beau- tiful ideas in order to explain them to parishioners.

I had also determined from talking to people and reading the church's own internal documents relating to the Process that my father's discernment process had been irregular. He should have had more than two and a half meetings with his vocations commit- tee. And posing follow-up questions to him by e-mail was entirely out of keeping with the idea of a prayerful discernment. You can't hear either God or a person over e-mail—technology betrays us sometimes.

Another thing I had learned was that the diocese of Ohio seldom invoked the modified ordination process known as canon 9, "On Local Ministry"—what my father once described to me as the bishop "deputizing a priest, the way a sheriff might do in a frontier town in the Old West." Because he was older and had no "careerist" ambitions in the church, my father had hoped to be considered for this quicker, less formalized process, whereby a candidate is ordained to serve in a specific parish (and not anywhere else in the church), which, because it's rural, in crisis, poorly funded, or has a distinct "ethnic composition, language, or culture," would not otherwise have access to a priest (or an appropriate priest). The seminary requirements are significantly reduced under this canon, as are the requirements that a person serve as a transitional deacon for a year before ordination to the priesthood. The retired military officer who had first caught my father's attention all those years ago had been ordained to serve as an unpaid volunteer assistant rector in his own parish—probably under canon 9.

This is a controversial canon, which my father didn't know when he started out, and a number of dioceses are dead set against invoking it. And in fact, a recently concluded internal review of "Title III—On Ministry" has recommended that canon 9 be eliminated entirely and replaced (or reconstituted) with a more flexible overall standard of formation that honors both "locally formed" and "seminary-trained" priests.[19]

So I had learned all these things—these disparities between his understanding of the process and the actual process, all of which I thought had critical bearing on what had gone wrong in his application. I hoped he would be comforted to know that everything else aside, his application had been punctuated with land mines that ranged from administrative politics (the debate over canon 9) to matters of technique, style—but that didn't necessarily reflect on his spiritual "fitness." On a long drive back from the aforementioned mattress store, I prepare to share my new knowledge with my dad.

"I think maybe I might have figured out some of the things you're supposed to say," I cautiously venture. *Cautiously* because it is already the second day of my visit and he hasn't so much as uttered the word *priest*.

Silence. "To the vocations committee," I clarify.

"Fuck them," he says.

More silence.

"They want me to roll over and die," he continues, "because they said 'no.' They want me to prove that there's nothing else in the world I can do except for this."

I think to myself that he's got a point, although nobody's phrased it like that; the whole idea of calling as everyone has explained it to me begins and ends with the conviction that there is no other conceivable way to express yourself.

"Why should you have to prove that the only possible thing you can be is a priest in order to be a good priest?" he continues. "How does one thing connect to the other? In order to be a good priest you have to die if you can't be one? That's just wrong."

What's happening in this moment in the car—a precociously antiquated Chevy pickup, with one operational taillight, two permanent spare tires mounted on the rear axle, a faulty brake line that means sometimes you have to stand up and put the full weight of your body on the pedal to make the car stop, a cracked windshield, the heater blasting to keep the engine from overheating, and two twin-sized mattresses loaded in back—is that it's slowly dawning on me that I've been so focused on learning what the church means by calling and what the church looks for in its clergy that I've never stopped to question the basic premise: what right does *any* institution have to subject someone to this kind of judgment?

There's an element of witch trial or McCarthyism in this evaluation process where the standards for reaching a conclusion are both so subjective and stand so utterly outside the control of the person under examination. And it's true. How is needing to be a priest so badly that you'll forsake your privacy and dignity, compromise your character and achievements, dissolve into paralyzing tears in front of the jury, believe you might die if they don't find in your favor—how is that what you need to be a priest? Since when does "your great yearning" constitute a job qualification? What distinguishes "great yearning" from "perverse ambition," for example?

I simultaneously realize this afternoon in the car that my dad is bailing. Which introduces into the equation the equally troubling possibility that he never had a divine call. If he was really meant to be a priest—even if it was merely something he wanted and not something he was summoned by higher powers to do—he wouldn't let himself be waylaid by one initial summary judgment. After all, taking the discernment process in its entirety—that preliminary committee of three was only the tip of the iceberg. They weren't even the palace guards; they were the road signs that read, "Guards Ahead." Maybe whatever he had in him driving this pursuit, he didn't have in sufficiency. Of course, a person does get stronger along the way, like a snowball, as he gathers encouragement and experience. One is always most vulnerable at the beginning—and naïveté is perhaps all one has to offset that attenuated vulnerability. But my father's naïveté had turned sour.

Thomas Merton's vocation was diffused early on by the negative judgment of one Franciscan, who believed that Merton couldn't become a monk for "legal" reasons (the murky stuff of Merton's debauched youth). When Merton's "failure" continued to haunt him a year later, friends told him that if he'd been dissuaded from his calling so easily, maybe it was never real. In 1941 Merton wrote to a friend, "When you started out . . . by saying that any person who asked all those questions probably wanted to be a priest, you (1) surprised me, (2) woke me up to the fact that maybe I am very bad at being abstract about anything, (3) you scared me. The priest business is something I am supposed to be all through and done with. I nearly entered the Franciscans. There was a very good reason why I didn't, and now I am convinced that Order is not for me and never was. So that settles that vocation."[20]

"There are plenty of other things that I can do," my father says. "This is the only business going that makes you crawl and beg and long to be in it—but it's no less racked by triviality and hypocrisy than any other business."

The conversation stops there, because he's unhappy, verging on angry; and I'm confused, verging on unhappy. I am wondering whether the vocations committee simply didn't hear my father's calling because he didn't have one. And I am also wondering whether the whole "discernment" affair wasn't just a cruel and fantastical way of telling him they didn't like him for the job.

If you have a calling, it's part of you. It grows with you—or you grow into it. Because the monks didn't take him, Merton went away, convinced this meant he didn't have a calling to be a monk. But he kept working on what he did want. He kept living as a Christian, and got better at it, and he got better at forgiveness (self-forgiveness). And then one day his old professor said, "If you take their word for it that you don't have a calling, that probably means you don't."

If you don't want it badly enough, then it's not part of you. Yearning isn't persistence so much as helplessness in the face of yourself and your desires.

My father is right. It's perverse to insist that you can't be a good priest unless it's the only thing that you could ever imagine doing with your hopes and your talents. It makes the whole adventure a kind of inbred, navel-gazing compulsion. What it should be (I think) is a legion of good, Christian, holy people offering their gifts and practice in the service of their deep shared faith.

> Saint Francis once asked a bishop for permission to preach in his diocese. I am in no need of anyone to help me in my task, the bishop coldly replied. Francis humbly withdrew, but in less than

an hour he was back again. What is it, brother, you require of me this time? asked the bishop in surprise. My Lord, Francis said to him. When a father drives his son out of the door he returns by the window.[21]

Not even a month after penning that letter, Merton wrote his friend again: "You see, I have always wanted to be a priest—that is, ever since my conversion. When someone told me that there was an impediment against my ever being ordained, I was very unhappy, and really, since then, I had been really quite lost, in a way. I knew I wanted to belong to God entirely, but there didn't seem to be any way particularly suited to fill up everything in me that I had hoped would be filled by the priesthood." He goes on to describe the peculiar inner conflict that was keeping him from trying again:

> First, I had been told it was a total, complete, irrevocable impediment in such strong terms that it seemed fantastic even to question them. Second, the devil made use of this to try and kid me that all this thinking about a religious vocation was just a silly, dramatic self-indulgence, and that I would never really be able to stand up under the life, in actuality, and that I had best forget all about it. Well, I could not forget about it, but I stalled around, having argued myself into such a state that it was almost impossible to do anything: and all along I had been arguing with myself instead of praying, which of course didn't help matters, but definitely guaranteed that I would end up in what you refer to as a "pretzel": and what a pretzel![22]

Two weeks after, Merton left for the monastery at Gethsemani where he entered the order of the Trappist monks.

Later that evening (once the mattresses had been hauled inside, dinner eaten, and everyone settled in cozily to watch TV), the phone rang. It was Elizabeth, calling from Canada, where she's recently started teaching. They've been spending half the year there and half the year here and commuting a lot in between, tricking out their teaching schedules and school arrangements so that the family spends as little time as possible apart. The house in Ohio is small and the whole first floor is a doughnut around the stairway to the second floor. So my dad took the call in the far side of the doughnut, talking quietly so as not to disturb my TV watching. Elizabeth is trying to figure out whether the Canada thing is going to work out in the long term. She's had other job offers and they could move to a new state, or stay the course and keep splitting their time until my father retires. It's a complicated professional decision and it's primarily Elizabeth's decision to make, but she's ambivalent and wants to know if my father has any strong personal feelings on the subject. I lower the TV—which I'm not watching anyway—so as not to disturb their conversation. I can hear him talking.

His strong feelings are that he really likes their church in Canada, likes their priest, and has had a number of conversations with her over the last year. Now that they've been members of the church for a while, and she's gotten to know him, she wants to introduce him to the bishop, whose "style" my father admires. Up in northern Canada, there are a lot of mission churches on Cree reserves that desperately need priests. My father's strong feelings are that he would like the family to stay in Canada so that he can pursue the priesthood there.

It strikes me now that a pretzel is often the most precise—and consequently the most beautiful—way to describe very important emotions.

Issues of authority are central to understanding the priesthood—how it operates and who is brought into it—and central to understanding how difficult it is to accept principles of divine discernment in contemporary America. The philosophical fire of our forefathers, and so much of our immigrant culture, is born, after, all from the ethos of dissent. We don't answer to a higher authority; we are our own authority. "Whoso would be a man," preached Ralph Waldo Emerson, "must be a nonconformist."[23]

The hierarchical structures of both the Episcopal and the Catholic Church represent a direct challenge to the American sensibility—a challenge that requires some real mental acrobatics to make those same structures palatable to the average self-determined citizen. Not only do priests wield authority, but they also answer to it, and all aspects of the designation of authority are tied up with the degree to which a priest or bishop is understood to have a divine mandate. Put that little bundle of bramble into a democratic context, and the matter gets even more complicated. There isn't a great deal of space allowed in American life for divine mandate to be the operational tool of a large institution.*

Despite the sweeping reforms of the Second Vatican Council, the sixteenth-century vision of the priesthood continues to bear unmistakable influence today—particularly in more conservative religions. As historian Richard P. McBrien wrote in 1988, "Priests are still regarded by many Catholics (including not a few priests) as having unique spiritual powers independent of any pastoral commitment to a particular congregation or community." That phenomenon seems to be more closely linked to the psychology of parishioners than it is to doctrinal history. It shouldn't be said that *only* Catholics ascribe a higher order of holiness to their priests—or wish they could. Yet, for American Catholics tensions between democratic (or at least representational) and monarchical governing models have been thrown into stark relief by the recent pedophile scandal.

Father Thomas Doyle, who was awarded the totemic first annual Priest with Integrity Award by Voice of the Faithful—the Boston-based Catholic lay group formed in the wake of the pedophile scandal—laid this out in his acceptance speech:

---

*Of course, I make this comment in the spirit of national character, and as Max Weber once pointed out, "the appeal to national character is generally a mere confession of ignorance." My appeal is made in the name not of lumping disparate people together, but rather to illuminate a possible difference between two social systems—not a lumping but a discernment.

What we see happening around us are the initial death throes of the medieval monarchical model of the church. This was and is an institutional Church based on the belief that a small, select minority of the educated, the privileged, and the powerful was called by Almighty God to manage the temporal and spiritual lives of the faceless masses, on the presumption that their unlettered and squalid state meant that they were ignorant and incapable of discerning their spiritual destiny. This is 2002 and not 1302, and that model is based on a myth that is long dead![24]

For the four thousand Catholics gathered for the Voice of the Faithful conference in Boston's Hynes Auditorium, nothing could seem more blaringly evident than what Father Doyle (a former staff member at the Vatican's U.S. embassy and a canon lawyer) had to say. Thunderous applause greeted the speech, and one enthusiastic listener hollered out, "Doyle for Pope!"—which made four thousand people laugh out loud. Despite the remarkable popular energy for reform that Voice of the Faithful harnessed that day, everyone present was painfully aware that the contest for pope totally excludes the laity.*

As foreign as the notion may be to freedom-loving Americans, the Episcopal and Catholic Churches both have chains of authority. It is according to this authority that the decision is made who can be a priest. I think that this is one of the hardest concepts to accept in this discussion. In America, you can be anything you want to be if you want it hard enough—anything but a priest.

·   ·   ·

*In the wake of Voice of the Faithful's high profile campaign for reform, pundits were quick to remind the media that American Catholics make up only 6 percent of the worldwide Catholic population, suggesting that it was something of a fantasy to think that the movement might have any influence on the Vatican. The stonewalling that the group experienced from American bishops in 2002 would support that hypothesis. However, a Voice of the Faithful spokesperson reminded me that although Americans are a relatively small minority in terms of numbers, they control 60 percent of worldwide financial contributions. So their "voice" is hardly marginal.

When a person takes his heart in his hand to his church and says, "I want to be a priest," an enormous intellectual, emotional, organizational, historical, and spiritual mechanism is put in motion. The church's answer, yes or no, represents an amalgamation of all these forces. The church has the secular authority to set standards, make decisions. It invokes a theological and historical tradition to determine these standards. It brings intellectual and emotional faculties to bear on your intellectual and emotional faculties. It speaks for God—in effect, if not in reality—but admits that it makes mistakes. If the church says, "I can't hear your call to ordained ministry," you must understand that buried in that complicated response is the *possibility* that you don't have one.

The Protestant reformer John Calvin drew a critical distinction between an external call and the "secret," interior call. The external call "belongs to the church," which simply means that if you believe in the authority of the church—by which I mean the corporate body of Christians, not the executive director—and if they don't call you to serve them, then you simply don't have a call.

In a dialogue called *The Teacher,* Augustine tells his son, "God is sought and prayed to precisely through our unexpressed interior wants, by a call within, in the temple whose consecration he desires." Augustine's "temple" isn't cultic; there are no blood sacrifices performed there. It is the "temple of the soul, the bedchamber of the affections." God already knows what's in there—there's no need to explain it to God, or to pray with words. "Of course, priests talk," he adds, "not that God should hear, but that men should, who, when they hear, are jointly reminded of their dependence on God."[25]

When a person within a Judeo-Christian context speaks of vocation as duty to the self, the notion is neither vague nor mystical, and yet it is complicated. It is not vague because within that tradition, God is part of the self, inside of the self, and so duty to the self implies, even *means,* duty to God. The Jewish scholar Arthur Hertzberg focuses the practice of religion, the essence of faith, on duty: "It is nonetheless an essential of the faith that the regimen which has been ordained for the religious practice of the Jew is God-given. This people was chosen to be a corporate priesthood, to live within the world and yet apart from it. Its way of life is the appointed sign of its difference."[26] This word *calling* doesn't in fact come into the daily practice of Judaism. It is instead associated with the enduring covenant by which God called the Jews to be a priest-people. The religious practice itself is a response to this single call, and a fulfillment of the covenant.

Richard Niebuhr identified the principle of covenant as fundamental to colonial American history, leading, significantly, to the formation of American democracy. The covenant posited a "world as a peculiar kind of society in which all parts are bound to each other by promises." Niebuhr went on to question

> whether our common life could have been established, could have been maintained, and whether it can endure without the presence of the conviction that we live in a world that has the moral structure of a covenant and without the presence in it of men who have achieved responsible citizenship by exercising the kind of freedom that appears in their taking upon themselves the obligations of unlimited loyalty, under God, to principles of truth-telling, of justice, of loyalty to one another, or indissoluble union.[27]

The idea of covenant fed also the idea of communal sin—and communal redemption. A chosen, or saved, body of believers, who sin en masse and seek redemption for the community is known as communitarian. Communitarianism intersects uncomfortably with individualism (the idea that salvation comes through personal religious revelation) throughout Protestant belief systems.

The Puritans, for example, related their hard life in the outposts of colonial America to the story of the Israelites in the desert. They understood themselves to be called to redemption as a body. But to enter "the body," a person had to have a conversion. That conversion had to be presented to the Puritan church and recognized as legitimate by those who were already converted. Conversion in those days wasn't a glowing rebirth but a battle for the soul between God and Satan played out as humiliation, despair, penance, and depression. This process of recognition was a primitive discernment process—though the frontier Puritans would never have used such a Catholic word.

Puritan minister Jonathan Edwards built a theology around the concept "By their fruit ye shall know them, not by their root" (religion is in the practice, not in the sentiment), and the fruit he was referring to was the testimonial to religious conversion as much as it was an ethic and lifestyle. The early American conception of public testimonial—conversion and evangelicalism—went hand in hand with the idea of building an upright, or benevolent, society. The expression of conversion by "many souls" was a revival of the idea of bringing Christianity to the world—a re-creation of the life of Jesus and his disciples, saving souls in the wilderness and building a new redeemed society. Conversion can be understood, according to William James, to mean that "religious ideas, previously peripheral in [a man's] consciousness, now take a central place, and that religious aims form the habitual centre of his energy."[28] The second conversion that leads a person to pursue ordained ministry is an attenuated extension of this religious experience. His public testimonial—in this instance, the discernment process—thus bears witness to his conversion experience, or acceptance of his divine internal calling.

The themes of interior and exterior religious experience, individualism and communitarianism, are all vying for dominance in the idea of calling and the practice of discernment in the Episcopal Church.

In Christianity, according to Karen Armstrong, the personal relationship between God and man "is characterized by love. But the point of love is that the ego has, in some sense, to be annihilated." Duty to the self becomes, in that context, not strictly egocentric or individualistic.

In *The Spirit of Capitalism,* Max Weber asserted that Martin Luther was the first to bring the idea of calling as a "life-task" into modern religion. "Fulfillment of duty in worldly affairs," wrote Weber, "inevitably gave everyday worldly activity a religious significance." A person's calling was "the fulfillment of the obligations imposed upon the individual by his position in the world"; this constituted an "outward expression of brotherly love." Most important, this conception of calling has a leveling effect. All callings have "exactly the same worth in the sight of God." Weber points out that the biblical source of Reformation ideas about calling come principally from Paul, and describes a biblical period during which everyone assumed that the world was about to end, and final judgment was imminent. Since the world was about to end, it was a fruitless waste of energy, hubris, and an imposition on the charity of brothers to try to change the circumstances that God had set out. "As the Lord hath called every one," said Paul, "so let him walk."

According to Weber, Luther's understanding of calling solidified around calling as a divine ordinance that man has to adapt to. But Reformation theology had extended this idea to include the notion that "work in the calling was a, or rather *the,* task set by God." In Weber's project, which is to demonstrate how Protestant ideas laid the societal groundwork for pure capitalism, Luther is merely the impetus ("the translator" of the Bible who brought his own spirit to the text), while John Calvin is the protagonist.

In a less-politicized elaboration of Weber's hypothesis, Armstrong explains in *The History of God* that Calvinism, "once discarded, can be expressed in secular ways." She goes on to point out that "this has been especially true in the United States. Many Americans who no longer believe in God subscribe to the Puritan work ethic and to the Calvinist notion of election, seeing themselves as a 'chosen nation,' whose flag and ideals have a semidivine purpose."[29]

Armstrong distinguishes between Calvin—who embraced the mystery of God and the paradox between divine justice and divine love—and Calvinism, which went on to make airtight the theory of predestination. God was all-powerful and man could do nothing to change his lot or realize salvation.

Calvin, building on Luther and engaged in the Reformation project of redefining ordained ministry, drew a critical distinction right through the heart of the idea of calling. In the spirit of third-century Christianity, the call of a man to ministry belongs to the church. In the spirit of individual salvation, a man has a private, interior call which he alone is responsible for answering. Calvin located the kernel of mysticism in man's individual search for Christ (an Ignatian idea). As to the role of ordained ministry, Calvin wrote,

> In order, therefore, that any one may be accounted a true minister of the church, it is necessary, in the first place, that he be regularly called to it, and in the second place, that he answer his call, that is, by undertaking and executing the office assigned to him. . . . I speak of the external and solemn call, which *belongs to the public order of the Church;* passing over that secret call, of which every minister is conscious to himself before God, but which is not known to the church. This secret call, however, is the honest testimony of our heart that we accept the office offered to us, not from ambition or avarice, or any other unlawful motive, but from a sincere fear of God and an ardent zeal for the edification of the Church.[30]

In Calvin's theology (Calvin's Calvinism), the notion of calling was specifically associated with the community's sponsorship of a candidate to the priesthood. Internal call was just that, internal, and the expression of it was not part of the selection process. The importance of articulating internal call as proof of worthiness for holy orders entered the selection process in colonial America's Calvinism, where the call to ministry was considered an advanced degree of the conversion experience. As the public testimony of conversion was a cornerstone of Puritan spirituality, revivalism, and subsequently evangelicalism, so, too, the public testimony of the secret call to save souls became an inextricable feature of the ordination process.

Because the foolishness of God is wiser than men; and the weakness of God is stronger than men. For ye see your calling, brethren, how that not many wise men after the flesh, not many mighty, not many noble are called: But God hath chosen the foolish things of the world to confound the wise; and God hath chosen the weak things of the world to confound the things that are mighty.

—1 Corinthians 1:25–27

In the early days of photography, when chemical emulsions were sluggish and shutter speeds were manual, people posing for portraits would have to sit very, very still for seconds, even minutes on end, in order to keep the picture from coming out blurry. This is what made photography both realistic and painterly. Now, with hair-trigger shutter speeds and souped-up silver, the moment is caught in an instant—and in that same instant, the moment is past. That's what makes photography, today, poetry.

Since no one is sitting very, very still for me, my portrait can be only both blurry and an instant past. As I write, the Episcopal Church is in the midst of overhauling its ordination process. On a much more comprehensive scale, the church has been looking at the same issues I have. The revisions will have an impact on people's lives and futures and the shape of the church to come. The church started its review long before I did, and will continue until new canons are written and implemented over the next several years.

The revision will probably not, however, have any impact on my father's petition. With a heavy emphasis on regularizing the standards of initial screenings across the country, had they been in place before my father made his application, they might have ensured that his vocations committee spent a full six months working with him—instead of a month and a half. And he certainly would have had several more face-to-face meetings. If, on the other hand, my father changes course and decides to direct his talents toward "lay ministry," the broad, all-embracing mandate of the revisions—which includes a more formal honoring of the different forms of leadership participation—might possibly provide him with a greater sense of real affirmation from the church. Specifically, the commission says: "Our relationship with God and our relationships in the world express our Christian identity. Each calling has full and equal dignity. The Canons should reflect this vision of ministry." Proposed revisions include expansion of "licensed ministries" (a new moniker for "lay ministries") to include pastoral leader, worship leader, preacher, eucharistic minister, eucharistic visitor, and catechist—any number of which might quench my father's particular yearnings.

The shape of these revisions will come out of the recommendations of a specially formed national advisory board called the Standing Commission on Ministry Development (SCMD). This commission was born in 1997 for the primary purpose of reviewing and proposing revisions to the canons, "Title III—On Ministry," and the discernment process (as well as other charges that included surveying the eleven Episcopal theological seminaries, assessing opportunities for the continuing education of clergy and lay professionals, and the theology of confirmation).* Their report was published as my research drew to a close. And significant changes to the Process I've described can be anticipated between 2003 and 2006 based on their recommendations. As I said: blurry and an instant past.

The Process as we know it has now been in operation for twenty-five years, a generation. Since its inception, the Process has been subject to constant adjustments—the ironing out of ambiguities, the

---

*The SCMD had an extensive mandate, and because of simple time constraints the focus of their work over the last three years and of their 2003 report to the general convention has been on Title III and the theological institutions.

streamlining of systems, and the modernization of language (to be inclusive). Eventually it became clear that canons probably shouldn't be subject to rolling adjustments and potentially inconsistent corrections. And that after twenty-five years, the Process itself had become institutionalized enough to withstand objective revaluation. What's more, many of the ideas that fed the formulation of the original system have by now become dated. The SCMD used as their point of departure two internal documents: the 1996 Stafford Falkowski survey, "The Implementation of the Title III Canons: A Review of Diocesan Practices," and the report "Toward a Theology of Ministry," authored by the same Standing Commission on Ministry Development, which was approved by the Seventy-third General Convention in 2000. Sister Catherine Grace isn't the only person who has described the Process as flaming hoops. In its opening statement, the SCMD acknowledges with concern that over the course of their research they heard that "the present ordination process has too many hoops for candidates and discourages young and minority aspirants."

Broadly speaking, the most visible changes* that the SCMD recommends are these: First, the elimination of the transitional diaconate as a requirement. In order to reinforce the "distinct ministries of Deacons and Priests," the commission suggests that people be ordained "directly to the order to which they are called." Second, the elimination of canon 9, on the "local ordination of priests" (the special-circumstances fast track described earlier), and totally revising the requirements for formation to be flexible enough to accommodate special circumstances and alternative modes of formation. These revisions will consolidate more control

---

*The commission also has recommendations that will affect the spirit of Title III, but are less "visible"—such as expanding "non-discrimination provisions," increasing the number and importance of "lay ministries," and incorporating continuing education or "ongoing formation" into church life for the ordained as well as for the laity. The effect of these changes will be seen more after implementation and continued practice than as an immediate consequence of canon revision.

over formation to dioceses—so that each diocese can create a system that suits its local needs.

With this increased control, the commission also hopes to return more authority and burden of responsibility to the bishop (so that bishops won't be inclined to leave the bulk of ordination procedures and decisions to the committees). In terms of actual preparation for priesthood, the committee states that "our most important discovery has been that the Bishops are the primary teachers of the Church and they are the principal gatekeepers of theological education in the Church. In fact," they continue, "this has been the pattern since the earliest days of Christianity. No other persons or groups rival the Bishops in this historic role. The bishops of the church, acting individually, are our Episcopal accrediting agency for the Episcopal Church. The opinion is strong that they should continue to act in this capacity."[31] A good example of this role for bishops is provided by Bishop Waynick of Indianapolis, who meets with her postulants monthly to instruct them in the Book of Common Prayer and in church polity, and how to translate these ideas in terms that are comprehensible to parishioners.

The committee also recommends a more even and streamlined process that doesn't subject a candidate to a harrowing, three-year-long succession of evaluations and approval seeking. Lastly, the commission calls for more and better discernment and formation: "Clarify the importance of discernment and formation for all the baptized, and the responsibility of dioceses, congregations, and other communities of faith, to provide support for discernment and formation," placing "discernment and formation at the center of Christian life and community."

This last recommendation reflects on a number of the issues already discussed here. The pivotal idea is that discernment should be a part of everyone's practice, in the sense that everyone has a call (and a cosmology or worldview), which will determine how they live their Christianity and how they make life decisions. In putting forth this recommendation, the commission emphasizes that all calls are equally valuable in the eyes of the church—and that through the process of discernment, people will gain a stronger sense of that. Importantly, this provision points to the *discernment* as a kind of methodology.

Over the course of my research, the discernment-training group Listening Hearts Ministries, run by Suzanne Farnham, came up often. Listening Hearts is not specifically an Episcopalian organization, but the Episcopal Church increasingly makes use of their principles, techniques, and training sessions. It would stand to reason that the commission also made use of these popular Listening Heart strategies as they thought about the way discernment is practiced across the country, and that their ideal of discernment largely matches the one proposed by Listening Hearts, which was formulated in the spirit of Ignatius's *Spiritual Exercises* and his *Rules for the Discernment of Spirits*. Almost everyone I met with was familiar with Listening Hearts, and most were excited about its program. Several of the people I interviewed, on the other hand, had attended Farnham's seminars and dismissed the methodology as "common sense"—which it is. Many of the techniques outlined in the training program are based on ideas so fundamental to Christian practice and history that it's easy to see why people found the material to be "obvious," "self-evident," "common sense." But common sense isn't all that easy to come by, and Listening Hearts' modern formalization of the discernment process provides a way of incorporating standards of common sense throughout the church so that at least everyone is—as they say—on the same page.

The idea that there are legible signs with which to identify a call is explained like this:

> Not only is every call unique, but the hearing of every call is unique also. One sign that God may be calling is a certain restlessness, a certain dissatisfaction with things as they are. Other signs of God's call may be a sense of longing, yearning, or wondering; a feeling of being at a crossroads; a sense that something

is happening in one's life, that one is wrestling with an issue or decision; a sense of being in a time of transition; or a series of circumstances that draw one into a specific issue.[32]

(Cautioning against the tendency to be too schematic in the interpretation of signs, Farnham cites an example from Quaker lore: "One text some Quaker sects used to confirm God's call was that a 'true' call was always contrary to one's own will. The assumption that to 'cross the will' meant taking up the cross of Christ often produced absurd results. For example, some Friends walked naked in the streets because it was contrary to their own will or inclination.")[33]

The "Guide" to discernment proposed by Listening Hearts is fundamentally an elaboration of how to create an environment in which trust and mutual respect, prayer, listening, and open-mindedness are the operative principles. Humility, the importance of scripture, discipline and perseverance, urgency, and perspective are all attitudes to keep in mind during discernment. Specific attention is paid to the discernment of call to ordained ministry, and several comprehensive appendices provide "tools" for engineering discernment sessions.

It seems clear that if these guidelines are followed, some kind of resolution will surely be reached in a way that demonstrates total respect and sensitivity to the person seeking assistance. This recasts "discernment" as we've been talking about it as a potentially wonderful process. It also seems clear that a group of respectful and sensitive people, oriented toward the goal of helping a peer work out a difficult spiritual question, could easily arrive at more or less the same system without using the program. This is because the techniques that Listening Hearts espouses—trust, listening, concentration, prayer, and patience—are indeed both commonsensical and compassionate. The church has apparently adopted this vision of discernment as an ideal, a perfect model for providing an equitable and useful process.

In that spirit, the most important qualification for a discernment session is (inexplicably) buried at the end of Appendix 2: "Types of Questions to Raise When Serving in Discernment Groups":

> When discerning what may be a call to ordination it is particularly important that the group await a strong and clear consensus to confirm that the call is perceived by both the candidate and the corporate body. Since genuine discernment depends on a willing and open heart, *mandating discernment could violate its nature.* Therefore making discernment groups available for aspirants is preferable to requiring the use of such groups. Furthermore, because strict confidentiality is a crucial condition for honest sharing, a discernment group *cannot be expected to issue a report* to anyone. Any communication must necessarily come from the candidate. Screening is best seen as a *separate and complementary* endeavor [my emphasis].[34]

My emphasis, which brings me to *my* point. The distinction between discerning the will of God in terms of a candidate's call to ordination and the screening of a candidate's eligibility for such a position raises the possibility of a misnomer (at best) and a psychologically damaging abuse of power (at worst) systemically employed throughout the ordination process. There is currently a screening process for the priesthood that is either called "discernment" or is modeled on discernment—yet it does not follow the rules of discernment. If you accept that Suzanne Farnham has developed a basically good model for providing spiritual guidance in a group setting and that spiritual guidance is the best means to sorting out a candidate's path—his or her "internal call"—then you must also accept Farnham's premise that God's will and the candidate's internal call cannot be a *mandatory* phase in the screening process for ordained ministry.

Take it one step further. Church screening of candidates for the priesthood (or diaconate) cannot include God's will as a prerequisite, because God's will cannot be known on demand—as so many members of the church's governance have openly acknowledged to me.

That means that by one interpretation it is dishonest of a diocesan discernment committee to include calling language—in the sense of discerning that secret call—in either their rejection or acceptance of a candidate. It's playing fast and loose with the divine.

I've wondered whether the task of filling vocations within the church shouldn't simply be liberated from the burden of couching decisions in terms of God's fiat. Likewise, the ordination process should not cloud the language of calling—which is a beautiful way of reflecting on individual path and responsibility within Christian life. Screening should be based on quantifiable qualities (also for the sake of maintaining ethical standards of equitable treatment) and should be devoid of reference to God's will. In the humble opinion of this virtuous pagan, the church should allow for John Calvin's critical distinction between the public call of the congregation or the church and the secret call "of which every minister is conscious to himself before God . . . the honest testimony of our heart that we *accept* the office offered to us."[35]

This conclusion is not as radical as it might seem at first glance, nor is it at all divorced from the critically theological backbone of church policy. According to the first canon of Title III, "Of the Ministry of All Baptized Persons," the church accepts that every one of its members is divinely called. It is the individual task of each member (in consultation with a priest, a spiritual director, or a discernment group) to thoughtfully and prayerfully identify (or discern) the substance of his or her own ministry. This brings us back to the idea of the baptismal covenant, the importance of which the church is continuously trying to enhance.

The Episcopal Catechism specifies, "The ministers of the church are lay persons, bishops, priests, and deacons."[36] In *Listening Hearts,* Suzanne Farnham explains, "All Christians are called to minister both to one another and to those around them by participating in God's work in the world."[37]

Even if you eliminate the divining of a person's call from the screening process, the *sacred* recognition of the divine work of the priest will always be preserved in the rite of ordination—when the ordinand makes vows to the church and God, and the church sanctifies the ordinand's manifest desire to serve the church.

An individual's first responsibility is to identify whatever he or she construes to be his or her true call. "Never ask if meaning it, wanting it, warned of it," wrote the poet Gerard Manley Hopkins, "—men go." "Every true call," writes Farnham, "is a call to obey God; indeed, the word *obedience* derives from the Latin *audire,* which means 'to listen.' "[38]

Listening will mean that when an individual identifies his calling to ordained ministry, he will obey, by presenting his case to the church. The church has no obligation to honor that case. If the church doesn't believe that the individual is a good candidate for the priesthood, then it invokes its public right to call whoever it wants to ordained ministry. But that doesn't mean that by rejecting the candidate it invalidates the candidate's own discernment. That doesn't mean that it claims to hear "the same voice" saying something entirely different.

I'm not convinced that acceptance into the priesthood should even partially be based on divine interior call. For that sets up a paradigm something like that famously incoherent "being a little pregnant." If there is a divinity guiding our individual paths, then there is a divine call for each and every one of us. The church is in the unique position of being able to provide this ideally wonderful discernment process—where everyone arrives, according to Farnham's instructions, at the same conclusion.* Why compromise discernment by

---

*Couched in notably different terms, Saint Ignatius gives the same instruction in his *Spiritual Exercises:* "To assure better cooperation between the one who is giving the Exercises and the exercitant, and more beneficial results for both, it is necessary to suppose that every good Christian is more ready to put a good interpretation on another's statement than to condemn it as false. If an orthodox construction cannot be put on a proposition, the one who made it should be asked how he understands it. If he is in error, he should be corrected with all kindness. If this does not suffice, all appropriate means should be used to bring him to a correct interpretation, and so defend the proposition from error" (chapter 22).

folding a bastardized version of it into the screening process? Offer both. Keep them separate. Keep them both based on principles of respect and compassion. Know that both fellowship and screening are ministries of the baptized. The church shouldn't put itself into the position of challenging people's discernments. The church should not claim to hear God louder or more clearly when it refuses an applicant who says, "God has called me to the priesthood." There's no point in engaging in a playground shouting match—"He did not!" "Did so!" "Did not!" "Did so!" Rather, the church can assert and has asserted that ministry takes many forms—and what the church needs in the ranks of its ordained clergy is a separate matter, which the church itself will discern in its own process.

I'm speaking broadly. I don't mean to suggest that my father's call was denied, or that he was drawn into anything like a playground shouting match, although other people have had that experience. No one ever suggested that my father didn't have a call. He was sent away as we've seen because the committee couldn't hear his call. However, it's tempting to speculate that if he'd had a discernment, and sat around for hours talking about his call with compassionate peers who knew how to ask hard questions, and knew how to discuss the answers, he might have been better prepared to remove the obstacles that were keeping others from hearing his call. He would have had some practice explaining himself. He would have already articulated his call before he reached the point where discernment was bound up in judgment or screening. This confusion of processes sets up a situation where the church authority that a candidate subordinates himself to deals a mystical, mantic card that not only confuses the issue of discernment but confuses (and undermines) the issue of authority.

"Outside the Exercises, it is true," wrote Saint Ignatius,

> we may lawfully and meritoriously urge all who probably have the required fitness to choose continence, virginity, the religious life, and every form of religious perfection. But while one is engaged

in the Spiritual Exercises, it is more suitable and much better that the Creator and Lord in person communicate Himself to the devout soul in quest of the divine will, that He inflame it with His love and praise, and dispose it for the way in which it could better serve God in the future. Therefore, the director of the Exercises, as a balance at equilibrium, without leaning to one side or the other, should permit the Creator to deal directly with the creature, and the creature directly with his Creator and Lord. (chapter 15)

Finally, a distinction probably should be drawn between identifying a corps of clergy to serve the church and the identification of prophets. Nowhere is it said that priests are (necessarily) prophets. Many of the calling stories used to apply to discerning priests (the call of Moses, Jeremiah, Peter, and Paul) are prophet stories. And they offer useful models for individual discernment. But the church has no business (nor should it have any interest) in claiming to identify and legitimize prophets. Farnham explains that "we normally relate to some people in a group more readily than to others. Psychologically, we tend to turn off the people we most need to hear. The people to whom we are least attracted often have the most to teach us. If we identify those to whom we are least drawn, we can make a special effort to listen to them attentively."[39] In effect, this is a description of a prophet, who bears a difficult message—not of a priest, who helps you comprehend a difficult message. Recognizing prophecy might be an operation appropriate to discernment, but not to governance.

The church is beholden to identify and defend the qualities and abilities of its chosen leaders, and to establish comprehensible selection criteria, acknowledging all the while that all of the baptized have a divine calling. The church is the body of Christ, and the administrative vision of the church is a necessary worldly vessel to serve the body of Christ, and out of respect for that precept the church should not confuse its administrative vision or obligations with God's will.

I suffer because of Vietnam, of the ghettos, of Poland, of my inability to express what should be expressed.

—CZESLAW MILOSZ

October 24, 2002, one hundred armed Chechnyan rebel fighters took a Moscow theater hostage during the performance of a popular musical. There were over eight hundred people in the theater, and after releasing a number of children and hostages, the rebel fighters said that they would blow up the theater, the 750 remaining hostages, and themselves, if Russian occupying troops weren't withdrawn immediately from Chechnya. After a standoff that lasted four days, Russian president Vladimir Putin ordered an elite military force to pump poison gas into the theater, knocking into unconsciousness or killing its occupants, then to enter and shoot the rebels who weren't already dead and remove the unconscious hostages. All one hundred rebels and 117 hostages died in the rescue operation. The theater was saved. Russian occupying forces remained in Chechnya with a renewed injunction to eliminate the rebel threat. Russia temporarily reversed its position against American plans to invade Iraq, joining in the "war on Terrorism," its sights set on the terrorist threat within its own occupied borders.

In the course of this tragedy, which lasted less than a week, the rest of the world was able to observe any number of people, both self- and popularly elected, playing God—or playing nature, if you prefer to think of it that way. Not one of them had been subjected to the rigorous discernment process that the religious bodies we've been examining have developed to select their own servant leaders. Not one of them underwent a battery of psychological exams to determine if he or she was suffering from a God complex—that instability of the ego that would bring a leader, a person in power, a person wielding a gun, grenade, or poison gas tank to confuse themselves with God or any supernatural controlling force. In the case of the Islamic fundamentalists, the confusion comes from the idea that

God himself had ordained this act of war, the homicides and suicides—a confusion exacerbated by the desperation of an occupied people—whereby God had already abandoned them to the occupiers. In the case of presidents and their militia, the separation of church and state (established and enforced in the name of religious tolerance) leaves no place for God. Thus there is, in some perverse inversion of the formula, no risk that a leader might confuse himself with God, no risk he might suffer a power complex or instability of ego. Although some of our American presidents have been charismatic (Franklin Delano Roosevelt, John F. Kennedy, William Jefferson Clinton), and many have been zealots and firebrands (Lyndon Baines Johnson, Theodore Roosevelt), and some have even had a sense of mission that could be described as vocational (Woodrow Wilson, Thomas Jefferson), it is impossible to identify a president who was *called* to the office. That is why we established term limits.

There are plenty of people with God complexes who work in politics. The rigorous screening that religious leaders are subjected to seems in every way to suggest a real concern for the well-being of the people to be led. The more primitive and apparently fairer selection of political leaders by popular election doesn't nonetheless suggest quite the same level of concern. And yet when we hand over control of the political body to someone—no, we're not giving them our souls—we're giving them power over our physical bodies. For better and worse, political leaders make decisions about life and death, whether it's how they decide to allot welfare money, the decision to save most of the hostages, or the decision to go to war.

In a *New York Review of Books* essay published to coincide with Timothy McVeigh's execution, Garry Wills wrote,

> Far from stigmatizing or humiliating the inmate of death row, we now provide him with a long and costly process meant to ascertain guilt, with free legal aid if he cannot afford his own, with counseling and family visits, with reading of his choice and TV, a last meal to his specifications, a last request, religious attendance,

guaranteed burial, a swift and nearly painless death. We shut up his last hours from the general public, and act as if this secret rite will deter by some magic of mere occurrence. We treat the killing as a dirty little secret, as if we were ashamed of it. Well, we should be ashamed.[40]

Days before McVeigh's execution in the summer of 2001, I found myself in conversation with a nondenominational minister. "I don't know," said the minister offhandedly, "if I should talk about the execution in my sermon this Sunday. Maybe I should just let everyone enjoy their weekend instead."

Upon hearing the minister's ambivalence about whether to subject his congregation to discussing the federal execution, I turned to him and asked, "How could you possibly not talk about it?"

Religion is in many respects born out of a desire to comprehend mortality. Nature is both indiscriminate and unforgiving in its acts. Nature's field, writes Czeslaw Milosz, "is the world as mathematical necessity." Random acts of nature can seem calculating in their cruelty. Acts of violence by man are incomprehensible—or beyond what we would like to comprehend. Religion imposes some order to the contingency. It offers us at least some shapes with which to organize all the apparent randomness—salvation, divine retribution, kingdom come. It teaches that Life is larger than any single physical body— and that every physical body represents Life in its fullness. ("Do not fear those who kill the body but cannot kill the soul," Matthew 10:28.) Those shapes provide emotional and intellectual comfort.

"According to the Gospels," explains the Italian cardinal Carlo Maria Martini, "neither physical nor psychological life (which the Greeks termed bios and psyche) holds supreme value. It is the divine life (zoe), as communicated to man, that holds supreme value." Martini explains that these three Greek words for "life" have distinct usages in the New Testament. He quotes John: "He who loves his life [psyche], loses it, and he who hates his own life [psyche] in the world will keep it for eternal life [zoe]" (John 12:25). And he quotes Jesus:

"I am the way and the truth and the Life" (John 14:6). "This explains," he continues, "the Christian conception of the value of
physical human life—the life of a person called upon to participate
in the life of God himself. For Christians, respecting human life . . .
is not an amorphous sentiment . . . but rather the fulfilling of a specific responsibility, that of a physical living person whose dignity is
not determined by benevolent judgment on my part, or to humani-
tarian impulses, but by divine calling."[41]

"We are all only human," says Bishop Bob Johnson, "and are essentially helpless at times, and unless we're willing to admit that, we're
living in some kind of fantasy. In some cases, you just can't kiss it and
make it better." A minister has unique access to the lives of his or her
parishioners—sharing not only the momentous occasions, such as baptism or marriage, but also death, illness, secrets, depression, doubts. It is
a position of enormous privilege in terms of intimacy, and of massive
responsibility. Clergy are constantly "on call," charged with being available during moments of unbearable difficulty. One priest told me the
story of having in a single day attended to three tragic deaths—a sick
young boy, a mother who died in a car accident, and an older man (a
longtime friend and parishioner) who suffered a heart attack. He said
that he found himself alone in his car, on his way from one hospital
to another, weeping, railing against God, and questioning the whole
system—but once he arrived at his destination he had again to be a
cornerstone of support for those who were grieving. Part of being
able to endure the grief of others is remembering that you are only
human, and you are there in the simple service of another human.

Henri Nouwen's analysis of Christian leadership is born out of
theology and comes down to methodology. *The Wounded Healer* was
written, after all, for practical use by ministers. "The Christian
leader," wrote Nouwen, "must be in the future what he has always
been in the past: a man of prayer, a man who has to pray, and who
has to pray always."[42] Leadership is fundamentally a relationship
between two people. In ministry, at least one of the two prays.

"Because of what this work requires in terms of energy and interaction, persistence and patience," explains Bishop Cate Waynick of Indianapolis, "there has to be a fire burning inside of the people who come to it—the way New York is filled with actors—who are doing something else 'for now,' but who know that they're going to be fulfilled when they get on that stage. And it calls for discipline. Ministry in the church is a kind of work that simply has to be rooted in prayer. I ask myself when I interview a candidate for the priesthood: Is this a person of prayer? Is this a person who can really commit to that discipline?"

Christian leaders, continues Nouwen, must have "a deep-rooted faith in the value and meaning of life" at all times, and have an "outgoing hope, which always looks for tomorrow, even beyond the moment of death." Reverend Hannah Anderson describes this as intentionally living in the "liminal space—the 'now but not yet' time of life. A priest lives in the liminal space between two realities: the world we can see and the world we believe in, which is yet to come into its fullness."

In *The Wounded Healer,* Nouwen tells the story of a young seminarian sitting awkwardly at the hospital bedside of a tobacco farmer. The enormous cultural and emotional differences between the two create a situation where neither is able to articulate much of anything. The farmer, facing a dangerous operation, fears death. The extreme isolation of his life, however, doesn't offer him very much to live for. The seminarian can't find the right words to comfort the man, or even to build a relationship with him. Nouwen explains that scrutinizing the dialogue between the two, you find that there was really nothing the seminarian could have *said* differently to comfort the man. Instead, what was needed of him was to establish some sort of human connection, to become a person for the sick man in an impersonal environment, to be *a face* waiting for him in recovery, or accompanying him in death: a companion. "Nobody can offer leadership to anyone unless he makes his presence known—that is, unless he steps forward out of the anonymity and apathy of his milieu and makes the possibility of fellowship visible."[43] A minister is someone who has the capacity to express more than anything else that "I am here. I will be here tomorrow and the day after tomorrow."

One of the questions posed to my father during the e-mail portion of his vocations screening was "How would you comfort someone who has had a death in the family?" His answer was something that I read with particular attention, because I've often morbidly wondered how and if my father—physically so far away—would be there for me if I were to experience a loss. His response to the committee was initially bewildering to me. He said, "You should stay quiet. The worst thing you can do is say, 'I know how you feel.'" He said, "You should offer love and comfort—physical comfort, like tea or hugs, if that's what's needed." He said, "You have to follow up— the other worst thing you can do is not follow up."

I remember thinking, *Tea and follow up?* And why must you be quiet? But of course he was saying what Nouwen said. It's not about the words. ("I know how you feel." "God loved your father—that's why he took him early.") Words get lost in a time of tragedy—they misfire, provoke anger, or fall senseless around someone awash in tumultuous emotions. It's about the presence, a loving presence, a comforting presence, and a presence that promises endurance. "I will be here tomorrow, and the day after tomorrow." This is the vow taken by a man with the courage to make promises, knowing they will be kept.

For the sake of argument, let's say that there are two classical ways in which people are tested that intertwine: the devil's way and Job's way. The first is a kind of tempting: to deviate from that which you know is right, a test of the self. This is the kind of testing that my father considers a wrestling with one's own worst qualities. This is "the devil made me do it" and this is the classic narrative of man against himself. The other kind of test is Job's test. This version amounts to the enduring of that which seems in excess of what one thinks should be expected of one. The necessary premise of this kind of test is a vision of things as they should be. If you have an idea of how things should be, then you are in a position to determine that things are *not* how they should be.

Everyone has a vision of how things should be—how crystal clear that vision is will vary from person to person as much as the vision itself will vary from person to person. We all have an operative ideal version of life. While the first kind of test might be characterized as moral, and the second existential, both are ongoing and determinative factors of how we live our life and how we construct our ideal. Thinking in terms of testing is a way of acknowledging the constant flux of moral circumstance and existential predicament—an operation of reconciliation between life and life. It is a system of growth, inasmuch as life is not static, and one is either assimilating experience into growth or else one is living purely responsively, untethered, a weightless object subject to the play of the wind.

We value difficult experiences because we discern growth therein. We're grateful in the long view for things that complicate our organism, that give us breadth, enrich our capacity for empathy—not just for other people and their worlds, but for the sheer unruly experience of living.

Calling is an individual sense of place and purpose. It's a self-defined truth applied to our activity in the world. My father is right to challenge a version of *calling* that consists of "being able to convince a committee of strangers that you will roll over and die if they don't let you become a priest." But it is equally true that if you've come to identify what you think you should be doing—if you are firm in your understanding of what the Reverend Donald Cozzens describes as "my truth in God's plan"—you will be hard put to stop wanting it or practicing it. This isn't rolling over and dying if your ambition isn't legitimized. Rather it's arriving at a point where you *already* are what you express as your calling—

where your understanding of who you are has become inextricable from you.

My father could, as he points out, expend his good intentions elsewhere. He could be a volunteer fireman, a hospice worker, or write a music theory textbook—but he doesn't. Over the years he has faithfully attended mass, he has played the organ on Sunday, sung in the choir, been a lector, taught Sunday school, studied and discussed becoming a priest with those close to him. It is important to him when people in the congregation tell him that they already think of him as a priest, because in a sense they're recognizing him for what he is.

If my father is never legitimized as a priest, if he is never ordained, then he will continue doing what he does and in time he may decide that *this* is what he was called to—this mishmash of activities that many people appreciate and some call priesthood. He'll recognize what is already part of him.

A friend who is a postulant in the Episcopal Church told me this story. She went to Radio Shack to buy an answering machine. The clerk assisting her seemed both terribly distracted and woefully uninformed about answering machines. She selected a basic model without his help and hurried out of the store with her purchase to finish her Saturday errands. But she couldn't stop thinking about the young man at Radio Shack, and over the course of the day, she became increasingly worried about him. So she returned to the store and confronted the clerk, asking him simply if he was all right. He admitted that he wasn't. He explained that he had wanted to be a pastor, and his church (not an Episcopal church) had just rejected him from the ordination process. He said that the only thing in his life that he ever thought he knew for sure was that he had a calling to ordained ministry. Now that he'd been definitively rejected, he was confused. He didn't know if God had abandoned him, misled him, or just had never been there in the first place. He felt so lost and depressed that he was carrying a gun with him and thinking about killing himself. My friend stayed and talked to the boy. She told him that she was studying to be a priest and so she sympathized with what it meant to want that, and to feel like it was your only path. She also told him that it was impossible that God had abandoned him— otherwise why was she there? Why else would she have come into that store that morning? Why else would she have come back?

I don't think of this as a story about the mysterious ways of God or divine intervention. It's not about a suicidal young man, or the emotional risks of applying to the priesthood—it's about my friend. It's a simple testament to a person who embraced her calling, who was paying attention when it was important to do so, who didn't ignore a nagging feeling, and who knew to be there for someone in trouble. It isn't about calling. It's about listening.

It wouldn't ever occur to me to describe my father as a wounded healer, but he has indeed soldiered on the battlefield of life. A child of midcentury America—immigration, war, Vatican II, and boom— he has an institutional memory and *sense* of history that brings weight to bear on all the systems that now are in place. He under- stands that "good" needs to be defended and tradition needs to be protected; not because it's familiar, but because it's proven, because it provides roots, and a sense of continuity integral to the religious idea. He's witnessed man's influence and man's transience—in both the public sphere and as it was brought to bear on his own life. He's experienced the folly of temporality. He has been swept up in the moment, and found himself midstream, unanchored. In Catholic tradition, the symbol of the anchor means hope. How can some- thing that represents staying fixed to one place, an anchor, possibly represent moving into the future, progress—hope? Because progress depends precisely on continuity, on a link to the past, a sense of his- tory, where we've come from, and a foundation in tradition the ves- sel that carries history. The word *secular* itself comes from the notion of temporality, living according to free-floating time, in the moment, disassociated from notions of past and future. My father by his own description frolicked in secularism, and chose to move beyond it.

"Here, perhaps, is where I part ways," writes Nobel laureate

Czeslaw Milosz, "with many people with whom I would like to be in solidarity but cannot be. To put it very simply and brutally, I must ask if I believe that the four Gospels tell the truth. My answer to this is: *Yes*. So I believe in an absurdity, that Jesus rose from the dead? . . . by that response I nullify death's omnipotence. If I am mistaken in my faith, I offer it as a challenge to the Spirit of the Earth. He is a powerful enemy; his field is the world as mathematical necessity, and in the face of earthly powers how weak an act of faith in the incarnate God seems to be."[44]

Czeslaw Milosz—the Polish poet whose Catholic identity is so deeply rooted in lived experience ("I suffer because of Vietnam, of the ghettos, of Poland, of my inability to express what should be expressed") that he awed the awesome Thomas Merton. Milosz doesn't ultimately have the confidence in mankind's brilliance that many of us would realize that we have, if we were to reflect on it. And if we reflected on it, many of us wouldn't have the weight of history that Milosz, who was born in 1911, bears to color our reflection—the annihilation of Warsaw by bombs, the massacre of Jews by Nazis, Catholics by the Communists, the second annihilation of Warsaw under Soviet rule, Vietnam, and the student uprising in California where he was a university professor (it was "a revolution against the squares" he complained; "they should learn instead pity and compassion for the squares"). Man is mammal in Milosz's vision—mere mammal, somewhat vexed by his own animalism. Man's big brains build systems that are too perfect to live by—history, socialism, democracy, religion. Man invents the systems and then fails them. "Thousands of young people in Poland," he wrote in a letter to Merton in 1961, "are torn between their emotional religion and the Church's teachings which do not provide them with answers understandable to them. Thomism? 'Irrefutable' proofs of God's existence? . . . Pascal was right when he said that a belief in God is of little use for a Christian. . . . I realize that nothing is more important than to find a common language with those who 'search in despair,' through poetry, prose, any means."[45]

The searching, the need to understand and be understood, is the passion that drives Milosz's Catholicism. It is a passion that recognizes the search, but denies fulfillment. This is Christianity as discipleship—the oldest form of ministry. It is in a sense the very *fallibility* of the religious system, its "absurdity," its weakness in the face of "earthly powers," that convinces him to continue believing.

There is a thread to grasp at in this tempest of opinions, truths, folly, and rhetoric; it is the thread around which religion builds its work. Life has a purpose, that purpose bears a responsibility, which is responsibility toward Life. There are 613 commandments in the Torah; they can be famously reduced to one, as expressed in this story: One day a heathen approached the great Rabbi Hillel and told him that he would be willing to convert to Judaism if the master could teach him the whole of the Torah while he stood on one foot. Hillel replied: "Whatever is hateful to you, do not do to your neighbor. That is the whole of the Torah, the rest is commentary—go and learn it."[46] Jews call this mitzvah, Christians call it ministry, I might call it humanity—everyone in faith is beholden to it.

You shall love your neighbor as yourself; I am the Lord.
—Leviticus 19:18

ACKNOWLEDGMENTS

I would like to thank Rene Steinke and Andrew Bachman for their insight, reading lists, letters of introduction, and friendship from this book's earliest stages onward. I am deeply indebted to those who generously gave me their time and experience in conversations and correspondence: Sister Catherine Grace, Bob Johnson, Hannah Anderson, Anne Richards, Douglas Brown, Garret Gentry, Stephanie Paulsell, Ismar Schorsch, Amy Eilberg, Catherine Waynick, Bud Holland, Monsignor Francis Kelly, Svea Frazer, Jodi Mikalachki, Diane Cook, Chuck Ransom, David Lee Carlson. For various kinds of hospitality and generous support, I would like to thank my cousins Ronna and Don Honigman, Ralph Simpson, the MacDowell Colony, the Bogliasco Foundation, Kim France, Monica Sarsini, and Frances Lansing. For her wisdom, openness, and advice, I would like to thank Anya Royce. My dear friend Ann Gagliardi was a heroic and astute first reader; Peter Steinke a generous last reader. This project wouldn't have been possible without the encouragement and enthusiasm of many people in Italy and New York, and I extend heartfelt gratitude to my extraordinary and far-flung community of friends and neighbors. I would like to thank my editor, Molly Stern, for her stubbornness and faith; and my agent and precious friend, Ira Silverberg, for being my rock. I would like to thank my extended family for constancy and affection, and my immediate family for trusting me with their stories. Although they don't appear (much) in these pages, I am most grateful to Benjamin Anastas and my mother, Arlene Zallman. Their love and intelligence are deeply embedded in every word.

NOTES

PART ONE: *My Father*

1. Donald Cozzens, *The Changing Face of the Priesthood* (Collegeville, MN: Liturgical Press, 2000), 4.

2. Mary McCarthy, *Memories of a Catholic Girlhood* (New York: Harcourt Brace Jovanovich, 1957), 27.

3. Cozzens, x.

4. Will Herberg, *Protestant, Catholic, Jew: An Essay in American Religious Sociology* (Chicago: University of Chicago Press, 1983), 2.

5. Michael W. Cuneo, *The Smoke of Satan: Conservative and Traditionalist Dissent in Contemporary American Catholicism* (New York: Oxford University Press, 1997), 16.

6. Richard Hofstadter, *Anti-Intellectualism in American Life* (New York: Vintage Books, 1963), 138.

7. Cuneo, 10.

8. Thomas à Kempis, *The Imitation of Christ,* edited and translated by Joseph N. Tylenda, S.J. (New York: Vintage Spiritual Classics, 1998), 95.

9. Thomas à Kempis, 7.

10. James Joyce, *A Portrait of the Artist as a Young Man* (New York: Viking Press, 1964), 203.

11. Cozzens, 32.

12. Cozzens, 32.

13. Cozzens, 16, citing Häring.

14. 1989 Girl Scouts Survey, American Religion Data Archive (ARDA), Penn State; see www.arda.tm.

15. Shelton Waldrep, "Introducing the Seventies," in *The Seventies,* edited by Shelton Waldrep (New York: Routledge, 2000), 4, quoting from George Lipsitz, *The Sixties: From Memory to History,* edited by David Farber (Chapel Hill: University of North Carolina Press, 1994), 230.

16. Henri J. M. Nouwen, *The Wounded Healer* (New York: Doubleday, 1972), 72.

17. Nouwen, 85.

18. Judith Wallerstein, Julia Lewis, and Sandra Blakeslee, *The Unexpected Legacy of Divorce: A 25 Year Landmark Study* (New York: Hyperion, 2000), 91.

19. Aristotle, *Poetics,* section 8, cited in M. H. Abrams, *A Glossary of Literary Terms,* 5th ed. (Orlando: Harcourt Brace Jovanovich, 1988), 141.

20. Joan Didion, *The White Album* (New York: Pocket Books, 1980), 11.

21. Pope Benedict XV, quoted in Omer Englebert, *The Lives of the Saints* (New York: Penguin, 1995), 25.

22. Stephen Clissold, *The Wisdom of Saint Francis and His Companions* (New York: New Directions Books, 1978), 13.

23. Clissold, 12.

PART TWO: *Calling and Discernment*

1. Frederick Buechner, *Listening to Your Life: Daily Meditations with Frederick Buechner* (New York: HarperCollins, 1992), 186.

2. Simone Weil, *Waiting for God,* translated by Emma Crauford (New York: HarperCollins Perennial Classics, 2001), 23.

3. Rowan Williams, "Vocation" (2001), Appendix 5 to Lord Dearing's report on church schools, *The Way Ahead;* PDF file available at www.natsoc.org.uk.

4. Suzanne G. Farnham et al., *Listening Hearts: Discerning Call in Community,* rev. ed. (Harrisburg: Morehouse Publishing, 2002), 107.

5. Karen Armstrong, quoted in "Not-So-Holy Matrimony," *The Guardian* (London), June 30, 2003.

6. Ignatius of Loyola, *The Spiritual Exercises of St. Ignatius,* translated by Louis J. Puhl, S.J. (New York: Vintage Spiritual Classics, 2000), 8.

7. Thomas à Kempis, 191.

8. Alister McGrath, *Reformation Thought: An Introduction,* 2nd ed. (Grand Rapids: Baker Books, 1993), 221.

9. Ralph Waldo Emerson, *The Complete Essays and Other Writing of Ralph Waldo Emerson* (New York: The Modern Library, 1940), 14.

10. W. Clark Gilpin, *A Preface to Theology* (Chicago: University of Chicago Press, 1996), 125.

11. Joyce, 171.

12. Richard P. McBrien, *Ministry* (New York: HarperCollins, 1988), 22.

13. Marion J. Hatchett, *Commentary on the American Prayer Book* (New York: HarperCollins, 1995), 505.

14. Farnham, 3.

15. Weil, 23.

16. William James, *The Varieties of Religious Experience: A Study in Human Nature,* edited by Martin E. Marty (New York: Penguin Classics, 1985), 223.

17. Sir Isaiah Berlin, *The Proper Study of Mankind: An Anthology of Essays* (New York: Farrar, Straus & Giroux, 1997), 185.

18. John Henry Newman, *Selected Sermons, Prayers, and Devotions,* edited by John F. Thornton and Susan B. Varenne (New York: Vintage Spiritual Classics, 1999), 303.

19. James, 239.

20. Hofstadter, 86.

21. Sidney E. Mead, "The Rise of the Evangelical Conception of the Ministry in America (1607–1850)," in *The Ministry in Historical Perspective*, edited by H. Richard Niebhur and Daniel D. Williams (New York: Harper & Bros., 1956), 231.

22. Hofstadter, 67.

23. James, 24.

24. Roland Barthes, *Sade, Fourier, Loyola*, translated by Richard Miller (New York: Hill and Wang, 1976), 52–53.

25. Thomas Merton, *New Seeds of Contemplation* (New York: New Directions, 1974), 98.

26. Karen Armstrong, *A History of God: The 4,000-Year Quest of Judaism, Christianity and Islam* (New York: Ballantine Books, 1994), 285.

27. Arthur Hertzberg, *Judaism: The Key Spiritual Writings of the Jewish Tradition*, rev. ed. (New York: Simon & Schuster/Touchstone, 1991), 56.

28. Arthur O. Lovejoy, *The Great Chain of Being: A Study of the History of an Idea* (Cambridge, Mass.: Harvard University Press, 1936), 8.

29. Thomas à Kempis, 191.

30. Elaine Pagels, *Beyond Belief: The Secret Gospel of Thomas* (New York: Random House, 2003), 92.

31. Pagels, 102.

32. Pagels, 102.

33. Pagels, 103.

34. Pagels, 109.

35. Hofstadter, 27.

36. Louis Menand, *The Metaphysical Club* (New York: Farrar, Straus & Giroux, 2000), xi–xii.

PART THREE: *The Process*

1. Nathan Humphrey, ed., *Gathering the NeXt Generation: Essays on the Formation and Ministry of GenX Priests* (Harrisburg: Morehouse Publishing, 2000), 15.

2. Hertzberg, 300.

3. Hertzberg, 304.

4. Guy Davenport, *The Hunter Gracchus and Other Papers on Literature and Art* (Washington: Counterpoint, 1996), 38.

5. Thomas Merton, *The Seven Storey Mountain* (New York: Harcourt Brace & Company, 1999), 293.

6. Father Walter Cuenin, quoted in Paul Willkes, "The Reformer," *The New Yorker*, September 2, 2003.

7. Council for the Development of Ministry, *The Implementation of the Title III Canons: A Review of Diocesan Practices*, compiled by Rev. William S. Stafford and Rev. Lawrence Falkowski, photocopy (New York: Episcopal Church Center, 1996).

8. Stafford and Falkowski.

9. Farnham, 47.

10. Statistics on religious affiliation from the American Religion Data Archive (ARDA), Penn State; see www.arda.tm.

11. Mead, 231.

12. McBrien, 32.

13. Clissold, 53.

14. Nouwen, 25.

15. Parker J. Palmer, *Let Your Life Speak: Listening for the Voice of Vocation* (San Francisco: Jossey-Bass, 2000), 4.

16. Palmer, 4.

17. Armstrong, *History*, 41.

18. Hertzberg, 97.

19. John Chrysostom, *Treatise on the Priesthood,* The Nicene and Post Nicene Fathers Series I, vol. IX, edited by Philip Schaff, D.D., LL.D. (1889) 3:1. Available at www.ccel.org by Calvin College, Grand Rapids, Michigan.

20. Robert Faggen, ed., *Striving Towards Being: The Letters of Thomas Merton and Czeslaw Milosz* (New York: Farrar, Straus & Giroux, 1997), 164.

21. Nouwen, 16.

22. Nouwen, 40.

23. Nouwen, 41.

24. Nouwen, 77.

25. Christopher Martin, "Introduction," in Humphrey, ed., *Gathering,* xv.

26. Martin, xxii.

27. Richard Kew, in Humphrey, ed., *Gathering,* 4.

28. Beth Maynard, in Humphrey, ed., *Gathering,* 84.

PART FOUR: *Polemics*

1. Arthur Hertzberg, *The Jews in America: Four Centuries of an Uneasy Encounter* (New York: Simon & Schuster, 1989), 382.

2. Hertzberg, *Jews,* 379.

3. Weil, 127.

4. Leo Baeck, *This People Israel* (New York: Holt, Rinehart and Winston, 1964), 31.

5. Hertzberg, *Jews,* 234.

6. Weil, 105.

7. Weil, 76.

8. Wills, 339.

9. *The Letters of William James* (Boston, 1920), vol. II, 100, cited in Hofstadter, 39.

10. Alexis de Tocqueville, *Democracy in America,* translated by Henry Reeve, revised & corrected 1839 (electronic edition deposited by the American Studies Program at the University of Virginia, 1997), vol. II, chap. 5, "How Religion in the United States Avails Itself of Democratic Tendencies."

11. Quoted in Joan Didion, "God's Country," *The New York Review of Books,* November 2, 2000.

12. "Roundtable on Religion in Politics: Stephen Carter, Barbara Ehrenreich, Stanley Fish, Michael Sandel, Judith Schaeffer, and Nomi Stolzenberg," *Tikkun*, December 31, 2000.

13. Armstrong, *History*, 211.

14. David Grossman, "Introduction," *The Second Book of Moses, Called Exodus: Authorized King James Version (Pocket Canon)* (New York: Grove Press, 1999), xi.

15. Grossman, ix.

16. Author's 1999 interview with Crace for *BOMB* magazine.

17. Weil, 70.

18. Weil, 77.

19. January 2003 report from the Standing Commission on Ministry Development of the 73rd General Convention (A073, "Revision of Title III Canons").

20. Thomas Merton, *The Hidden Ground of Love: Letters of Thomas Merton on Religious Experience and Social Concerns,* edited by William H. Shannon (New York: Farrar, Straus & Giroux, 1985), 7.

21. Clissold, 60.

22. Merton, *Hidden Ground,* 9–10.

23. Emerson, 122.

24. Thomas Doyle, acceptance speech for the Priest of Integrity Award, Voice of the Faithful Conference, Hynes Convention Center, July 2002; transcript from Voice of the Faithful Web site, www.votf.org.

25. Garry Wills, translator, *Saint Augustine's Childhood: Confessiones,* vol. 1 (New York: Viking Press, 2001).

26. Hertzberg, *Judaism,* 27.

27. Gilpin, 132.

28. James, 96.

29. Armstrong, *History,* 279.

30. Wilhelm Pauck, "The Ministry in the Time of Continental Reformation," in *The Ministry in Historical Perspective,* 138–42.

31. "Report of the Theological Education Task Force," Standing Commission on Ministry Development (January 2003).

32. Farnham, 11.

33. Farnham, 24.

34. Farnham, 95.

35. Pauck, 138–42.

36. "An Outline of the Faith, or Catechism," The Book of Common Prayer (1979), 855.

37. Farnham, 18.

38. Farnham, 13.

39. Farnham, 61.

40. Garry Wills, *The New York Review of Books,* June 21, 2001.

41. From *Che cosa crede chi non crede,* letters between Cardinal Carlo Maria Martini and Umberto Eco, my translation (Rome: Atlantid Editoriale, 1996).

42. Nouwen, 47.

43. Nouwen, 65.

44. Czeslaw Milosz, "If Only This Could Be Said," in *To Begin Where I Am,* edited by Bogdana Carpenter and Madeline G. Levine (New York: Farrar, Straus & Giroux, 2000), 320.

45. Merton, *Hidden Ground,* 118.

46. Hertzberg, *Judaism,* 167.

INDEX